METHODS OF INSTRUCTION

OR

THAT PART OF THE PHILOSOPHY OF EDUCATION WHICH TREATS OF THE NATURE OF THE SEVERAL BRANCHES OF KNOWLEDGE AND THE METHODS OF TEACHING THEM ACCORDING TO THAT NATURE.

BY

JAMES PYLE WICKERSHAM, LL.D.,

STATE SUPERINTENDENT OF PUBLIC INSTRUCTION OF PENNSYLVANIA, LATE PRINCIPAL OF THE PENNSYLVANIA STATE NORMAL SCHOOL, AND AUTHOR OF "SCHOOL ECONOMY," ETC.

"The method of nature is the archetype of all methods."—MARCEL.

"Man cannot propose a higher and holier object for his study, than education, and all that appertains to education."—COUSIN'S PLATO.

PHILADELPHIA:

J. B. LIPPINCOTT & CO.

Entered, according to Act of Congress, in the year 1865, by

JAMES PYLE WICKERSHAM,

In the Clerk's Office of the District Court of the United States for the Eastern District of Pennsylvania.

As a Tribute of Respect

To the men and women now constituting the Teachers' Profession in America, characterized as they are by learning, worth, and devotion to a work among the most noble that human effort ever aspired to accomplish — the right education of the whole people of the nation — who for their heavy labors receive small recompense save the consciousness of doing good,

The Author,

Whose desire it has been to be worthy of a place as a co-worker among them, whose hope it is to aid in elevating and dignifying the Profession to which he and they belong, and whose reward it will be to have secured their approval of his work, begs leave to dedicate this book.

PREFACE.

The author of this volume published, about a year ago, a book entitled "School Economy." In the Preface to it, the statement was made that other volumes were contemplated, but that their publication depended very much upon the reception of the one then offered to the Profession and the public. The commendations of that book were so numerous and hearty, and its sale so rapid, that the obligation was soon imposed upon the author of redeeming his implied promise, by printing the volume on "Methods of Instruction," which was then announced as being almost ready for the Press.

The present work, like the former one, is based upon lectures delivered to classes of students preparing themselves for teachers, but much additional matter is introduced here, that was not contained in the original lectures, for the purpose of rounding out the whole into a more perfect system, and making the book more acceptable to all classes of teachers. As it now stands it is hoped that it will be found to embody principles well worthy the attention of the Philosopher as well as of the Educator, and that its merit may be such as to make it a standard work in the profession whose interests mainly it is designed to serve.

It will be observed that the word TEACHING is used to designate all that belongs to the profession, whose aim it is to educate mankind. The words Law and Medicine have a similar relation to those professions whose objects it is, respectively, to preserve social order, and to cure the sick. Pedagogy, is the term generally employed by the Germans to express what I now call Teaching, but this word has an unpleasant association in this country, which unfits it for that purpose. Teaching was divided in the Preface to the "School Economy," into four divisions, viz.: School Economy, which treats of the preparation for, and the organization of, the school, and the conditions of its efficient working; Methods of Instruction, which treats of the nature of knowledge, and the methods of imparting it; Methods of Culture, which treats of the nature of man, and the methods of educing from it all possible perfection; and the History of Education. To the matter composing the first three divisions I have sometimes thought shorter, but, perhaps, not more expressive, names might be applied, as follows: SCHOLASTICS, instead of School Economy; DIDACTICS, instead of Methods of Instruction; and HUMANICS, instead of Methods of Culture. The first is, perhaps objectionable because it has already been appropriated, though not much used; the second is very expressive, and is now applied somewhat indefinitely to Teaching in general; and the third, in a slightly different form, has associations of long standing, which render it a fit term to express the object-matter proposed to be embraced by Methods of Culture. Throughout this work, however, the forms of expression first chosen will continue to be used.

The labor expended in the preparation of this book was very great. It formed a daily subject of thought for the past ten years, and much of it was written over three or four times. This is hardly the place to confess how often the task was about to be abandoned from the disproportion felt to exist between its magnitude and the limited powers that could be summoned to execute it; but it was as often resumed, and is now completed —completed, but not perfected, for it is not presumed that nothing erroneous or imperfect will be found in the work. It would have been easy to fill five hundred pages with matter concerning the methods of teaching the several branches of knowledge considered independently; but in that case the book would have been a mere collection of fragments, and not at all a scientific treatise. It might, indeed, have been more popular, but it would have been unfaithful to the great theme discussed; so at the risk of losing readers, patient effort was made to grapple with the subject in its broadest relations. Great difficulty was met in condensing the materials. It would have been much easier to write several volumes on the subject than one. The thinking reader will appreciate this labor.

Criticism is anticipated from those who would measure all knowledge by the standard of utility, or confine it to the few branches which seem to impart most skill in transacting the world's affairs, but this will be borne with patience, if what is written shall secure the approbation of those who see in education the means of developing all the powers of the human soul, and furnishing it with that instruction which is not only profitable on earth, but which leads up towards the world of light and love.

Teachers of the most limited scholarship will find much matter in the book that they can readily make use of in the every day work of their schools; but some such teachers will likely complain that they meet with things which they cannot understand. This, perhaps, will not be the fault of the book. The doctrine of education cannot be discussed as a Philosophy without using philosophical principles and philosophical language. Works on Law and Medicine rise to the level of the subjects of which they treat, and lift the earnest student up with them. Teachers must adopt a higher standard of learning. They must acquaint themselves with the fundamental principles of Teaching. They must learn to think. And, besides, this book was not written for the babes of the profession, but for the men —not for those who are satisfied to tramp forever the tread-mill of routine and get no farther and rise no higher, but for those who aspire to gain broader and clearer views of the Philosophy of Education and to guide the work of teaching by their light. Teaching, when rightly done, is not a mere process of imitation or a piece of guess-work. Its rules and precepts are not even the generalizations of successful practice, but they are founded upon the universal and necessary laws which condition matter and govern mind.

As a preparation for the successful study of this book, it is necessary to understand the several branches of knowledge of the methods of teaching which it treats; and also to be versed in the sciences which directly appertain to mind—the Psychological Sciences. In the broadest sense it requires the whole of Science to constitute the basis upon which Teaching must rest. The solution of the problem of man necessitates the solution of the problem of nature, for to understand him all else must be understood. And yet this conception is so far above the practice of the profession, so much beyond the reach of many who are called good teachers that I scarcely venture to present it. When I think of the low ends we aim at in education, and the unworthy means and imperfect methods we use to accomplish them, I tremble to think we are teaching and know so little. God, forgive us if we mar thy noblest work. We are ignorant, and would be humble. Thou alone canst know the difficulties that surround our task.

The plan of this book was formed during the year 1855. To fill out the plan much reading as well as much thinking has been done; but to tell to-day what was obtained by the first process and what by the second is an impossibility. Wishing to do justice to everybody, no claim that may be fairly made to any idea in it will be disputed; and it is hoped that something may be left even when all claims are satisfied. Nothing, however, has been taken from others and used without digestion. All the facts and principles found in the book, come whence they may, have been fused into a common whole. This whole — this collecting and uniting of the scattered fragments of thought concerning education — this *system*, is what the author asks credit for, if credit be deemed his due.

The question is a disputed one as to whether Teaching is a science or an art. The settlement of this question depends wholly upon the definitions of science and art. Teaching seeks an end without itself, and this is a characteristic of art. It comprehends many scientific principles which admit systematic arrangement, and this is a characteristic of science. It applies those principles in the form of rules or precepts in the accomplishment of its ends, and this again exhibits its relationship to the arts. All the principles of Teaching come to it second-hand. They are first found in the material or mental sciences, and are used in Teaching to furnish a ground for its methods of procedure. But as a body of truths they are among the broadest and noblest that the human mind can contemplate, and consequently place Teaching side by side, as the peer of the proudest professions known to men. Teaching has the same claims to be considered a science as Jurisprudence, Medicine, or practical Ethics; for all these are constructed in a manner precisely like Teaching. All of them borrow their principles, and all of them use these principles in the effort to attain their respective ends. Perhaps, as Mill following Comte suggests, "There ought to be a set of intermediate scientific truths, derived from the higher generalities of science, and destined to serve as the generalia, or first principles, of the various arts." Some such generalia relating to Teaching are given in this book under the head of Conditioning Principles. These and other principles like them constitute the claim Teaching has to be called a Science. If the claim is not well founded with respect to Teaching, it cannot be well founded with respect to any other profession. I am quite willing to consider Teaching an art, but it is an art based upon scientific principles that should always guide its practice. Let teachers forever discard the degrading idea that the highest and holiest work in which men can engage on earth, the right education of the human soul, is a mere mechanical employment that can be learned by imitation—is a thing so easy that no special preparation is required to do it. Let them hold to the truth, though their pearls be trampled on by vulgar feet, that Teaching lays under contribution all science and all art in working out the grandest end that human conception ever realized — the perfection of the race.

With grateful thanks for the kind reception accorded to his first volume, the author now hopefully trusts his second to the same generous hands.

J. P. W.

STATE NORMAL SCHOOL, January, 1865.

CONTENTS.

INTRODUCTION.

TEACHERS REQUIRE SPECIAL PREPARATION.

CONDITIONING PRINCIPLES.

PAGE

PAGE

BUILDING THE FOUNDATION.

CHAPTER I.

INSTRUCTION IN THE ELEMENTS OF KNOWLEDGE.

CHAPTER II.

INSTRUCTION IN LANGUAGE.

CHAPTER III.

INSTRUCTION IN THE FORMAL SCIENCES.

CHAPTER IV.

INSTRUCTION IN THE EMPIRICAL SCIENCES.

CHAPTER V.

INSTRUCTION IN THE RATIONAL SCIENCES.

CHAPTER VI.

INSTRUCTION IN THE HISTORICAL SCIENCES.

CHAPTER VII.

INSTRUCTION IN THE ARTS.

METHODS OF INSTRUCTION.

INTRODUCTION.

TEACHERS REQUIRE SPECIAL PREPARATION.

EDUCATION as a science comprehends the laws of the physical and mental constitution of man, and its relations to those means by which he can receive instruction and culture.

Education as an art consists in selecting and applying the means used for imparting instruction and culture.

Like other sciences, education can be studied; and, as in other arts, acquired skill as well as native talent is essential to success. To attain a knowledge of the science and proficiency in the art of education, it seems evident at a glance that special preparation is necessary; but as this position has been questioned, it is considered advisable to introduce the following work by some considerations in its favor.

Until within a few years, the common schools of this country were taught almost exclusively by persons who had never studied professionally, who, indeed, were generally ignorant that any preparation could be made or was needed to enable them to discharge their duty in the work of teaching. Academies and colleges were not much better off in this respect; for, though those who taught in them possessed a higher degree of scholarship than the teachers of common schools, they could justly claim little more professional knowledge. The public seem to have been satisfied with this kind of guess-work teaching. Instructors of youth were allowed to enter upon their business without having served even that period of apprenticeship deemed necessary for those who make hats or coats, build houses, or shoe horses. They were everywhere employed with little regard to their literary, and less to their professional, qualifications. These strictures are not so applicable to the present condition of our educational affairs as to their condition a few years ago; but notwithstanding schools for the training of teachers exist in most of the Free States, and other means of obtaining knowledge appertaining to teaching are readily accessible, the great body of American schools are still taught by persons who have neither attended Normal Schools nor availed themselves of any other means of professional improvement.

That special preparation is necessary for teachers will appear from the considerations which follow:

1. The Teacher must understand the true Object of Education. — The lowest idea of the object of an education embraces only its advantages in acquiring that knowledge which may be used in obtaining food, clothing, shelter, protection, or in carrying on some kind of business. An idea of the object of education to this extent may be obtained, perhaps,

without any special preparation, it may result from the pressure of circumstances; but education has an object far higher—an object that is not limited by the mere necessities of life. The great end of education is to perfect man, physically, mentally, morally, religiously. To do this truth must be sought and loved for its own sake, discipline must be valued for the permanent strength it imparts to the soul, longings for the high and the holy must be made to spring up in the heart, and all his powers must be so directed as to attain true manhood for man. To realize all this even in thought is difficult, to realize it in life is the great problem which it is our mission on earth to solve. No teacher can work effectively without a well-defined object, and no teacher can fully conceive the highest object of education without long and careful thought. To do so, he must study with profound attention the natu e of man physically and mentally, and his relations to the world in which he lives, to his fellow-men, and to God.

2. The Teacher must understand that upon which he operates.—No man can operate skilfully upon a thing the nature of which he does not understand. The farmer must understand the nature of the soil he cultivates; the blacksmith, the iron he fashions; the potter, the clay he moulds, before either can produce the most advantageous results. The human mind is certainly not less easy to comprehend than are soils, iron, or clay, that the teacher can be safely relieved from the special professional labor and study required of farmers, blacksmiths,

and potters. True, like them, he may work like a machine, or work by imitating others, but such blind methods of procedure, unworthy of a man in any avocation of life, become almost criminal when applied to the education of human beings whose success in this world and happiness in the world to come he may jeopardize.

3. The Teacher must understand that with which he operates. — The subject-matter of knowledge comprehends the world of matter and the world of mind. The teacher has all created things from which to select means to be used in the work of education. No man can make a judicious selection of these means, and be prepared to present them in their proper order and proportion without long and careful study. The physician spends much time and thought in selecting and compounding his medicines for the body; it is not more easy to prepare those which are designed to be administered to the mind. Indeed, the selection of the best course of study for a child is a problem as difficult as any with which the human mind ever tried to grapple.

4. The Teacher must understand how to conduct the operation. — A man may understand the nature of the thing upon which he intends to operate, he may understand the means with which the operation is to be performed, and still want a knowledge of the method of performing the operation. It is the teacher's duty to train and instruct children, and he can have no intelligent method of doing this

without making special preparation. He can no more dispense with a knowledge of the method of operating than can the man who navigates a ship or builds a railroad. If methods of teaching were merely mechanical, founded upon no fixed principles (and this is not the case), they could not be successfully imitated without special preparation; for such is the law with this whole class of operations. Besides, facts show that the possession of knowledge does not imply ability to impart it. It is self-evident that one person cannot impart to another what he does not know himself, but it is maintained here that good scholars do not always succeed in becoming good teachers. Persons who have been well taught must have learned something concerning the methods by which they were taught, but they cannot intelligently follow these methods in their own practice unless they have carefully studied all their details, and the principles upon which they are founded. Like passengers on board of a rail-car or steamship, pupils may make swift speed toward their journey's end without noticing the way along which they travel. Methods of teaching cannot be well studied incidentally; they have a philosophy of their own, and should be made a definite object of study. Skill in teaching, it is true, may be acquired by school-room experience without special instruction beforehand; but this is always done at much risk to the teacher, and with much loss to the pupils. No man has more need to profit by the experience of others than the teacher, for no man's mistakes are less easily remedied. Teaching talent may seem in some inborn, but this is true also in respect to particular individuals in all professions, and cannot be fairly adduced as an argument against special preparation for those not so highly favored by nature.

5. THE TEACHER MUST KNOW HOW TO MANAGE AND GOVERN A SCHOOL.—Discipline gives power. One hundred well-drilled soldiers are worth more on a battle-field than several hundred raw recruits. The captain of a vessel, the superintendent of a factory, the commander of an army, must acquire professional skill by discipline; knowledge of the principles of school-management and school-government, and skill in applying them, must be acquired in the same way. Progress can be hoped for in teaching only as teachers make use of the experience of their predecessors as a starting-post for their own investigations. Where wise and good men tell us how to avoid falling into errors, it is great folly to shut our ears to their advice. Nor can natural aptitude for managing and governing a school be relied upon, any more than natural aptitude for practicing medicine or law can be relied upon in those professions.

Some additional reasons will be given in favor of special preparation for teachers. They belong to a different class from the preceding, but are scarcely less convincing:

1. SPECIAL PREPARATION ON THE PART OF TEACHERS IS NECESSARY TO CONSTITUTE TEACHING A PROFESSION.—If scholarship is the only requisite for the teacher, then all scholars are teachers, or may properly become such whenever the prospects of success in

more desirable fields of effort become discouraging. Teaching would thus be a kind of common ground open to all, and admitting the limitation of no professional lines. As a consequence, teachers would attach little importance to, and have little interest in, their work; there would be little unity of effort among them, and a general want of that class feeling, or *esprit du corps*, which is always essential to the building up of any profession, and without which teaching can neither attain the rank among the professions hoped for by teachers, nor meet in the value of its results the reasonable expectations of the public.

2. SPECIAL PREPARATION ON THE PART OF TEACHERS IS NECESSARY TO MAKE TEACHING A PERMANENT BUSINESS. — At present no other kind of business is subject to so many changes as teaching. It is certain that of those who have charge of our Common Schools one year, not more than two-thirds, in some places not more than one-half, remain to take charge of them the succeeding year. Such frequent changes do not take place in any other pursuit, and they are partly, at least, accounted for in the teachers' profession by the opinion which is held by many that "anybody" can teach. The consequence of this opinion is that thousands are still found occupying the position of teacher who never intend to become permanent teachers, but who teach merely to replenish their exhausted funds, to enjoy opportunities for self-improvement, to put in time while waiting to engage in some other kind of business, and are restless under the

irksome necessity that confines them to the school-room. A well-taught school by any of these classes of persons must be an exception to the rule. They have made no special preparation to become teachers, and they do not intend that either their livelihood or their reputation shall depend upon their success as such; and actuated by none of the usual motives that prompt to earnest effort, they cannot be expected to evince much interest or exhibit great skill in teaching. In proportion as men expend time, labor, and money in fitting themselves for a particular kind of business will be their indisposition to abandon it, and never until the public recognize the truth that teachers require special preparation, will communities be freed from the evils consequent upon the frequent change of teachers, and the profession of teaching relieved of the horde of intruders who now disgrace it and reduce to a very low amount the remuneration it affords.

3. Efforts for the Special Preparation of Teachers have been attended with satisfactory results.—Prussia has tried the experiment of training teachers upon a large scale, and both government and people think it has been successful. Austria, France, and England have their schools for teachers, and find them essential to the well-working of their systems of education. Such men as Dinter, Cousin and Brougham have advocated the establishment of Normal Schools. These schools have also been established in many of our American States; and though they have encountered much opposition,

they have everywhere met with signal success. The public have seen teachers who have made special preparation at Normal Schools work by the side of those who have not made such preparation; with the shrewdness characteristic of our people a comparison of their respective merits has been made, and the conclusion is best expressed in the liberal patronage which such schools receive and the hundreds of thousands of dollars which are annually expended for their support.

The reasons just stated are sufficient to show that teachers require special preparation, and their statement seems appropriately to introduce a work on Teaching which aims to aid in that preparation. If any teacher, or any one who designs to become a teacher feels the want of the preparation which it has been shown teachers need, he is invited to study the subject as presented in the following pages; and it is hoped he will not only find that which will increase his ability to discharge the duties incumbent upon the teacher, but that which will elevate his idea of the importance and dignity of the teachers' profession.

CONDITIONING PRINCIPLES.

Human perfection is the grand aim of all well directed education. The teacher has ever present with him his ideal man whose perfections he would realize in the children committed to his care, as the sculptor would realize the pure forms of his imagination in the rough marble that lies unchiseled before him. Embraced in this great end of education there are several subordinate ends, that of gaining knowledge, that of attaining discipline, that of lifting up the mind to the contemplation of pure beauty, truth, and excellence, and that of fitting ourselves to perform in the best manner possible all our duties to man and to God.

Granted, that this is a true conception of the end of all education, and the object-matter which must form the foundation for a system of teaching, will comprehend: 1st. The nature of the thing to be operated upon, or *educational capabilities;* 2d. The nature of the instrumentalities which may be used in operating upon it, or *educational means;* 3d. The manner of performing the operation, or *educational methods.* A system of agriculture is likewise divisible into three parts; that which treats of the soil, that which treats of the means of fertilizing or working it, and that which treats of the methods of applying the means to the desired end. A system of Medicine, too, consists essentially of the sciences of Anatomy and Physiology, Pharmacy, and the Practice of Medicine.

In a system of teaching, the thing to be operated upon is man; the means wherewith to operate are found in everything that can be made to bear an objective relation to man; and the methods according to which the operation must be performed can have a basis nowhere but in the relations the mind and body sustain to each other and to the great universe.

The whole subject admits treatment from two stand-points: 1st. *The nature of man and the methods of educating him according to the laws of that nature;* 2d. *The nature of the several branches of knowledge and the methods of teaching them according to the laws of that nature.*

Proceeding from the first of these stand-points, we commence with the study of man, learn his educational necessities and capabilities, and conclude with an exposition of the methods by which he can best be educated. Proceeding from the second stand-point, we commence by an examination of the means which may be made use of in the work of education, the several branches of knowledge; inquire into their relations and conditions, and close the investigation by presenting the methods by which knowledge can be best imparted. The whole subject of teaching may therefore be divided into two great parts, appropriately called METHODS OF CULTURE and METHODS OF INSTRUCTION. If the two classes of methods thus arrived at are found to harmonize, no further verification of their truthfulness is needed.

The subject of Methods of Culture may be treated of hereafter, but, in the present volume, it is my intention to consider only Methods of Instruction. Care will be taken, however, to verify conclusions in all open ways before announcing them.

The methods adopted in the work of teaching may be right or they may be wrong. Just so the horticulturist can stimulate his plants to a more active growth or he may destroy them, the lawyer may gain or lose his cause, the physician may cure or kill his patient; and even the mechanic may operate upon his wood, or clay, or iron by skilful or unskilful processes. Immortal minds are committed to the teacher's charge. If he adopt right methods of teaching he can make those minds bear an image worthy of their heavenly origin and destiny and of Him who created them; but if he pursue wrong methods they may be marred and debased until they become the most lamentable of all spectacles, wrecked and ruined human souls.

Starting with the obvious fact that there may be right and wrong methods of teaching, I proceed to take the first step in the search for those that are right by stating some of the principles which all such methods must observe, and which have been denominated CONDITIONING PRINCIPLES.

Methods of intellectual education must be conditioned on the one hand by the nature of mind, and on the other by the nature of knowledge; the subject, therefore, will be considered in two sections. The first will embrace a statement of principles that belong rather to Methods of Culture, but whose guiding light cannot well be dispensed with in the department of education now under consideration. Upon an examination of these principles, it will be seen that the two sources from which they are drawn yield the same fruit—one set of principles corresponding with the other—and a basis for the science of teaching is found either in mind or in nature, is both Psychological and Cosmological. In order that the student may better appreciate the beautiful correlation existing between the two sets of principles, the corresponding propositions will be numbered alike.

This classification of principles, it ought to be remarked, is intended to embrace only the most important of those which appertain to intellectual education—it is not exhaustive.

I. Principles Inferable from the Nature of Mind.

The nature of a thing acted upon always governs in some measure the methods of acting upon it. If soils were differently constituted, farmers would be under the necessity of changing their modes of cultivation; if the diseased human body was unlike it now is, a corresponding modification would be necessary in systems of medical practice. The same process that will put in motion particles of air or water will not separate those of quartz or granite. Wood and iron cannot be worked in the same manner nor with the same tools. Hence *educational principles are inferable from the nature of mind, and among them are those which follow:—*

1. The Intellectual Faculties can receive Cul-

TURE ONLY BY JUDICIOUS EXERCISE.—No means are known whereby the faculties of the mind can be developed but by exercising them. By the potent spell of the magic word Exercise, is evoked all human power.

The proof of this proposition is found in multitudes of facts. The senses grow more acute by using them. The memory is improved by remembering, the reason by reasoning, the imagination by imagining. All these powers, too, become weak if not used. These facts may be learned from each person's own experience, or from observation upon others. The law inferred from them is fixed and universal.

Exercise, however, in order to strengthen must be judicious. Too much or improper exercise will weaken the mind's powers instead of giving them strength.

2. THE HUMAN INTELLECT EMBRACES A NUMBER OF DISTINCT FACULTIES EACH OF WHICH REQUIRES A DIFFERENT KIND OF CULTURE.—It is acknowledged that the body may be made strong without giving strength to the mind, that our intellectual, emotional, and executive faculties can, as classes, receive an independent culture. This law holds good of the distinctive faculties that make up the human intellect. It requires one mode of culture to educate the senses and the perceptive powers, another to strengthen the memory, and still others to develop the powers of recollection, imagination, comparison, and reason. Each intellectual power differs from the others in its nature, in its mode of operation,

and modes of culture must adapt themselves to these differences. He would be like a blind man leading a blind man who should attempt to teach, ignorant of this great law.

3. Human Beings have been created with different Tastes and Talents to fit them for performing different Duties or for occupying different Spheres in Life.—That children differ in tastes and talents every parent and every teacher is agreed. The Bible intimates the same fact. The reason probably is that, as in nature's system each necessary office was designed to be filled by a qualified officer, men differ because their social duties or their spheres in life are different. But, whatever the reason, the fact is certain, and is of great significance to the educator. It teaches him that he must plan his system of Teaching with reference to the peculiar tastes and talents of children.

Doubtless, certain kinds of general knowledge and certain kinds of mental discipline may be considered indispensable for all; but, in addition, every true teacher should consider it a privilege to furnish each one of his pupils an opportunity for the development of his special powers. The aim of education is not to make all men move in the same plane—to create a social dead-level. Protestations have been made against the prescribed, unvaried course of instruction in institutions of learning, and not always without reason. Such men as Lord Byron, Hugh Miller, and Dr. Kane were restless while made to pursue those branches of study in which they felt little interest, and indulged by stealth those special talents which God had given them. Educate together from their youth up such men as Plato and Aristotle, Kant and Gœthe, Newton and Burns, La Place and Lamartine, Benjamin Franklin and Patrick Henry, and they might be made more alike, but would the world profit so much by their genius? A wise system of education aims to render available all the mental force of the world. The mechanic may contrive and the merchant make his ventures, the farmer watch his harvests and the statesman promulgate his laws, the naturalist search and the philosopher speculate, the poet kindle the fires of genius upon their intended altars, and the prophet pluck down manna from Heaven to feed soul-hungry mortals—the world needs them all, and teachers must not attempt to thwart what God seems to have designed. But in all this it must be remembered that special talent may result from education as well as be the gift of nature. No fact is more open to the notice of an observer of the phenomena of mind than that mental force may be directed artificially to certain faculties which grow strong by use, while others are dwarfed for want of exercise.

4. The Perceptive Powers are Stronger and more Active in Youth than the other intellectual faculties and thus furnish a basis for the superstructure of Knowledge.—A child is merely an animal until there is awakened in him the power of self-consciousness. After this I can find no time when all his faculties are not active in some degree; but his perceptive powers are the strongest and most

active during the whole period of childhood and youth. Any one who will observe children can scarcely doubt this fact. They like to see and hear things. What is new or strange attracts them. How rapidly they learn the form, color, size, and other qualities of things! What an immense number of facts they acquaint themselves with as they play in garden or yard, walk through field or meadow, or pass along street or highway!

We do not, as some have taught we do, derive all our knowledge from experience; but no psychological truth is more obvious than that we cannot know anything without experience. For the attainment of certain necessary, regulative truths, experience may furnish only the *occasion;* but its necessity to the knowing process is not less real when it stands directly as the source of our knowing than when it stands indirectly as the occasion of it—when it determines the limits of our knowledge than when our knowledge transcends its limits. Experience therefore may be said to form the basis of knowledge.

Convincing reasons may be found in what has now been said, in favor of enlarging experience as much as possible by taking advantage in the work of education of the strong and active perceptive powers of the young. Let teachers make them acquainted with things, facts, phenomena, that they may have a broad basis upon which to erect the superstructure of knowledge.

5. Commencing with the Perceptive Powers, the various Intellectual Faculties Increase in

Relative Strength in the following order: Memory, Recollection, Imagination, Understanding, Reason.—It must not be understood that the first named of these faculties attains maturity while the others remain in a state of inactivity. Probably, a child in the simple act of refusing to put its hand against a hot stove to-day because yesterday it was burned in doing it, makes use of all the faculties it ever will possess. Still these faculties are relatively stronger at some periods of life than at others, and this fact cannot be overlooked in teaching.

As used here, Memory is the power of retaining knowledge; Recollection is the power by which we awaken what lies dormant in the mind; Imagination is the power the mind has of holding up vividly before itself the thoughts which it has recalled into consciousness; Understanding is the power by which we judge of relations; and Reason is the power that gives birth to those necessary and universal principles which control all thinking. It is proper to remark that this classification is essentially Hamilton's, and the definitions are, in part, his.

It is evident that knowledge must be retained before it can be recalled, that it must be recalled before it can be held up for contemplation, that it must be held up before the mind before its relations can be judged of, and that the whole thinking process must go on before it can be controlled or regulated. Logically, therefore, the activities of the several faculties do follow an order of succession, but practically the whole goes on simultaneously

Still, as before stated, these activities differ relatively in degree during the different periods of life.

Next to the Perceptive powers the Memory is the most vigorous intellectual faculty possessed by the young. It is the granary of the mind. Let it be well filled while it can be, as from its stores all the other faculties must take their materials.

A little later the faculties of Recollection and Imagination are developed in full strength. Both are engaged in lifting up the elements of knowledge from the depths of the Memory and placing them in vivid pictures before the mind. The forms of the Imagination are, however, at first rude and fanciful, being yet unchastened by the higher powers of Judgment and Reason.

The Understanding is the working power of the mind. It studies the relations of wholes to parts, parts to wholes, and things to one another. It classifies, generalizes, reasons. This power, although manifesting itself in a little child, does not attain maturity until the age of manhood.

The Reason rules the mind. As soon as a child is conscious of the identity or difference of two objects, he must use his Reason; nor can he take a single step in any intellectual process without its aid. But, while this is true, Reason can never assume full sway until all the other intellectual faculties perform their work. A commanding general cannot wield the whole power of his army unless every subordinate officer and every private does his duty. None but a man intellectually full-grown can make a right use of his Reason, and the most difficult of all Philosophies is the Philosophy of Reason itself.

6. THE HUMAN MIND POSSESSES TWO SOURCES OF KNOWLEDGE, THE SENSES AND THE REASON, THE PRODUCTS OF WHICH DIFFER IN KIND.—That we derive knowledge through the senses, no one doubts. It consists, in the first place of facts, which, however, may be elaborated into systems of science. Knowledge thus derived may be called *empirical* knowledge, because its source is experience.

That we possess knowledge which we do not derive through the senses must be evident to all who will consider the matter. Our idea of space, for example, is not merely the sum of all the spaces embraced in our experience, but it transcends all possible experience. So of the idea of time. We can acquaint ourselves with things that are very great in extent—the earth, the distances of the heavenly bodies, the profound abysses penetrated by the telescope, but still we know that all these are limited, *finite*, and we cannot help believing that there is something more, the unlimited, the *infinite*. No experience can show us that two straight lines cannot enclose a space, or that two parallel lines will never meet, and yet we know that such is the case. We may, indeed, have no *adequate* conception of the absolute or the infinite, of a creation, of God, or of immortality; but certainly we have ground for thinking that there is something uncaused, something unlimited, that the universe had a beginning, that God is, and the human spirit is immortal. In every direction the intuitions of the Reason overleap the boundaries of experience, and furnish, at least, a ground for enlightened faith. As the Reason is the source of the kind of knowledge now referred to, it may be called *rational* knowledge.

Empirical knowledge includes all that concerns the qualities and quantities of things, the relations of substances and attributes, and causes and effects, and systems of inductive science. Rational knowledge includes the universal and necessary principles which condition the whole of the mind's operations, which form the foundation of all Philosophy, properly so called, and upon which must rest all firm faith in "things unseen."

The value of what has just been said will be appreciated by the many thinking teachers who lament the materialistic tendencies of some of our modern systems of education. All the knowledge that can be gained through the senses may be, but why should we close up that other fountain of the soul from which comes knowledge richer and purer? It will do us good to remember that "Man cannot live by bread alone."

7. In acquiring Knowledge the mind first distinguishes its objects in kind, then in quantity, and afterwards in their relations. — Perhaps the distinguishing of an object in kind involves somewhat of the processes of distinguishing it in quantity, and in its relations; but the arrangement as expressed is as correct as any serial arrangement of mental phenomena can be, and will be found to have much practical value in the work of education.

A child first noticing objects, retains only that general impression of them which enables him to recognize them among other objects. Long afterwards, it may be, he attends to them more closely, makes accurate measurements of the qualities he observes, or determines their quantities. Still later he learns to inquire into causes, to look for ends, to estimate uses.

Our investigations concerning what is new to us follow the same order. Take a crystal: we first distinguish it from other things; then count its faces, measure its angles, test its structure; and afterwards search for the causes which may have been operative in its formation. Take heat: we bring it under observation as a distinct object; we invent thermometers to measure it, and then busy ourselves in finding a theory that will account for its facts.

The genesis of science is in accordance with the same principle. Astronomy, in its beginnings, consisted of the loose observations ignorant men could make with the unaided vision. In course of time observations became more numerous and more exact until measurements were attempted; and finally the speculations of Copernicus and Galileo, and the great discoveries of Kepler and Newton made the study of the stars, a science. Some facts, belonging to the science of chemistry, must have been possessed by the most ignorant savages; these greatly multiplied would naturally attract the attention of men in more highly civilized communities, who would set about determining their nature, their quantity; and, by-and-by, laws would be discovered and a science begin to emerge from the confused mass of materials. The other sciences have grown up in the same way.

8. THE RATIOCINATIVE FACULTY IN ELABORATING

SYSTEMS OF SCIENCE PROCEEDS INDUCTIVELY OR DEDUCTIVELY, ANALYTICALLY OR SYNTHETICALLY.—I use the expression ratiocinative faculty to designate a specific application of the faculty of the Understanding.

Starting out with the products of the Senses and the Reason, two modes of dealing with them are possible. We can commence with particular phenomena, and proceed to find the general laws which comprehend them. This is Induction. It is a process of involution.

We can commence with general or universal truths, and proceed to find the particular truths which are embodied in them. This is Deduction It is a process of evolution.

All reasoning must be either inductive or deductive. We can take wholes and unfold their parts, or we can take parts and unite them into wholes, but all thinking in judgments must assume one or the other of these forms. Logicians use but two kinds of syllogism, the inductive and the deductive.

Analysis and synthesis are the servants of induction and deduction. Analysis is the separation of a whole into the elements which compose it. Synthesis is the composition of a whole from the parts which belong to it. An observer noticing a phenomenon which he wishes to understand, simplifies it by division, and then infers the law that controls it. Thus his power of induction is aided by analysis. Or he may have discovered a number of different laws relating to phenomena and desire to combine them all into a system of science, and this can be done only by the process of multiplication. Thus his power of induction is aided by synthesis. The general or universal principles with which deduction begins imply in their very names the existence of special or conditioned principles, from which they can be discriminated only by a process of analysis. Thus analysis aids deduction. A deductive science like Geometry is made up of a system of truths depending upon axioms, definitions, and preceding demonstrations, and is a work of synthesis. Thus synthesis aids deduction.

Systems of science, therefore, must be elaborated by the methods of induction and deduction aided by those of analysis and synthesis, and the methods used in constructing systems of science must also be used in teaching them.

9. The Acquisitive Powers of the Mind in getting Knowledge operate according to certain Laws of Suggestion.—The laws of suggestion are operative in the search for original knowledge. We begin to make observations upon a particular object, directly it presents itself in another point of view, and then in still another; and thus we are led forward in a series of successive steps. Or from one object, we may pass to another, and then to others, neglecting many but selecting some, which upon an examination of the train will be found to follow one another according to some principle of suggestion. Series of experiments, too, are mostly carried on in the same way, the first suggesting the second, and the second the third, and so to the end. That the mind thus proceeds in getting knowledge by means of observation and experiment there can be no doubt Suggestion of a different kind may lead

it on from one set of reasonings to another, but still this higher work of the mind may be considered as proceeding according to the same law.

The laws of suggestion are operative in the study of acquired knowledge. It is associated facts that most attract children and most engage their attention. Present them as isolated statements and they will be forgotten, weave them into a narrative or story, and they impress themselves on the memory forever. The advance in study is most rapid where the facts to be learned are systematically arranged, when all the parts of the sciences under consideration follow one another in a logical order.

It follows from what has been said that teachers should understand the laws of suggestion, and take advantage of them in imparting knowledge.

10. The Reproductive Powers of the Mind by means of Laws of Association enable it to recall its Knowledge and to hold it up in vivid Pictures before it.—Every one is aware that his thoughts are not isolated, but that each is a link in a chain. It is proper to speak of a train of thought. Some circumstance suggests a thought, that suggests another, and so on in a ceaseless flow. Or we can hold up before the mind one conception or element of thought, and immediately other conceptions or elements of thought crowd about it and appear in connected or related clusters.

Sir William Hamilton says that "thoughts are associated, or able to excite each other: 1st, if coexistent, or immediately successive in time; 2d, if their objects are conterminous, or adjoining in space;

3d, if they hold the dependence to each other of cause and effect, or of mean and end, or of whole and part; 4th, if they stand in a relation either of contrast or of similarity; 5th, if they are the operations of the same power, or of different powers conversant about the same object; 6th, if their objects are the sign and the thing signified; or 7th, even if their objects are accidentally denoted by the same sound." These laws may be reduced in number, but they seem more easily applied as stated. They must condition the whole work of imparting knowledge. Questions cannot be asked by a teacher, nor can answers be given by pupils skilfully without observing them. They determine the order of arrangement in both science and art.

11. THE PRODUCTIVE POWERS OF THE MIND ENABLE IT TO MAKE NEW DISCOVERIES AND NEW INVENTIONS.—Facts disprove the doctrine of those who maintain that there is nothing new, that what seems new is but the revival of the old which had been forgotten. Ideas may not be innate, but we have innate powers of mental production. There can be originality in this sense, that one man may think something that no other man ever thought. Apparent chance may present a fact, or occasion a circumstance, which a thousand men will pass by unheeding, but at last one comes that way to whom its language is intelligible, and the world is blessed with a new discovery, or a new invention—a law of gravitation or a steam-engine. The mind has productive powers. It is not like a mirror reflecting back only what is presented before it. It is an active principle, capable

of guiding its own exertions, capable of making plans, capable of searching for truth and of applying it to new uses, and expressing it in new forms. Such powers ought not to rust away in inactivity.

12. THE HUMAN INTELLECT GROWS ONLY BY ITS OWN INHERENT ENERGIES.—All true education is a growth. The mind is not a mere capacity to be filled like a granary, it is a power to be developed. It is no *tabula rasa*—no blank sheet of paper to be written upon, but it has innate activities which prompt it towards its end, and cause it to modify all with which it comes in contact. The horticulturist puts his seed in good soil, surrounds the plants with circumstances most favorable to their growth (a proper degree of heat, light, and moisture), protects them from injuries, and expects his crop. He knows that the life-principle which God placed in the seed needs but opportunity to grow. The mind must receive a like culture. When the human body needs food the healthy appetite craves it, and if taken into the stomach without such craving, it is apt to clog the system rather than to nourish it. Neither can the mind be forced to digest its food. Even an unprofessional diagnosis reveals the fact that there are many cases of mental dyspepsia in our schools. A desire to know is the mental appetite, and the gratification of this desire must be a primary condition for all normal growth of the intellect.

13. THE ACTS OF MEN DO NOT DERIVE THEIR MORAL QUALITY FROM THE INTELLECT.—The best fruit of the intellect is science, and the principles of science

cannot be said to be right or wrong—they are simply truths. The intellect, indeed, enables us to comprehend moral as well as other truths, but, in the mere comprehension of a moral truth, I can detect no moral element.

It must not be inferred, however, that intellectual culture has no relation to moral and religious culture. It is intellectual culture that renders moral and religious culture possible. The intellect is the eye of the soul, and all our seeing earthward and heavenward is done by it. It is the intellect that reveals God in His works, in His Word, and in the human soul. A man may be pious and know little of the principles of science, but he must have sources of light within himself.

The culture of the intellect must precede all other culture. We must acquaint ourselves with acts before we can judge whether they are right or wrong. We must know that God is, before we can love him. A knowledge of the important Psychological fact, that the intellectual capacity of the mind acts of itself in the presence of its objects, and that the emotive and executive capacities await the action of the intellect, would have enabled missionaries to understand, long before they found it out by costly experience, that schools must precede churches in heathen countries in order to make their labors most effectual. The principle is applicable everywhere.

14. The Intellect of Man has Limits which no Extent of Education can enable it to pass.—In all human reasoning something has to be taken for

granted. The most profound logic can neither take us back to a beginning nor lead us forward to an end. Looking backward, successions in nature seem like an endless chain of effects and causes, and, looking forward, they seem like an endless chain of causes and effects. We can think successive periods in time or points in space until the imagination grows weary with the vast summation, but still there is more beyond. We can mount the great ladder of successive causes until our heads grow dizzy, and yet we fail to form an adequate conception of the absolute. Finite ourselves we cannot measure the infinite.

All that is said in the preceding paragraph is true, and yet it does not express the exact limitations of human thought. We cannot measure the infinite, but *we can think in all directions beyond the finite.* Our idea of space is not filled by the sum of all experienced spaces, nor our idea of time by the sum of all experienced times. We feel that there are more links in the chain of causation than can be counted. We cannot indeed by searching find out God, but we can know that He exists. "A Deity understood" says Sir William Hamilton, "would be no Deity at all." The highest effort of reason is to furnish a ground for faith. We have a clear view up to the boundaries of the finite and the relative, and then we are permitted—glorious privilege!—to *know* that the infinite and the absolute, the unconditioned—lie beyond. The conviction that we have power in thought to overleap the conditioned, results from no mere blind consciousness, as some have said, but it is *certain knowledge.* We see the light but we cannot approach or analyze it. Our reason gives us a firm ground for belief in the existence of God, but here we must be content with an imperfect knowledge of Him.

II. Principles Inferable from the Nature of Knowledge.

I mean by knowledge the means made use of in the work of education. These means exist both in the form of ascertained and unascertained truth. A teacher may content himself in making his pupils acquainted with what knowledge he finds in books and what he knows himself, or he may lead them to try their strength in wrenching new truth from nature; but whether ascertained truth be taught or unascertained truth be sought for, the nature of the truth employed will vary the methods of imparting it. The principle that the methods of operating upon a thing are modified by the means used in the operation, is susceptible of many illustrations. The farmer considers the nature of his fertilizers before he adopts a method of applying them upon his fields, the physician regards the properties of his medicines in his methods of administering them, and the mechanic handles his jack-plane in one way and his hand-saw in another. That the teacher must perform his work in obedience to the same principle will be abundantly proven to one who will consider the propositions which follow.

1. The several branches of Knowledge can be made to furnish the Intellectual Faculties with

Exercise proper in kind and quantity.—The intellectual faculties grow only by exercising them, and bountiful provision is made for such exercise. It is furnished by noting the vast multitude of facts and phenomena with which we become aquainted ourselves or of which we learn from others, and by the study of Natural Science, Language, Mathematics, Metaphysics, History. In this manner the Senses, Perception, Memory, Recollection, Imagination, Understanding and Reason can all receive due exercise. All this will be clear to any one who will analyze a branch of knowledge, and learn how its several parts adapt themselves to the different intellectual faculties. The intellectual faculties, however, will not grow stronger without effort. A merely passive state of mind weakens it. We must knock at the door of knowledge before it will be opened. We must smite heavily the rock of truth before its fountains will gush forth their waters for the thirsting spirit. Nature everywhere ignores the indolent. She eats away their strength as rust destroys iron. Nor will it do to look on while others work. No Sedan chairs can be used for carrying passengers along the paths that lead to the temple of knowledge. Labor is the inexorable condition of success in study.

Knowledge, too, is easy or difficult and thus adapts itself both to the weak and the strong. Many of nature's facts and phenomena appear openly to the senses, but more require careful searching to find them. She allows some truths to lie loosely upon the surface, but others she conceals deep down in her very heart. Both a child and a philosopher may observe an apple fall from a tree, or a soap-bubble float away in the sunlight, and each find suitable intellectual exercise in so doing. The great is everywhere found in the little, and the little in the great, that the intellect in its several stages of growth may have exercise proper in kind and quantity.

2. Educational Means can be found adapted to give Culture to every Capability of Mind. — A plant is beautifully adapted to the circumstances that surround its growth. It needs mineral elements, and its little rootlets seek and find them in the soil. It feeds on gases, and millions of minute pore-mouths suck them in. It needs moisture, and the rain falls about it. It needs heat and light, and the sunshine warms its roots and plays among its branches. So, too, an adaptation exists between our intellectual wants and the means of supplying them. Each distinct intellectual faculty requires a different kind of culture, but educational means are as diversified as the wants they are intended to supply.

We have senses, and there are things to be seen, and heard, and handled. We have perception, and there are objects and phenomena that constantly, and on every hand, attract observation and court examination. We have memory, and the world is full of things to be remembered—the object-matter of science and art, the words of language, the facts of history, the products of all that the mind does. We have recollection and imagination, and the stores of the memory must be brought forth, held up for contemplation, and represented in new forms. We have understanding, and the whole work of elaborating systems of science—forming classes, making generalizations, and demonstrating principles, must be done. We have reason, and we know there is something beyond the conditioned, universal, and necessary principles, and a Being with infinite perfections, God. If any intellectual power lacks in discipline, it is not because means are wanting adapted to the purpose.

3. No God-constituted difference of Mental Constitution is left unprovided for in the Wealth of Means which the Creator intended to be used for the Purposes of Education.—All men are not naturally alike in taste or talent. To discharge the various duties of life different kinds of ability are required. Unity in diversity seems to be Nature's greatest maxim.

If God made men unlike, did He provide means for preserving the difference? It cannot be doubted that some men are peculiarly fitted to observe and investigate the works of nature, and to build up systems of natural science; and is not their field of labor boundless? There are men who seem specially endowed with a talent for Mathematics, can they ever exhaust the laws which may be evolved from number and form? There are men whose penetrating glance can pierce the shifting phenomena of sense, and perceive the very foundations and ends of things, Philosophers—and surely things have foundations and ends. Are there no materials left out of which Poetry and Music can be made? none that the artist can express on canvas or in marble? Has God so fully revealed Himself that prophecies are no longer possible?

The answer to all these questions is easy. The creation is infinite in all directions. No one man can explore the whole of it. No one man can perform all the world's work. If all men were similarly endowed with talents, or gifted with tastes, there must come a time when all progress would cease. Divide labor, let each do what he can do best, give all employment, and this field of life will bring forth its most abundant harvests. With such an arrangement need any one be idle? Not until the finite becomes the infinite.

Much is said in works on education in regard to the harmonious culture of our mental faculties. If it is merely meant that all our faculties should receive due culture, the sentiment is faultless; but if it is meant that each individual should receive an even culture, that the powers of his mind should be balanced, that the chief business of education consists in suppressing talents where talents have been given, and attempting to create talents where talents have been denied, I must be permitted to enter my protest against the doctrine. The interests of science and the duties of life no less than our diversity of gifts forbid it.

What is above said applies to the difference required in the education of the sexes. Individuals may learn whatever they are capable of learning. The tastes and talents God gave to women they may use as well as men; and just so far as their tastes and talents differ from those of men should their education differ. It need scarcely be added that all women can find fit food for their mental appetites as well as all men.

4. NATURE PRESENTS TO THE INQUIRER, FIRST THE CONCRETE, AND THEN THE ABSTRACT; FIRST THINGS, AND THEN WORDS OR SIGNS FOR THINGS; FIRST FACTS AND PHENOMENA, AND THEN LAWS AND PRINCIPLES; FIRST WHOLES, AND THEN PARTS AND COLLECTIONS OF WHOLES —THUS INDICATING TO THE TEACHER THE PROPRIETY OF CONFINING HIS ELEMENTARY INSTRUCTION MAINLY TO LESSONS ON OBJECTS WHOSE PROPERTIES CAN BE DIRECTLY PERCEIVED, FOR THE PURPOSE OF MAKING THE EXPERIENCE OF THE YOUNG AS EXTENSIVE AS POSSIBLE.—The perceptive are relatively the strongest intellectual faculties possessed by the young, and they are the first to be made use of in the search for knowledge.

Nature presents to the inquirer first the concrete and then the abstract. This is true of course with respect to all objects of Natural History; but it is also true of the so-called abstract sciences. The first step in Arithmetic was counting the fingers or counting something else. The first step in Geometry was the measurement of land. The first Music was the song of birds or the tones of the human voice.

Nature presents first things and then words or signs for things. All that we know of the origin of language goes to confirm this view. Many correspondences are found in the primitive languages, and some in all languages, between the sounds of words and the things signified by them. Qualities were noticed and then names applied. The Bible tells us, too, that animals were brought before Adam to see what he would call them.

Nature presents first facts and phenomena, and then laws and principles. The genesis of all science is confirmatory of this statement. It is true that when a science reaches a certain stage of advancement and its laws and principles become well-established, they can be applied to new facts and phenomena; but science in its earlier stages of growth is now alone in question.

Nature presents first wholes and then parts and collections of wholes. The whole of an object must be observed before it can be analyzed into parts; and the mind must pass from one individual whole to others before it can make a synthesis of the collection.

If these statements are true, they must have an important bearing upon elementary education. Nature plainly indicates the first steps in learning. To attempt to teach in contravention of her plan is to damage the intellect under training, and to lay a foundation upon which science can never rest securely. The great aim of elementary education should be to communicate the elements of knowledge—to make more extensive the experience of the young.

5. Nature opens up her Truths in a certain order and that order must be followed in Investigation and Study.—The elements of all knowledge are cotemporary in origin. A child may begin the study of all branches of science, for in their beginnings all seem equally simple. Progress in science

is from a united base to divided branches, or from the homogeneous to the heterogeneous. The observations a child may make as he stands in a garden or walks through a meadow will serve as the first steps in all kinds of learning. From this root several trunks spring, and divide and subdivide like the branches of a tree.

The object-matter of knowledge is arranged like successive strata, that beneath not being approchable except by passing through that above. First, we find qualities and facts disconnected and fragmentary. They lie upon the surface. Deeper down we find other facts and other qualities. Second, we notice the likeness and unlikeness of things. They appear to us in clusters or classes. The differences we notice first are very apparent, but identity and difference extend down to the very heart of things. Third, we begin to see that particulars can be reduced to generals, that individuals belong to classes, and species to genera, that many phenomena are the result of a single law. No limits can be fixed to this work. Fourth, seeing effects, we search for causes. We inquire why? and wherefore? We construct syllogisms and carry on processes of reasoning. No end can be found to the chain of causation. Fifth, we realize that something exists that no process of reasoning can reach—that we can think things that we could never know by experience; that we can catch glimpses, at least, of the infinite, the pure, and the perfect. Here we find God, and our work is done.

I cannot claim that what has just been said is an accurate expression of the order in which the mind proceeds in acquainting itself with the object-matter of knowledge, for I well know that more or fewer steps may be made; but I think it will convey to the mind of the reader with sufficient clearness the great educational truth under consideration.

The contents of a text-book must be arranged in accordance with the law now stated. In commencing the study of a branch of learning, it is clear that there is a first step which should be taken, a second that ought to follow, and this introduces a third; and so a whole subject, to be properly studied, must be made up of a series of logically connected parts. A pupil enters school knowing something. The teacher must acquaint himself with what his pupil knows, and then detach from what is unknown to him appropriate matter, and link the known and the unknown together.

6. The Empirical and the Rational Sciences require Different Methods of Instruction.—Knowledge has two sources, the Senses and the Reason. All science based upon the evidence of experience may be call Empirical science, and all science based upon the intuitions of the Reason may be called Rational science. Methods of teaching these two classes of sciences are different.

An Empirical science differs from a Rational science in its *data*, in its *end*, and in its *processes of reasoning*. The data of an Empirical science are facts; its end is the attainment of general laws, and its processes of reasoning are inductive. The data of a Rational science are necessary and universal principles or ideas, its end is the attainment of particular principles, or less general ideas, and its processes of reasoning are deductive. Chemistry is an Empirical science, and Geometry, including its axioms and definitions, has the form of a Rational science; to those acquainted with the nature of both no further exposition is necessary.

There are two modes by which an Empirical science may be taught. By the first, facts are presented, and then the laws that may be inferred from them. By the second, an hypothesis may be assumed, and afterwards search may be made for the facts by which it can be tested; or laws, fully established, may be stated to the unlearned in the form of propositions, and the facts upon which they rest adduced to prove them. In the more advanced stages of an Empirical science, it is possible to anticipate the existence of unascertained facts from a knowledge of the general laws which must control them. In the first mode there are given facts to find laws, and in the second there are given laws, either ascertained or hypothecated, to find facts.

There are likewise two modes of teaching a Rational science. The necessary and universal principles which form the data of such a science may be first communicated, and this may be followed by the demonstration of the particular truths contained in them. This is the first mode. A particular truth or principle may be assumed, and the proof of it be sought for in the necessary and universal principles of which it is a part. This is the second mode. The first mode consists in the evolution of the contents of axioms, definitions, intuitions of the reason; the second consists in demonstrating particular truths, by showing their conformity with universal and necessary truth.

The two modes of teaching an Empirical science differ from the two modes of teaching a Rational science. Take the modes first named with reference to each, and compare them. The source of our knowledge of facts is the Senses, the source of our knowledge of universal and necessary principles is the Reason. When we infer general laws from particular facts we proceed in one way, inductively; but when we attempt to analyze the pure products of the Reason we proceed in quite another, deductively. The conclusion in one case is but the generalization of experience and cannot extend beyond the facts observed, while in the other the conclusion is exact and positive knowledge.

The same differences will appear if we compare the two modes last mentioned. Starting out with an hypothesis or an ascertained law in Empirical Science may be the same as commencing with the assumption of a particular truth in a Rational Science, but here the similarity between the two modes of procedure ends, for proving a principle by facts differs very materially from demonstrating it by reasoning.

7. The First Form of Instruction must be Qualitative, next Quantitative, and then a Comparison of Relations.—Things are known only by their qualities. They are the Alphabet of nature. They are the medium of introduction between that which is to know and that which is to be known.

The first form of instruction must be qualitative.

Mark how a child learns. He perceives that things are hard or soft, large or small, few or many, long or short, tough or brittle, hot or cold, white or black, red or yellow, heavy or light, sweet or sour, without at all stopping to measure their several degrees. He distinguishes objects from one another by their kind of qualities. He will learn for instance to distinguish a horse from a cow before he can distinguish horses or cows from one another. The same thing may be inferred from the language of a child, as his first speech is made up of words which stand for *man, dog, clock, cat,* &c., &c. He even uses *pa* and *ma* in a general sense. All this goes to prove the truth that stands at the head of this paragraph, and suggests lessons on objects, lessons on form, consistency, color, and the qualities of things generally.

The second form which instruction should take is quantitative. After having observed a quality we soon begin to limit it—to limit it in space, in time, and in degree. We inquire how large or how small? how long or how short? how much or how little? We invent weights, measures, coins. It is evident that to learn quantities requires closer, more precise, better defined thought than to observe qualities; and such thought is necessary to build up a science. When children have learned the qualities of objects, let them be made to attend to them more closely, to *quantify* them. They should not merely name the form of an object, but tell its length, breadth and thickness; not merely say that a thing is large or small but state how large or how small; they should be taught to measure in ounces and pounds, in pints and quarts, in shades, in degrees, and in numbers.

After instruction has passed through the qualitative and quantitative stages, its further progress must be by a comparison of relations. We discriminate qualities and measure quantities by comparison, but this kind of comparison is not a comparison of relations. We employ such a comparison when we compare causes and effects, means and ends, and the inherent identities and differences of things; and such a comparison is only possible when we are in possession of the qualities and quantities used as data in our reasoning. All works of science, properly so called, are the results of a comparison of relations, and the teacher has, therefore, ample material for imparting the kind of instruction implied in the premises.

8. As conditioned by the Relations of the Object-matter of Knowledge, Methods of Teaching must be Inductive or Deductive, Analytical or Synthetical.—The whole objective world is made up of existences and the laws which control them. Science is made up of such of these as men have been able to observe and find out. Induction means ascending from facts to principles, and this method may be adopted in teaching.

When in the possession of the generalizations of induction, we can use them in the interpretation of new facts and phenomena, and this process is sometimes called deduction, but it is rather a part of induction and is so considered here. No science can be well taught without its use.

It has been shown that the intuitions of the Reason

enable us to apprehend certain necessary and universal principles and that these contain other principles embodied in them. Deduction, as I understand it, is the evolution of particular principles from necessary and universal principles, and as such must be the method of study in all the Rational Sciences. Properly there is no induction in Mathematics or Logic, and surely there is none in Ethics or Æsthetics.

As the inductive is the only method applicable to the Empirical Sciences, and the deductive is the only method applicable to the Rational Sciences, and as all science may be included in these classes, it follows that methods of teaching must be either inductive or deductive.

Apart from mere perception or intuition, every operation we are capable of performing upon the object-matter of knowledge may be generalized into the processes of multiplication and division. In our investigations of nature, she never presents herself to us in her minutest subdivisions. With solvents, dissecting-knives, and microscopes we must search for these. Earth, water, air, animal and vegetable organisms are made to yield up their hidden elements. This is the process of division or analysis.

Nature does not anywhere, to our view, complete herself. She ignores fractions. We see a number of her animals, her plants, her rocks, her stars, and infer the rest. We laboriously search out laws and truths and combine what we discover into systems of science; but, at best, we know little in comparison with what remains unknown. Science grows; every day adds something to the world's stock cf knowledge. This is the process of multiplication, or synthesis.

All knowledge, as presented in books for study, is a synthesis. The materials of which such knowledge is made up, however, must have been obtained mainly by means of analysis. If in teaching a science we follow the method by which it grew up, the process must be synthetical, but if we take it as it is, and divide and subdivide it into parts until we find the elements upon which it is based, the process is analytical. Both processes are equally legitimate, and both should be used in almost every lesson. Authors of text-books are accustomed to apply the terms analytical and synthetical to their works with very little judgment. Both analysis and synthesis must be made use of in writing a text-book on any subject, and in teaching it, and no other methods having the same aim are possible.

9. THE OBJECT-MATTER OF KNOWLEDGE, AS IT EXISTS IN NATURE, IS SO CONNECTED AND ARRANGED AS TO FACILITATE ITS ACQUISITION.—The suggestive powers of the mind and the connections of matter correlate. We can imagine a world with its parts confused, disjointed, fragmentary. In ours complete isolation is unknown. The motto *e pluribus unum* could nowhere be so well applied as to the universe.

It is the connections and relations of natural objects that render science possible. Surely there is a foundation in the things themselves for the formation of classes, genera, and species. If a student makes the acquaintance of one fact, that will introduce him to another, and so on in endless succession.

Nature is arranged like a suit of rooms, each with a door opening to the next, A student in sympathy with nature hears voices calling him, and sees hands beckoning him on at every step in his progress, and before him ever floats "the banner with the strange device, *excelsior*."

If the object-matter of knowledge, as it exists in nature, is so connected and arranged as to facilitate its acquisition, so may it be in text-books. A text-book ought to present a subject in its natural order and connections. One point, or one topic, or one lesson ought to suggest the next. It may be well in teaching sometimes to put questions concerning things apart from their connections, but it is best to first teach them in their connections.

10. THE MATTER OF KNOWLEDGE, AS IT LIES IN THE MEMORY, HAS CONNECTIONS AND RELATIONS WHICH INCREASE ITS AVAILABILITY.—If the connections and relations of knowledge are observed in acquiring it, it will preserve these connections and relations as it lies in the memory, and the same conditions that rendered its acquisition more easy, will also aid in making it available. In addition, however, there are other laws which apply to acquired knowledge that do not apply to the objective realities from which it was derived. Things originally disconnected or unrelated, may have been learned at the same time, or in such way as to link them together in the memory. Besides, the laws of association seem constantly operative in assorting the materials of knowledge as they exist in the mind. They bring like things together, and separate things that are

unlike. A well disciplined memory has a place for everything, and keeps everything in its place.

If the object-matter of knowledge, as it lies in the memory, has such connections and relations as have now been pointed out, they must make it more available. A man of business can settle an account in a few moments, it may be, if all the papers relating to it are kept together, but, if they are scattered about, hours may be occupied in doing the same work, and even then it may be done inaccurately. It is just so with the materials of knowledge as they lie in the memory. These materials are too vast to be dealt with as individual things, they can only be made available to the powers which recall and hold them up for contemplation, by forming them into trains, arranging them in clusters, uniting them in series, or associating them in classes. Teachers, who would not see much of their labor lost, must conduct their work mindful of these facts.

11. New Discoveries in Science and New Inventions in the Arts are still possible, and Methods of Instruction should prompt the Young to make them. — Discoveries are constantly being made in all departments of science. Never before was the progress of science so rapid. The harvest seems ripe, and every reaper is blessed with a share of fruit. And still all that has been done is little in comparison with what remains to be done.

What is true in the field of science is true also in the field of art. It may be that the same rapid progress is not apparent with respect to the Fine Arts, but it is especially manifest in all departments of the Mechanic and Useful Arts; and still every day human ingenuity brings to light some new invention.

I take it that education means something more than merely conning the facts and repeating the reasonings of text-books. If properly instructed, pupils will desire to look beyond what they have been taught, or what they have simply learned. They will feel that work has been left for them to do, and they will desire to do it. The highest aim of teaching is not to store the mind with the accumulated knowledge of ages, but to arm it with energy and skill; not to enable pupils merely to solve problems in Mathematics, construe sentences in Grammar, or answer questions in Philosophy, but to inspire them with a love of study, to awaken in their minds an animating, life-giving power, that does not rest satisfied with present attainments but is ever striving to open up new truths, to express new beauty, or to contrive new ways of lessening labor or effecting good.

Few, if any, great thinkers were ever made by books. A mathematician very inferior to Newton or La Place can follow the reasoning of the Principia or the Mécanique Céleste. Bacon and Locke are read by school-boys who talk flippantly of the Inductive Philosophy and the doctrine of Innate Ideas. When once conquered, nature's noblest truths grow comparatively tame. To secure the best mental discipline, we teach too much at second-hand. We rely too much upon books. We suffer the mind's productive powers to lie too nearly dormant. We follow too closely in the paths beaten by others to gain the advantage of that vigorous self-thinking, which is necessary to wrench new truth from nature. Those methods of teaching should be adopted which would throw pupils most upon their own resources, which would call out all the originality that they may possess, which would lead them to repeat the experiments and verify the conclusions of others, and urge them on to add their mite to the sum of human knowledge and human ingenuity.

12. Nature everywhere courts Investigation by a System of Attractions which enlist the Attention, and induce Increased Activity in the Powers by which we Remember, Reflect, Reason and Philosophize; and, therefore, Methods of Teaching should be Suggestive.—Pupils should not be made mere passive recipients of knowledge. Many teachers tell too much. They communicate facts, answer questions, solve problems, and their pupils receive their instruction in blank wonder or stupid indifference. With such teaching knowledge is merely received like grain into a granary or freight into the hold of a ship. Such teachers are like apothecaries or grocers, and simply deal out their stock in trade to their waiting customers. At the best they can only store the memory with facts which must lie there, cumbrous, undigested, and useless.

The search for knowledge should not be characterized by a blind activity on the part of the pupil. We have just seen that a teacher may aid his pupils too much, it is just as true that he may aid them too little. A due regard to the economy of the mental forces will not admit of their useless expenditure. Pupils without direction as to what or how to study may waste their time in fruitless efforts. A traveller in a strange city without a guide may easily lose his strength in ill-directed efforts to find his way, so a timely hint from a teacher may relieve a pupil from a difficulty that is wearing away his time and wearying his patience without conducing to any useful end. The teacher can guide his pupil without carrying him along, he can direct his work without performing it, he can pilot his bark without doing all the rowing.

Progress in study should not be merely mechanical. It is easily possible for pupils to go over studies without learning them. Their progress is measured too often by the quantity of the work looked at, rather than the quality of the work done. Some teachers are at great pains to relieve their pupils from the trouble of thinking. They are constantly watchful to remove every difficulty from their pathway, and, by leading questions, make them seem to know that of which in reality they are ignorant. If learning could be obtained in this way, the road to it would be a "royal" one—a kind of rail-road, ready-graded and well provided with cars and motive power, to transport swiftly along those who are in search of knowledge, and who meanwhile can sit or sleep.

In opposition to those methods of teaching which make the condition of the learner one of passive reception, one of blind activity, or one of mechanical progression, we say that methods of teaching should be suggestive—should prompt pupils to earnest self-exertion. Facts should be communicated in such a manner as to suggest other facts; one effort in reasoning, stimulate to other efforts; one trial of strength, induce other trials; one difficulty overcome, excite an ambition to triumph over other difficulties. The teacher should create interest in study, incite curiosity, promote inquiry, prompt investigation, inspire self-confidence, give hints, make suggestions, tempt pupils on to try their strength and test their skill.

Nature teaches according to the suggestive method. The phenomena of animal and vegetable organisms of earth, and air, and sky, are so many hints to induce man to investigate her mysteries. Grecian artists take a hint from plants and trees, and Doric and Corinthian columns adorn their country's proudest cities; Newton takes a hint from a falling apple, and the ponderous planets roll in harmonious grandeur about the universe, in obedience to his law of gravitation; Watt takes a hint from a hissing tea-urn, and we have the steam-engine; Hugh Miller takes a hint from the curious fossils which his boyish pranks exhumed, and the Old Red Sandstone of his loved Scotland spreads forth its treasures in a voice so eloquent that the whole world listens.

Nature teaches according to the suggestive method. She has her picture galleries, and her galleries of statues, her stupendous architecture, her rich museums, and her immense zoological and botanic gardens; to all the enjoyments of which she invites men eagerly, freely, without money and without price.

Nature teaches according to the suggestive method. She excites curiosity, courts investigation, asks to have her riddles read; sometimes, silently persuading the willing to examine her treasures, and sometimes compelling the indolent to study her laws by making obedience to them essential to their well-being.

(One of my best lessons in teaching was taught me by a robin. It was in my garden, and the mother-robin was teaching her young brood to fly. A little robin sat upon the nest and seemed afraid to move. The mother-bird came and stood by its side, stroked it with her bill, and then hopped to a neighboring twig and stood awhile as if to induce the little bird to follow. Again and again she repeated her caresses, and then hopped nimbly to the same twig. At length the little bird gained courage, and to the great joy of its mother, shook its weak wings, started and stood by her side. Another more distant twig was now selected, and further effort brought the little bird to it also. And so the process was repeated many times, until the timid fledgling now grown quite bold could sail away with its mother over woodlands, fields, and meadows.)

13. THE STUDY OF THE SCIENCES DOES NOT IN ITSELF LEAD TO VIRTUE.—Virtue may be defined as conformity of conduct to the rule of right, and a virtuous man is one who conforms his conduct to the rule of right. But the rule of right cannot be found to inhere in things—neither in their fitness, their harmony, nor their relations. No study of the sciences, however profound, can reveal it, although such study may prepare the way for its full appreciation.

Looking to the same conclusion is the fact that many great scholars have been bad men, and many good men have been poor scholars.

But while no searching among the sciences will discover the rule of right, we intuitively conceive an ideal of the perfection and worth of the human spirit. That there is a real thing corresponding to this ideal conception is most certain, although it cannot be made an object of scientific investigation. The right is to add perfection and worth to the human spirit, and study when pursued with this end in view is virtuous. Those means are virtuous which are legitimately used to attain virtuous ends.

In the light of what has been said it is easy to define the relation of intellectual education to wrong-doing or crime. The moral value of an intellectual education depends upon the end for which it is sought. It is bad if sought for selfish or wicked purposes. It is good if sought for the purpose of benefiting mankind, of dignifying the human character, or of honoring God; if sought to gain knowledge, to attain discipline—ends within itself, although among its gettings one will not find wisdom, yet its tendencies must be indirectly on virtue's side.

14. WHAT WE CAN KNOW IS EVERYWHERE BOUNDED BY WHAT MUST REMAIN UNKNOWN.—An apple falls from a tree in a garden. A wise man, watching it, is moved to search for the cause. He observes many similar phenomena, and ascertains that all of them are controlled by a common law. He calls it the law of gravitation, and finds, after careful investiga

tion, that its influence extends to the heavenly bodies and keeps the planets in their orbits. But can any one tell us what the law of gravitation is in itself? or what may be its cause? A Geologist may trace with indefatigable labor the changes through which our earth has passed; he may ascend from the present condition of things to that which immediately preceded it, and from that to the next, and so on until he finds the earth at first to have been without form and void, and with darkness resting on the face of the deep, or until it appears as a vast nebulous mass of fluid-matter floating in space, and yet be compelled to leave the whole mystery of creation unsolved. Who can define space? Who can measure time? Who can mount up to the beginning of things, or fathom their end? Who, indeed, can take up the ends of the thread of his own consciousness?

What we can know is everywhere bounded by what must remain unknown. But what can we know? We can know all that is finite and relative, although we cannot number the years it will take the race to do it. We can do more, we can know *that* there is an *infinite*, an *absolute*, a *God*, but *what* they are it is beyond our power to find out. Philosophy, mis-called so, has never been able to exclude from the human consciousness the idea that there is something that extends beyond all possible experience, that back of all phenomena there is some actuality in which they inhere, or from which they spring, that there must be a great First Cause. The human consciousness is right. This idea must be answered by a reality. It is impossible not to believe it. It must be or nothing can be. But while we have firm ground for faith in such a reality, we can construct no science of the unconditioned. What we know must be derived from Revelation. We see with human vision, but cannot understand without supernatural assistance.

If these views are true they will prevent an over-estimate of the extent and value of scientific attainments. They show that the knowable has limits; and they show, too, that even the basis of the knowable is faith. Science will thus learn to walk in the humble sphere God designed for her.

They will also furnish a ground upon which to establish the doctrines of Religion. They are equally at variance with Atheism on the one hand, and Pantheism on the other. They make certain our knowledge of the existence of God, but in limiting our knowledge of Him to this fact, they necessitate a Revelation, and leave room for the most exalted faith.

BUILDING THE FOUNDATION.

THE Naturalist finds classification necessary to enable him to handle the immense number of facts which observation brings to light in any one branch of science. It will surprise no one, then, that in a discussion concerning Methods of Instruction, which requires the whole object-matter of knowledge to be kept in view, some systematic arrangement of the various branches of knowledge is necessary as a preliminary condition.

A certain amount of knowledge is now in the possession of mankind. If we could determine the process by which it was obtained, or how it grew up in the mind, a great step would be taken in the way of ascertaining a correct method of teaching, for knowledge must be imparted in the manner it can best be learned. If History tells anything on this point, it ought to be consulted.

It is not a matter of indifference as to what kind of knowledge is first imparted. There is much which a child can understand, and much that can only be comprehended by full-grown men. In any particular branch of knowledge some things depend upon other things, and thus necessitate a series of connected steps in teaching.

In building a foundation for our proposed Methods of Instruction, it may be well to consider:

I. The Classification of Knowledge.
II. The Genesis of Knowledge.
III. The Order of Study.

The close attention of the student is invited to the discussion of each of these topics, as he will find therein a key to much that follows:

I. The Classification of Knowledge.

A classification of knowledge is possible from two stand-points. Its object-matter consists of the universal whole of things. The whole of things has its divisions and subdivisions — its kingdoms, classes, orders, genera, and species. It is for Philosophy to find the trunk, and trace out the branches of the tree of knowledge; or it is for Philosophy to find a principle of classification, and apply it. This stand-point is that of the objective relations of knowledge.

Laws control all our mental operations. Science could not result from lawless thought. If we could mark the point at which the thinking process begins and measure the successive stages of its unfolding, we might be able to classify knowledge from the order in which its several parts are evolved. This stand-point is that of the subjective laws of thought.

To a mind with infinite powers a classification of knowledge is possible, both from the relations of things and from the laws of thought; but the results of one mode would be the same as of the other. When men attempt to classify knowledge, they must proceed in the same way; but their imperfect understanding of the relations of things on the one hand, and of the laws of thought on the other must always render their results incomplete, if it does not cause them to be erroneous.

Since knowledge is the product of the mind within upon the world without, it would seem that there could be formed a classification of knowledge founded upon its historical development, which would be sufficient at least for practical purposes, combining, as it might, the advantages of both the preceding methods; but even here there is little agreement among those who have attempted it.

Before any systematic discussion respecting Methods of Instruction can take place, some scheme for the classification of knowledge must be adopted; and, seeing this, diligent search has been made to find one suited to the purpose. Many have been examined, but all of them seemed open to serious objection. Comte's is the best known classification of the sciences, made with respect to the matter of which they are composed. His classification is as follows: Mathematics, Astronomy, Physics, Chemistry, Physiology, Social Physics. The principle which determines the order of the. series is the relative degree of simplicity in the subject-matter. Without naming the several objections that may be made to this classification of the sciences as such, it is enough to show its want of adaptation to the purposes of teaching to say that the mental nature of no child will admit his being first taught Mathematics, next Astronomy, and so on to the end of the series. Hegel may be taken as the ablest representative of the class of Philosophers who classify the sciences with respect to the laws of thought by which they are evolved. But he begins with Logic, or the science of pure ideas — a science he has scarcely made clear to the wisest men, to say nothing of children. Herbert Spencer's classification of the sciences, founded upon the relative degree of abstractness in the matter of the various classes comprised in it, is more exhaustive, and, I think, more philosophical than that of Comte, but it cannot be used to any more advantage in teaching, as his first class comprises what is most abstract, while the work of instruction must commence with what is wholly concrete. Our own countryman, Rev. Dr. Hill, President of Harvard University, has arranged and expounded with great ability a classification of the sciences based upon the order in which the several sciences are developed; but, as has been already intimated, and as will be more fully shown hereafter, the *elements* of all the sciences are so nearly cotemporaneous in origin that it is practically impossible to fix their position in an order of time. A course of study, therefore, must commence with the elements of *all* the sciences, and not as Dr. Hill states in the order of his classes, Mathesis, Physics, History, Psychology, and Theology. It ought to be added, however, that, somewhat in violation of his own theory, as it seems to me, Dr. Hill advocates in practice the simultaneous study of the different branches of knowledge.

Failing to find in any of the schemes of classification known to me, those requisites which the discussion contemplated seems to demand, I will *group* into several great classes the matter taught in our schools, trusting to the Philosopher of a future day to accomplish what I now feel myself unable to do. These classes have been formed with special reference to teaching. *They differ most in the elements they contain capable of modifying Methods of Instruction.* Still, branches of knowledge have not been thrown together independent of what is considered to be their essential relationships, nor in the general arrangement is all reference to the order of growth in which knowledge is built up in the mind overlooked. It will be perceived, however, that these classes of studies often involve one another. From the nature of the case, it is impossible to form a classification to which this may not be made an objection. The principles of the various branches of knowledge necessarily overlap and interlace, for there is in reality but one science. Nature is a whole, and one science must be involved in all other sciences. It ought to be remarked further that the elements of all the sciences are, in their beginnings, equally simple. Nor can one science ever attain perfection without help from the other sciences. The simplest fact that can be observed must have a connection with the most profound truths. There is no proper hierarchy of the sciences.

The classes it is thought proper to make, are the following:

FIRST CLASS. — *The Elements of Knowledge.* — The elements of knowledge are the perceptions of the sense and the intuitions of the reason. Upon these, as a basis, all knowledge is built up.

By perceptions of the sense is meant whatever can be seen, heard, felt, or directly known by the senses — facts and phenomena. Included in this class are the color, form, size, weight, and number of objects; such qualities as hardness and softness, smoothness and roughness, sweetness and sourness, loudness and softness; and such phenomena as appear to the senses in the world about us.

By intuitions of the reason are meant those regulative principles of the human mind which render all experience possible. A child may be wholly unconscious of them, it may be a long time before he can give them verbal expression, but they are ever operative, universal, and necessary. It cannot be supposed that any mental operation, even the simplest act of perception, takes place without the control of law; and a careful analysis of such acts will reveal the fact that they involve certain universal and necessary principles which admit of statement. A very young child, for example, knows its mother, but the law of identity and difference, by which it does so, cannot, of course, be understood. A boy who has his ball in his pocket is quite sure it cannot be in the pocket of another boy, although he may not be able to appreciate the axiom that "A thing cannot be in different places at the same time." He knows, too, that a whole pie is equal to the sum of all the pieces into which it is cut, if he can find no fit expression for the principle that enables him to know it. Pages of illustrations might be given, but these are sufficient to show that the principles upon which the profoundest Philosophy must rest are found operative in the minds of children, and must be considered among the elements of knowledge.

All science must rest upon the basis now pointed out, but the arts have science itself for a basis; and soon after a child is in possession of the elements of the sciences, he begins to operate with, or upon, them in such a way as to produce what may be called the elements of the arts. He imitates sounds; he carves sticks, and moulds clay; he paints his face or clothes with berries; he builds houses with stones or blocks; he makes figures in the sand; indeed, it is not difficult to trace in the plays of children the rude beginnings of many of the arts which have now, in civilized countries, reached such a high degree of perfection.

The first of our classes then includes the elements of knowledge, the elements of the sciences, and the elements of the arts. The discussion of each class of knowledge might embrace the elements upon which it rests; but as teaching must begin by imparting a knowledge of the elements of knowledge in general, without regard to the class to which they belong, the plan adopted is considered the best.

SECOND CLASS.—*Language.*—Language might be classed among the arts, since, like them, it is in part, at least, the product of human skill. It might be classed with the Empirical sciences, since, like them, many of the laws which govern it have been derived from observation and experiment. And, again, it might be classed with the Formal Sciences, since its laws are often identical with the laws of thought. Its great importance, in an educational point of view, however, determines me to consider it by itself.

The class is intended to embrace all those branches of instruction which relate to the acquisition of skill in the use of language, or which treat of language as a science.

Third Class.—*The Formal Sciences.*—Two sciences are designed to be included in this class—Mathematics and Logic. Mathematics gives precise expression to the relations of forms and numbers, and Logic gives precise expression to the laws of thought. Matter could not exist but for Mathematical conditions, and thought is known to us only under Logical conditions. Logic is the more general of the two sciences, for Mathematical reasoning itself is subject to its forms; but their relationship is sufficiently obvious.

Fourth Class.—*The Empirical Sciences.*—Laws learned by induction are called Empirical laws, and the sciences composed of systems of these laws have received the name of Empirical sciences. Or, the Empirical sciences are the sciences which are made up of that knowledge of which experience is the *source.* Among these sciences are Geography, Chemistry, Natural Philosophy, Physiology, Zoology, Botany, Geology, Astronomy, Psychology, &c.

Fifth Class.—*The Rational Sciences.*—The basis of the Rational sciences is the self-evident, necessary, and universal principles which can be directly apprehended by the reason without the intervention of any discursive process. Or, the Rational sciences are the sciences which are evolved from those ideas of which experience is the *occasion*, but not the source. The term Metaphysics might be applied to the whole class; and of its subdivisions I will name but three: *Philosophy*, or the science of THE TRUE; *Æsthetics*, or the science of THE BEAUTIFUL; and *Ethics*, or the science of THE GOOD.

SIXTH CLASS. — *The Historical Sciences.* — History collects the facts relating to the life of man upon the earth, and presents them in systematic narrations. In its higher departments it essays to solve the problem of man's condition and destiny. Into all calculations respecting the Historical sciences, the elements of a free-will and a superintending Providence enter, and these render it necessary to place the Historical sciences in a class by themselves.

Events cannot be recorded or accounted for before they have occurred, and hence History complements all other sciences, and cannot be finished until all the future becomes the past.

SEVENTH CLASS.—*The Arts.*—Art in its beginnings may precede science, but in its more advanced stages it must always follow it. Says Mill, "Art necessarily presupposes knowledge; art, in any but its infant state, presupposes scientific knowledge; and if every art does not bear the name of the science upon which it rests, it is only because several sciences are often necessary to form the groundwork of a single art." This explains sufficiently well the place occupied by "The Arts" in our classification of knowledge. The class will be divided into the *Empirical* arts and the *Rational* arts.

II. The Genesis of Knowledge.

It is proposed to inquire how the human race came into possession of the knowledge they now have? Volumes would be required to push the inquiry to its limits; but it is hoped that enough concerning the subject may be stated in a few pages to throw considerable light upon Methods of Instruction. The growth of knowledge in the individual mind must correspond to its historic growth in the mind of the race.

Sufficient has already been said, or will be said in other connections, concerning the genesis of the "Elements of knowledge," and hence this topic will be omitted in the present discussion. The order followed in the discussion of the other topics under this head will be that of the preceding classification

The Genesis of our Knowledge of Language.—Several theories of the origin of language have been proven fallacious. It is now acknowledged that no ready-formed vocabulary could have been the gift of God. While some words, in all languages, are imitations of sounds heard in nature, the vast majority of them cannot be accounted for by any system of Onomatopœia. Interjections are, doubtless, found in all languages, but that all other parts of speech are derived from these has never been proven, and is past belief. The most profound of modern Philologists have reached the conclusion that man was endowed by his Creator with the *power of naming*, and that he exercises this power in the same way as a bird sings. Multitudes of words were produced in the early ages which perished, but certain root-words, four or five hundred in number, survived the "struggle for life," and now form the basis of all languages. These root-words are the generous parents of whole tribes of other words, which, by being modified in meaning, compounded and inflected, swell the number of words in some languages to eighty or a hundred thousand.

But a teacher is not so directly interested in questions concerning the origin of language as he is in those concerning the manner in which children, in ordinary circumstances, acquaint themselves with human speech.

I do not doubt that the same speech-forming instinct or faculty exists now as in the early ages of the world's history, and that if the race were to lose all knowledge of the words they now use they would produce new ones. But children do not create a new language, they merely acquire the power to use one already in existence. How do they acquire it? First, they notice objects or actions. Then they hear certain verbal sounds associated with them, and finally learn to imitate these sounds. They are aided in the whole process by an innate desire to know and to speak. An English child learns English because he hears English words and English forms of expression. Other languages are learned in the same way. The words a child first learns are those that stand for objects or actions which are most prominently presented to him, or in which he feels most interest. Of this class are *pa*, *ma*, *puss*, *dog*, *horse*, *door*, *hat*, *clock*, *bell*, &c., &c., or *run*, *walk*, *ride*, *turn*, *bark*, *sing*, &c., &c. The same principle holds good with regard to the manner in which the ability to use forms of expression consisting of two or more words is acquired. The parts of speech a child generally uses first are the noun and the verb, and those he next uses are the adjective and the adverb; and it requires much practice before he constructs whole sentences in talking.

It may be fairly inferred from what has been said that the best mode of teaching young children the use of language is to make their acquaintance with things as extensive as possible, and to allow them full opportunity of hearing things talked about, and of talking about them themselves.

THE GENESIS OF OUR KNOWLEDGE OF THE FORMAL SCIENCES.—There can be no doubt that Mathematics arose from very humble beginnings. I am not aware that any savage tribe has yet been found who had not some idea of number, but some are known to exist who cannot count beyond five. Pressed by necessity, primitive men began to enumerate *present* objects. Afterwards they desired to count *absent* objects, but finding the mental effort too great they resorted to counting their fingers as children do now, hence the application of the word, *digit*, to a number less than ten. When they did not count their fingers, they may have used pebbles, as is indicated by the word *calculus*, or sticks, or leaves, or grains of corn. Some nations were found to use *five* as the basis of their scale of notation, probably because five is the number of fingers on one hand; and many use *ten*, probably because that is the number of fingers on both hands. Weights and measures, too, arose in the same way. No one can be mistaken in the significance of words like *grain*, *pennyweight*, *carat*, *barleycorn*, *foot*, *span*, *hand*, *day*, *month*, &c., &c. It is clear that the art of numbering must have, for a long time, consisted in performing the simplest operations upon objects—must have been wholly concrete. By and by, however, the ability to use larger numbers was acquired, abstractions were performed, symbols were invented representing, at first, perhaps, only lines or strokes, or combinations of lines or strokes, more difficult calculations were made, and Arithmetic began to assume something of its present form.

The annual overflowings of the river Nile, in Egypt, rendered it difficult to preserve the boundaries of the lands owned by particular individuals, and it is said that Geometry was first used for the purpose of measuring land in that country, and hence derived its name. Doubtless the land was measured in Egypt, and the circumstance alluded to may have rendered it necessary to measure it with more than usual accuracy; but it is evident that some of the principles of Geometry must have been applied from the earliest dawn of the human intellect. They were used in constructing dwellings, in making domestic utensils, articles of clothing, and weapons of warfare, in overcoming resistances, and in calculating distances. Indeed, the idea of form must be cotemporary in origin with the idea of number, if it does not precede it, and both come into the mind at a very early age. The arts now referred to had probably made considerable advancement before any particular notice was taken of the Geometrical principles involved in them, but, by and by, their further progress rendered such notice necessary, and Geometrical truths began to be recognized. Other truths were found by demonstration to be contained in these, and a mass of loose Geometrical knowledge floated about in the minds of men, until such Philosophers as Thales, Pythagoras, Plato and Euclid reduced the whole to systematic order, and found fit expression for the universal and necessary principles upon which it is based.

Sir William Hamilton defines Logic as the "Science of the necessary Form of Thought." Abstract as is the conception of this science in the minds of Philosophers like Hamilton, and lofty as are now its claims, it is probable that its beginnings consisted in the simplest reasonings. Children reason now almost from infancy, and we may well suppose that men did so from the earliest times. The circumstances by which they were surrounded compelled them to think. They must be protected from cold and heat, they must have food, they must defend themselves from animals and from enemies of their own species, and all this required the exercise of reason. Doubtless, it was soon observed that some reasoned well, made safe calculations, managed skilfully. These were considered wise men, and often became trusted rulers. In the course of time many observations were made upon reasonings, their correct forms were in a measure determined, and sources of error were pointed out. If the History of Logic could be written, such fragments would be found among all people who have attained any considerable degree of civilization. They existed in ancient India, in Egypt, in Greece, and most likely in other countries of antiquity. It remained for the giant mind of Aristotle to collect them, and construct of them a system that has won the admiration of the world.

From what has been said, it seems likely that Logic at first consisted of descriptions of certain disconnected forms of thinking which men made use of in carrying on the common affairs of life; that afterwards these forms were compared and simplified; and that eventually they became entirely abstracted from the matter which had filled them, and Logic took its place along side of Mathematics as a Pure science.

THE GENESIS OF OUR KNOWLEDGE OF THE EMPIRICAL SCIENCES.—Efforts have been made to discover the origin of the sciences belonging to this class, and to write their history. Such efforts have been successful in accumulating a vast amount of valuable knowledge, but no one has ever been able to point out the time at which men first began to observe the facts upon which they are based. When well considered, this is not at all wonderful, since the very earliest inhabitants of the earth must have observed some of the phenomena of nature, and these observations of which no record could be kept became the basis of all knowledge.

Our American savages have among them no such thing as science, and yet they are in possession of many of the elements of the sciences. They have marked the places of some of the stars, and can calculate the lapse of time and the change of seasons. They can find their way through the forests, and have learned much concerning the properties of trees and plants and the habits of animals. They are familiar with the forms and motions of the clouds and the phenomena of rain, hail, snow, &c. They are acquainted with the processes of fermentation and distillation, and have noted those of growth and decay. Indeed, they are remarkably close observers of nature, and I do not believe that any science can be named of whose fundamental facts they do not know something. What is true of these untutored Indians is true of all tribes or nations of uncivilized men. Among them there is needed but the ability to colligate and generalize to commence the evolution of the sciences.

Children, too, become acquainted with a vast number of facts—facts belonging technically to all the sciences, especially the Empirical sciences; and these they can be taught when older to arrange into systems of science.

The history of science and the condition of the knowledge in the possession of uncivilized men and of children indicate that the Empirical sciences are merely the extension by means of reasoning of the accumulated facts which experience has made known. Common knowledge becomes scientific knowledge by classification and generalization. A common man becomes a philospher by learning to reason.

For the purpose of illustrating the position now taken, a few facts will be stated in the history of a single science, Botany. "In the accounts of rudest tribes," says Whewell, "in the earliest legends, poetry, and literature of nations, pines and oaks, roses and violets, the olive and the vine, and the thousand other productions of the earth, have a place, and are spoken of in a manner which assumes that, in such kinds of natural objects, permanent and infallible distinctions had been observed and universally recognized." In the early stages of man's career, however, plants and parts of plants received names as individuals and of course were not carefully noticed in their connections and relations. Then came a time when much inconvenience was felt from the use of loose and ambiguous terms and from the multitudes of objects which required naming, and men resorted to classification as a relief.

The first classifications of plants were very vague and unscientific. Among them were that which divided plants into *trees*, *shrubs*, and *herbs*; that of Theophrastus which divided them according to *size*, *use*, *place of growth*, *lactescence*, and *generation*; and that of Dioscorides, which arranged them according to their qualities, as *aromatic*, *alimentary*, *medicinal*, and *vinous*. It is easy to see in all these classifications, and in others like them, the attempt to systematize the results attained by the superficial observations of men. The work was rendered more difficult by the many qualities which an active fancy and a love of the marvelous had attributed to plants.

The kind of classifications just named was gradually displaced by others more systematic. The fanciful gave way before the real. Step by step, closer investigations revealed new facts, until, at last, such Naturalists as Linnæus and Jussieu were enabled to place the science of Botany upon the firm basis of the inherent resemblances and differences existing in the vegetable world.

The Genesis of our knowledge of the Empirical sciences generally, is believed to be fairly exemplified by the Genesis of our knowledge of Botany.

THE GENESIS OF OUR KNOWLEDGE OF THE RATIONAL SCIENCES.—We observe facts in the material world; upon investigation these facts are found to have certain relations which, when properly expressed, are called laws—the laws of matter. We observe, by means of our consciousness, facts in the world of mind; these, too, have their relations which can be expressed in the form of laws—the laws of mind. Thus are constituted the Empirical sciences. All such laws, however, are dependent, contingent, and subject to modification or limitation.

This is not the place to enter upon a lengthy discussion in order to show that we are in the possession of principles wholly unlike those which make up the Empirical sciences, and which, indeed, may be made to form the basis of a class of sciences by themselves; but among these principles I would place—

Certain Primary Ideas.—No one will maintain that our idea of space or time corresponds with our conception of the sum of our experienced spaces and times. Our conception of the infinite and the absolute is, at least, beyond our knowledge of the finite and the relative. The ideas which we have of the true, the beautiful, and the good, greatly transcend the perfections of any object which our senses have made known to us. We think of God, not merely as a projection of our own personality with all its human frailties, but as a Being endowed with all possible virtues, without spot or blemish.

And *Certain Generalized Intuitions.*—I mean by Generalized Intuitions, the axioms of Mathematics and Logic, the maxims of Philosophy, Æsthetics, and Ethics, and the foundation principles of all other sciences. I call them "Intuitions," because they are perceived by the mind directly, without the intervention of any discursive process. They are without doubt, an outgrowth of our Primary Ideas. I describe them by the word "Generalized," since, as it seems to me, they are not found, or do not come into the mind, except upon the presentation, or representation, of an object or a succession of objects, either material or mental. I distinguish them from Empirical laws because they transcend experience and are self-evident, universal, and necessary. Take the axiom—two straight lines cannot enclose a space, and its truth is perceived at once; but, although felt to be self-evident, universal, and necessary, such a truth would never have occurred to a mind wholly unacquainted with straight lines.

The Rational Sciences, then, are the sciences which treat of those Ideas which are the primary sources of knowledge, and those Intuitions which may be generalized into principles that are self-evident, universal, and necessary. What has been their manner of growth?

Primary Ideas, as previously stated, come into the mind upon the presentation or representation of some object. They are not innate in the sense in which power of remembering or reasoning is innate; but they necessarily attend the function of cognition.

These Ideas do not comprehend the infinite or the absolute, although a *belief* in the infinite and absolute is founded upon them. They are things of degree, widening as experience widens, but always transcending experience. Children and savages have ideas of space and time, of the true, the beautiful, and the good, which all the matter of their experience cannot fill; but they cannot fully realize these ideas or find expression for them. As men advance in knowledge their Primary Ideas become more clear and more comprehensive, and finally attract attention, and find articulate expression. Once held up before the mind as objects of study, philosophers evolve their contents and arrange them in scientific order, deduce from them certain definitions, axioms, maxims, and fundamental truths, and construct upon this foundation, as I suppose, all the branches of Metaphysics. It will be noticed that I base these sciences upon *such ideas as we can form* of the object-matter now under consideration. I do not maintain that a "*Philosophy* of the Unconditioned" is possible, but I do maintain that a Philosophy of such of our knowledge as transcends experience is possible, and I think I have shown how it originates.

THE GENESIS OF OUR KNOWLEDGE OF THE HISTORICAL SCIENCES.—History is an account of what man has done, and how, and why he has done it.

History may consist in a narration of facts, and in that case the Genesis of our knowledge of it is very obvious. All tribes of uncivilized men have their traditions. They are related by parents to their children, and by the old to the young. They contain some truth intermixed, doubtless, with much that is fabulous. When a people become a little more advanced in civilization, these traditions, in the form of myths or legends, are frequently sung or recited in verse by individuals who make a profession of it. They are sometimes commemorated by rude figures cut upon the surface of rocks, or by rough piles of stone. After having learned to write, it is not long till men begin to compose History; at first full of fancy and fiction, by and by it becomes more truthful, and assumes its proper place in Literature. Thus, the simple stories that may be told in the cabins or around the council-fires of a tribe of savages, become, in the course of centuries, the basis of the great tomes written by a thousand pens, which narrate in choice words and polished style the teeming events of the past.

History may be the exposition of a Philosophy, and then our study of it can only properly begin after we have acquired much other knowledge upon which it depends. The Philosophy of History is the Philosophy of man; and as he was the last of created things—the crowning glory of the whole, to understand him all else must be understood. A knowledge of him, indeed, is necessary to complete all other knowledge; but, in the order of things, we must approach the study of mind through the study of matter.

THE GENESIS OF OUR KNOWLEDGE OF THE ARTS.—Man undoubtedly was created with the power of making things. He was an artificer from the beginning. Birds build nests, beavers make dams, bees construct combs in which to store their honey, and the most primitive races of men were endowed with similar but higher mechanical powers. It is not possible to account for the origin and growth of the Arts without admitting that this *inventive, creating* instinct is the foundation upon which they are based. This power was probably stimulated into exercise by necessity. Food, clothing, protection from the elements and from wild beasts, were, at least, needed by the earliest inhabitants of the earth, and such wants must be supplied; and, doubtless, under their pressure the first rude Arts made their appearance. The kinds of food first used were nuts, berries and other fruits, and sometimes roots. Flesh did not come into use until later, and then it was eaten raw. No cooking was done in these early times. The primitive inhabitants of the earth clothed themselves with the leaves of trees or the skins of animals. Caves and hollow trees were the first houses, and clubs and stones the first implements of warfare. With these to start with, the human race commenced that career of progress which excites the wonder of all who contemplate it, but which can be illustrated here by only a few examples.

The Greeks classed Drawing, Writing, and Painting together, as having a common basis, and applied to them the common name γραφική, or Graphics. It is to be presumed that men would early endeavor to represent the strange forms which they saw about them. The first written communications with one another were probably of this nature. As a matter of fact a kind of picture-writing or picture-drawing, has been found to exist among a number of tribes low down in the scale of civilization. These rude drawings were sometimes colored, and thus came the first attempts at Painting. The colors, however, were put on with little skill, just as savages paint their faces or children daub pictures on paper. It was not till influenced by the fine scenery and polished culture of Greece that this difficult art assumed any thing like perfection. As Drawing, in the course of time, branched off into Painting, so also it was the source from which Writing was developed. Things were first represented by pictures, and as these, where frequently used, became very familiar, their forms were very much changed and greatly abbreviated to render them more easily and quickly made. By and by, some of them became symbolical, as a picture of a circle represented eternity, and one of a fox, cunning. Then the same characters, or the same characters somewhat modified, were used to represent monosyllabic words, and when these were compounded, syllables of these words. At last they were made to stand for sounds, and the Alphabet was invented. Thanks to some old Egyptian king, whose vanity built the Pyramids and inscribed them all over with hieroglyphics, for these same hieroglyphics tell, in unequivocal language, the story just related. Champollion and others seem to have found among them pictures representing things in every state of transition until they became letters representing sounds; that is, they found the same characters to be ideographic, verbal, syllabic, and phonetic.

Even in the most polished styles of Architecture it is thought the influence of the primitive abodes of men may be traced. The Egyptian style resembles *caves;* the Chinese, *tents;* the Grecian, *huts;* and the Gothic, *hollow trees*, or trees themselves, pine or fir. Trees driven into the earth in rows to support a covering may represent columns wider in diameter below and narrower above as trees are. The bases of columns may have been suggested by blocks of stone placed under wooden pillars to keep them from dampness, and the capitals by boards laid on the tops of such pillars to broaden the place of support for the structure which rested upon them. Sculpture in its beginnings had a close relation to Architecture. Stone, without doubt, was early quarried and cut for the purpose of building. Carvings for ornament on rocks and the walls of caves, succeeded carvings intended to preserve the memory of real forms or interesting events. These carvings were at first slight indentations merely presenting the outlines of the figures, afterwards they were cut out more fully and assumed the form of bas-relief, and finally we may reasonably suppose whole statues were chiseled out. Piles of stone were the first monuments, then came plain monuments cut from solid rocks in place, and these among the Greeks assumed the form of highly beautified sculpture representing gods and men.

Poetry and Music, closely related as they are, probably had a cotemporary origin. No tribe of savages has ever been found who had not forms of measured words and who did not indulge in singing them. The Poetry is often barbarous, and the Music.

a succession of discordant sounds; but they are the first rude beginnings of arts that have done much to elevate mankind. The first musical instruments were probably made of metals, as the Chinese gongs; of the skins of animals, whence our drums; of reeds or the bark of small trees, whence our pipes, flutes, and organs; and of strings, whence lyres, harps, and pianos.

Agriculture must have been practiced very early, but the implements used for loosening the soil were at first sharpened sticks, next came implements of stone, and after long ages those of iron. Some trade was probably carried on by all uncivilized nations, but it consisted merely in exchanges of articles used for food, clothing, or protection. Rivers were at first navigated on logs, which afterwards were hollowed out into canoes. A few of the properties of vegetables seem to have been discovered at an early day, and certain of them used for medicines among all primitive people.

Sufficient has now been said concerning the Genesis of our Knowledge to warrant a few generalizations which have an important educational significance:

First, *Knowledge as a whole seems to have been developed from the common observations of men stimulated by animal or spiritual wants.*—In the early history of the race, the pressure of animal wants seems to have done most to promote science and art; but in all times, and especially in highly civilized nations, men have been moved to the attainment of knowledge by the wants of their spiritual nature. This is the case whenever knowledge is sought for its own sake or with the end in view of making more perfect him who seeks it.

In addition to what has already been said in support of the main proposition, the opinion of the learned Philologist, Max Müller, may be quoted. He says, "However humiliating it may sound, every one of our sciences, however grand their titles, can be traced back to the most humble and homely occupations of half-savage tribes. It was not the true, the good, and the beautiful, which spurred the early philosophers to deep researches and bold discoveries. The foundation-stone of the most glorious structures of human ingenuity in ages to come, was supplied by the pressing wants of a patriarchal and semi-barbarous society."

I know indeed that it is argued by some, that Adam and his immediate descendents must have received knowledge as a gift from the Divine hand, inasmuch as no savage nation has ever been known to civilize itself. But this theory does not account for the fact that new discoveries and new inventions have been made, and surely all that is known concerning the evolution of the sciences and arts is against it. The correct theory probably is that God endowed the first men with the *power of gaining knowledge*, that he has continued so to endow man, and that all progress in learning and skill is owing to the operation of this power moved by causes in the condition and circumstances of men, and prompted at times, doubtless, by the direct agency of the spirit of God. It seems clear to me that the problem of human civilization is impossible of solution without an acknowledgment of the direct interposition of Deity in the affairs of men.

Second. *A Course of Instruction should commence with the General Elements of Knowledge.* — Children evince their knowledge-acquiring power by noticing objects, and learning their qualities and phenomena. They evince their art-producing power by changing the places of objects, and forming them into new combinations; by piling up blocks, building playhouses, cutting figures from paper, and imitating the words and actions of those about them. What has been said concerning the Genesis of our Knowledge goes to show that, as children acquire knowledge now, so men acquired it in the infancy of the race. It is, therefore, clear that instruction must begin with the elements of knowledge.

These elements should be made to comprehend as much as possible — should not be confined to a few particular branches, but be general. It is a great mistake to push children into the higher parts of any one study until they have learned the elements of many studies. For example, the principles of Grammar and Arithmetic are studied by many who ought to be studying the elements of the Natural Sciences, or other branches adapted to their mental condition. Thousands of children are thus mentally surfeited every year, and the result is a mental dyspepsia in early youth that entails, during their whole life-time, sad consequences upon its poor victims.

Third. *The second great step in a Course of Instruc-*

tion should be to acquaint pupils with Particular Branches of Knowledge. — A child learns facts and phenomena as they present themselves. He may, in a single day, learn such as belong technically to twenty different sciences and arts.

At its base all science is united, has only one trunk; but it soon begins to divide and subdivide into numerous branches. The homogeneous becomes the heterogeneous by a wonderful process of differentiation. The undefined elements of general science become the well-defined elements of particular sciences. And as is the growth of the sciences so must they be studied.

Branching from the same trunk, the sciences never lose their reciprocal relationship, and always shed mutual light upon one another, yet they are sufficiently distinct to admit of independent study. Beyond the elements, therefore, the several branches of science may be pursued, each by itself, all together, or a few at a time.

Educational institutions almost universally have what is called a Course of Study. Each pupil studies a few branches at a time, and when he is thought to have completed these to the extent desired, he commences others, and thus goes on until he has mastered the prescribed course. What use has thus sanctioned will generally be found the best policy.

If a pupil enjoy an opportunity of pursuing a course of study wisely arranged according to this plan, it will be well for him to follow it through Common School, High School, and College, and, afterwards, if the desire exist, and the way open, he may apply himself to some particular science or department of science. Considerable general knowledge must be possessed, and a good degree of mental discipline be attained, before fresh investigators can push their inquiries beyond the present limits of some existing science, or make discoveries worthy the name of a new one; and a life-time is too short to accomplish much in a wider, unexplored field of research than a single science affords. In fewer words, the plan proposed is this: teach, first, the elements of the sciences in general; next, teach in detail the most important principles of the several sciences composing a carefully arranged course of study; and last, let those who can, make themselves masters of some special branch of science, and push their inquiries beyond what is known respecting it. This is essentially the plan adopted in countries where learning has made the greatest progress; and it is the only plan which can secure to the student general scholarship under the greatest advantages, and, at the same time, afford him opportunity, with the fairest prospects of success, of fathoming the depths of some special science, and adding, in that direction, something to the sum of human knowledge.

Fourth, *A Course of Instruction should End by Teaching the Relationship and Harmony of all Knowledge.*—It would be a difficult thing to determine the lines which separate one science or one art from another. Knowledge is not composed of independent facts and principles, all its parts belong to one whole; and the Philosopher is always distinguished from the mere Scholar by his broad, comprehensive generalizations which mark the unity of created things and from which may be inferred the unity of the creating Mind.

No course of study can be considered complete until the logical relations of all its parts have been exhibited. Pupils pursuing different studies, treated of in different works by different authors, and sometimes taught by different teachers, are apt to overlook their relationship and harmony. Each branch becomes isolated, and pupils are required to study the details of particular sciences when they ought to be engaged in learning the principles of general science. It is hardly possible in school, for example, to teach, in full detail, any one of the Natural Sciences, but it is possible to teach the great, leading principles of all of them. The specific study of the sciences should, therefore, be followed by the general study of science. A course of study should not end in a number of points but in a centre. The skill of an architect cannot be fully appreciated while his work lies scattered in disjointed fragments, so the value of science is much lessened and its beauty much obscured to him whose study ends in contemplating disconnected facts, broken systems, and inharmonious expressions. Comte says: "The present exclusive speciality of our pursuits, and the consequent isolation of the sciences, spoil our teaching. If any student desires to form an idea of Natural Philosophy, as a whole, he is compelled to go through each department as it is now taught, as if he were to be only an Astronomer, or only a Chemist; so that, be his intellect what it may, his training must remain very imperfect. And yet his object requires that he should obtain general positive conceptions of all the classes of natural phenomena. It is such an aggregate of conceptions of all classes, whether on a great or on a small scale, which must henceforth be the permanent basis of all human combinations. It will constitute the mind of future generations. In order to this regeneration of our intellectual system, it is necesssary that the sciences, considered as branches from one trunk, should yield us, as a whole, their chief methods and their most important results. The specialities of science can be pursued by those whose vocation lies in that direction. They are indispensable, and they are not likely to be neglected, but they can never of themselves renovate our system of Education."

III. The Order of Study.

It was previously stated that the sciences do not admit of a serial arrangement. In their primary elements, all of them are equally simple, and in their ultimate principles all of them are equally difficult. They can be cultivated simultaneously, or they can be cultivated as they grew up, first, in the form of general elements; second, in the form of special sciences; and, last, in the form of the philosophy of science. Upon these points, however, sufficient has already been said.

In the discussion which is to follow, concerning methods of teaching the several branches of study, much care will be taken to point out the order in which the several parts of each branch should be taught, and this will render unnecessary an investigation of the same subject in this place. It is designed here to show what different studies or parts of different studies can be profitably pursued simultaneously. Our aim will not be to name these studies so much with reference to their logical relations among themselves as with respect to their adaptation to the mental condition of pupils when they engage in their study. Constant reference will be had to the Classification of Knowledge already presented.

Our education should never end, but that portion of our days which we appropriately devote almost exclusively to obtaining an education, may be called the school-time of life. Our school-time of life may be divided into four periods; the first embracing the time from birth to the age of five years; the second, from the age of five to ten; the third, from ten to sixteen; and the fourth, from sixteen to twenty-one. The first of these periods may be called *Infancy;* the second, *Childhood;* the third, *Youth;* and the fourth, *Manhood.* This classification will be of much practical value, but from the nature of the case it is a very loose one. The task we undertake is to name the branches of learning or the kind of study suitable for each period. A general statement is all that is practicable, and each teacher must work out the details for himself with the aid furnished him in subsequent chapters.

First Period. — *Infancy.* — The first care of a mother is to preserve her infant's health. The large number of deaths which occur during infancy proves such care to be necessary.

Not less important than the preservation of their health is the formation of the character of young children. Those traits of character which distinguish a child at five years of age are most likely to distinguish him through life. Much influence may be allowed to the laws of hereditary descent, their due weight may be given to the circumstances of the school and of general society, and it will still be true that whether an individual possess the virtues of industry, perseverance, honesty, manliness, bravery, kindness, piety, and the like, or otherwise, will depend mainly upon the home instruction, or rather *home-impressions*, which children receive during the first five years of life. But we are at present concerned only with the intellectual acquisitions which a child can make during the period of Infancy. These intellectual acquisitions have been expressed by the terms Elements of Knowledge, and are considered to form the bases of all we know. Such knowledge comes from an experience with objects, and is best learned, as will be shown hereafter, in series of lessons given without much regard to the scientific arrangement of their subject-matter. All classes of knowledge may be profitably embraced in a single lesson. Here, however, it may be best to point out what a child may learn during the period of Infancy concerning the elementary facts, phenomena, and forms of the great classes into which it has been deemed expedient to divide our knowledge.

An infant learns to speak. It is a wonderful process, and requires the guiding care of parents. The speaking instinct must be encouraged to manifest itself with the utmost freedom. The sounds of the language must be correctly uttered and proper forms of expression must be furnished, and the child's faltering tongue be taught to imitate them. If a child listen to good language, he will know no other. All bad habits of speech should be carefully corrected.

Number is an idea which we obtain very early. Before the age of five, a child may be taught to count objects, and to add and subtract small numbers by their means. He must be able to conceive forms in order to tell one object from another. He reasons, too, and should have his opportunities of so doing multiplied.

Before a child can speak, objects may be given to him, and he will learn many of their properties in playing with them. Well-selected toys may be made to furnish valuable information. The more he is allowed to hear and see, the sharper will be his senses and the more he will remember. It can hardly be said with sufficient emphasis that the kind of instruction most suitable for Infancy is that which is addressed to the senses and the powers of perception—that which can be best imparted by the direct presentation of objects and their phenomena or vivid pictures of them. The intense curiosity of children prompts them to seek what is new, but they notice things as individuals, not in their connections, and nature on the surface so presents them. The Empirical sciences are based upon the facts of experience, and, if allowed fit opportunity, a little child will become acquainted with multitudes of these facts.

During the period now referred to, the principles of the Rational sciences cannot be made the direct object of instruction; but it is very evident that they are operative in the minds of children. They recognize the truth of such axioms as "A whole is greater than any of its parts" in relation to particular things, although they do not generalize them or understand their verbal expression. They also can be trained in a degree to discriminate between truth and falsehood, beauty and deformity, and right and wrong. No part of elementary education can be of greater importance than that of teaching the young to make these recognitions and discriminations, but there is no part of it more neglected.

Nothing delights a child more than stories, narratives, and personal incidents, if related or read in language which he can understand. Good fruit could be produced by instruction of this kind.

Children can learn to sing almost as soon as they can learn to talk. At the age of three or four, they will draw figures on a slate or blackboard, cut paper, mould clay, build play-houses, and imitate many simple, mechanical contrivances. Such educators as Pestalozzi and De Fellenberg understood this want of children and provided for it.

SECOND PERIOD.—*Childhood.*—If during the period of his life between the ages of five and ten years, a child does not learn to speak well, it is scarcely likely that he will ever do so. Pure models should be furnished him; and he may be taught to speak foreign languages as well as his mother-tongue. Exercises in Pronouncing, Spelling, Reading and Composing, may be commenced and prosecuted during this period. The meaning of a great number of words may be learned if properly illustrated and explained. Lessons on classes of words may be given, but Grammar proper is a study too difficult for children under the age of ten.

During this period children can be readily taught to read and write numbers, and to perform the Mathematical operations of Addition, Subtraction, Multiplication, and Division, both of Integers and Fractions. These operations should be performed at first with objects, and both the mental and written forms of solution ought to be practiced. They may engage with great profit in the solution of simple problems involving these fundamental rules, but they cannot make much progress in reasoning about the relations of numbers. Pupils of this age, too, may be made acquainted with Geometrical figures and their properties so far as they can be exhibited to the eye by diagrams or blocks. Any except the simplest attempts at demonstration would be out of place. No generalization of the reasoning process can be understood by a child of ten years of age, and, therefore, theoretical Logic is beyond his reach. He can reason, however, and should be encouraged to use his powers in this respect. His questions should be answered, and he should be led to seek for the causes of things.

From five to ten years of age, the powers of the mind which are predominantly active are the senses, the perceptive faculties, the memory, and the fancy;

and these fit the mind for making observations and storing away facts. It cannot be doubted, therefore, that much time during this period should be spent in the study of the elements of the Empirical sciences. A child may be made familiar with thousands of interesting facts, and learn the names of thousands of interesting objects. He may thus be made acquainted with the elements of Geography, Botany, Zoology, Astronomy, Natural Philosophy, Physiology, and other sciences like them. The simple facts of this class of sciences seem to be particularly adapted to the capacity of children between the ages of five and ten, and peculiarly pleasing to their tastes. They are keenly alive to all that is new, or strange, or curious. Before the age of ten, however, it should be remembered, a child is not prepared to appreciate generalizations, abstractions, systems, or theories, and it is folly to attempt to teach them to him. Children cannot be made philosophers; but the condition of their mental nature admirably fits them for learning the names and more obvious properties of the multitudes of objects which the bountiful hand of God has scattered all about us as if His purpose was to furnish means of pleasing and instructing little children.

Rational science is beyond the capacity of children of ten years of age; but the principles upon which such sciences are founded, as previously stated, may be made operative in their minds. They operate, indeed, in the minds of all persons, however young or ignorant; but by a studied presentation of occasions calculated to call them into activity, the mind receives that discipline which eventually prepares it for their apprehension and systematic elaboration. The kind of instruction, therefore, that was considered proper up to the age of five must be continued to the age of ten and longer. Any attempt to teach a child of this age to account for principles which are to him simply instincts that guide his life, or to make him comprehend even the first steps of a systematically arranged Rational science, would prove a fruitless labor. As inductions from particular facts, such principles can be understood by a child; but as abstract principles, independent of facts but conditioning them, they can be comprehended only by mature minds. To open the minds of his pupils to the comprehension of these principles in the only form in which they can be understood, as a preparation for understanding them in that higher form in which they become our main reliance in solving the greatest problems of life, is the highest duty of the educator.

History, when presented in a form suited to their capacity, has great attractions for children. They like the play of life—like to read accounts of voyages, travels, and past events, and they do not forget what they read. They are especially fond of the novel and the marvelous. Fiction might be made highly useful in the work of education. A Fiction may be a faithful portraiture of life, and as such to be commended. The strong appetite which the young manifest for this kind of literature is not without its meaning. With judicious management it can be gratified without harm, and in due time will give place to other mental appetites, for which it is, in part, a preparation.

In the Arts, at this age, a pupil can be learning to draw and write. His Drawing ought to be confined to copying pictures, drawing simple objects from nature, and inventing easy patterns. He ought to learn to work, to imitate models, and to handle tools. It will do him good to visit shops and manufactories. He should be taught to sing, and may begin to take lessons upon some musical instrument. Pictures will delight him, but not those which represent some abstract idea, but those rather which exhibit life.

THIRD PERIOD. — *Youth.* — With respect to Language, instruction, during this period, should be continued in all that relates to Reading and Composition. The pupil's vocabulary of words should be enlarged by careful study. The Grammar of the English language may be commenced at ten, and, if other languages are to be studied, they may be commenced at the same age. Some progress may be made in speaking, reading, and writing our own and other languages before this age; but their formal study cannot profitably commence earlier. A course of reading in both prose and poetry should be continued through the whole period of youth.

In Mathematics, Arithmetic, Geometry, and Algebra can be completed by the time a pupil is sixteen years of age, at least so far as these subjects are treated of in our ordinary text-books. During this period, pupils must be carefully trained to habits of correct reasoning — they must be taught to observe the laws of Logic in their thinking. The higher generalizations of abstract Logic may be beyond their reach, but they can be made acquainted with the most useful forms of syllogism, and with the modes of discovering truth and exposing error.

Competent to classify and generalize, the youth of from ten to sixteen years of age may study the properties and phenomena of objects in connection with the laws that govern their relations. To do this he must not only observe, but he must search and make experiments; and he should be so taught that he may rise gradually from the sphere of scattered facts to the sphere of united systems. During this period great progress ought to be made in sciences like Geography, Physiology, Natural Philosophy, Chemistry, Botany, and Astronomy. The facts relating to them should be classified, inferences should be drawn, and a general preparation should be made for the full discussion of their highest principles.

The time for the study of the Rational sciences does not come to many before the age of sixteen. Instruction relating to them should, therefore, be continued in the spirit of that described as appropriate for the period of childhood. In addition, however, at about the age of sixteen, pupils may be taught the distinction between universal, necessary, and self-evident truths and such as are empirical. Forms of expression may be given to some of the grand maxims which constitute the basis of all science, and pupils be taught to realize their truth. Undefined standards of truth, beauty, and goodness can be applied with great profit. Progress can be made in the arts which depend upon the principles of the Rational sciences long before these principles themselves can be made an object of thought.

During the period of youth, History should occupy a prominent place among the studies of every pupil who desires a liberal education, or who desires to guide his own life by the lamp of past experience. First in importance is the History of one's own country, then that of other countries most closely related to it, or that of those which have played the most important part in the world's affairs. Biographies of the good and great will be read with avidity, and are well calculated to exert a favorable influence upon the young. The historical development of the several sciences will furnish matter of much interest. From these sources, vast stores of facts can be collected, and will furnish a basis for the generalizations which belong to the Philosophy of History.

Sufficient skill for the ordinary purposes of life may be acquired in Writing and Drawing during this period. Instruction in Vocal Music should continue, and if proficiency in Instrumental Music, Painting, or any other branch of an ornamental education be desirable, it can be most rapidly attained during the years between ten and sixteen. I think the Formal and the Empirical Sciences can be most effectually taught in connection with the application of their principles to the arts of which they are the bases. Sciences like Arithmetic, Chemistry, and Astronomy, excite much more interest in the minds of students when they see that they can be made practical — when they see their use in the arts. When the young exhibit special mechanical talent, or special talent in an art of any kind, that talent should receive special culture.

FOURTH PERIOD.—*Manhood.*—At the termination of this period, the scholastic course of study is supposed to be completed.

Suitable studies in language are Rhetoric, Criticism, Literature, and foreign languages, both ancient and modern.

Studies in the Formal Sciences should embrace the higher Mathematics and Logic. Their relations to other sciences should be pointed out, and an application of their principles should be made.

The more abstruse principles of the Empirical Sciences studied during this period, can be mastered; and such principles, and the relations of these sciences to one another, are proper objects of study for minds approaching maturity. Pupils may be encouraged to select some one of the sciences, and to prosecute original investigations with respect to it. The ambition to add something to the sum of human knowledge is a worthy one.

This period should be characterized by the study of the Rational Sciences, furnishing as they do the noblest themes for human thought, and the best means of mental discipline. It will be found, too, that their principles underlie all other sciences, and are necessary to their full comprehension. That teacher deserves the name of wise man, who, taking his pupils through many sciences, leads them at last to the firm conviction that *faith* is the only sure basis of all philosophy; and this, when well understood, is the spirit of all Metaphysical study.

History must now embrace the History of science and the History of philosophy, as well as reveal the principles that have ever worked changes in the affairs of men. Its highest province is to embrace all science and all art in its comprehensive narrations, and to trace out the causes and effects of human actions, and thus solve the problem of human life.

If it is thought proper to continue the study of Drawing through any part of this period, it may include the principles of Shading and Perspective. Mechanical and Architectural Drawing might, in some cases, be taught. The time to be devoted to Music must depend upon other circumstances than those which arise from its nature. This, too, is the case with other arts, such as Painting, which are considered more ornamental than useful. From the age of sixteen to twenty-one, the realities of life begin to press themselves upon the attention of the young man or the young woman. They select a profession, or seek to prepare themselves for some kind of business. They feel the need of a professional education; and such an education aims not to impart knowledge of the sciences, but skill in the arts. The highest of all arts is the *art of living well,* and to this art all science contributes. Exceptions apparently to the common order of things are the gifted sons of Genius — the great Artists of the world. To them we are indebted for the noblest creations of the human mind; and, though but one such person—poet or prophet—appear in a century, a broad system of education cannot be unmindful of the great fact.

What has now been written is intended to introduce a discussion of those detailed methods of instruction of which it is the special object of this work to treat. In accordance with the classification of studies already made, the remaining part of the volume will be divided into seven chapters as follows:

I. Instruction in the Elements of Knowledge.
II. Instruction in Language.
III. Instruction in the Formal Sciences.
IV. Instruction in the Empirical Sciences
V. Instruction in the Rational Sciences.
VI. Instruction in the Historical Sciences.
VII. Instruction in the Arts.

CHAPTER I.

INSTRUCTION IN THE ELEMENTS OF KNOWLEDGE.

What is meant by the elements of knowledge has already been explained. The elements of each branch of knowledge, or of each class of branches, might be treated of in connection with the discussion of the methods of teaching that branch or that class of branches; but practically these elements are not separated but combined in early education. A child cannot study the sciences, but he can study the general facts which form their bases.

The whole subject will be discussed in two sections as follows:

I. Informal Instruction in the Elements of Knowledge.

II. Formal Instruction in the Elements of Knowledge.

Under the first head it is intended to speak of that instruction in the elements of knowledge which a child acquires from parents, companions, and the circumstances that surround him, without any special teacher or any set lessons. Under the second the design is to discuss that kind of instruction which is now generally known by the name of Object Lessons.

I. Informal Instruction in the Elements of Knowledge.—How interesting to the educator is the infant soul in its efforts to attain freedom! Wrapt in sleep, how softly it awakens to a state of conscious existence! Closely folded within the depths whence it comes, how gently its tender germs seek the light! An angel sent from God, with what seeming hesitation it sets its delicate feet upon the rough earth!

We know not what impressions a child may have received before that time, but the beginning of its instruction may be dated from the moment it knows itself—from the moment it shows, by looks or actions, that it recognizes something apart from its own being. Commencing at this tender age, a child must receive instruction suited in kind and method to its capacity. Children exhibit in their mental manifestations and predilections the kind of instruction and training which they need. There are internal impulses which prompt them to satisfy their mental cravings. By carefully watching the outward play of these impulses, we may be guided in selecting the most appropriate means and methods of educating the young. "Follow the indications of nature," said Rousseau. In order to make the subject as definite as possible, the most important educational inferences which can be derived in this way, will be expressed in a series of propositions:

1. Children should be Allowed ample Opportunities for Exercising their Senses.—A child can exercise the senses of touching, tasting, and smelling before it can see and hear. Of the two

last named senses I am not sure which is first awakened, that of seeing or hearing; but when a few weeks old an infant will look at bright colors and seem pleased with certain sounds. When a little older, it will follow with its gaze the motions of objects which attract its attention, and smile at the sound of voices or of music. Soon after it learns to hold and handle things, and to play with them, and all the senses begin to develop themselves rapidly.

The maternal instincts of mothers generally teach them how to supply the intellectual wants of their young children. They suffer them to gaze at the lamp, or the open fire, at the sunlight as passing through openings in the window-blinds it plays upon the floor or about the curtains, at the bright colors of flowers, buttons, or clothing. They allow them to look through the casement at what they can see in yard, garden, street, or field. They amuse them with talking and singing, with rattles, little bells, or gingling keys. They place in their hands numerous playthings differing in size, shape, texture, and color. They let them look at animals in motion, vehicles passing on the highway, and trees moved by the wind. No better mode of awakening the slumbering intellect of a child than this could be pointed out. It needs but to be applied with more intelligence. Mothers might place before their infants a great variety of objects presenting marked contrasts in color and sound; they might select and change their playthings with more judgment, and make more attractive the world of nature about them.

The mental growth of a child from the time it

becomes conscious of the existence of objects around it until the time it can walk is truly wonderful. Its power of discriminating colors, sounds, and consistencies is greatly increased. Its senses are rapidly developed. It becomes alive to all that is passing around it, and exhibits a strong inclination to touch and handle all objects within its reach. It learns to walk, and then commences the active exercise of its newly found powers. Drawers are opened, baskets upset, cupboards and closets explored, flowers plucked. The child seeks objects about the kitchen, parlor, shop, yard, garden, and, if allowed, on the highway or in the street. It is wide awake, and knowledge seems to be taken in through every pore.

This is a precious season in which to sow the seeds of knowledge. Mothers especially at this time enjoy opportunities of pouring instruction into the opening mind. Says Harriet Martineau, "If the mother is at work, and the children are running in and out of the garden, it is only saying to the little toddler, 'Now bring me a blue flower; now bring me a yellow flower; now bring me a green leaf.' At another time she will ask for a round stone; or a thick stick; or a thin stick. And sometimes she will blow a feather, and let it fall again; or she will blow a dandelion-head all to pieces, and quite away. If she is wise she will let the child alone, to try its own little experiments, and learn for itself what is hard, and what is soft; what is heavy, and light; hot, and cold; and what it can do with its little limbs and quick senses. Taking care, of course, that it does not injure itself, and that it has objects within reach in sufficient variety, she can do no better, at this season of its life, than to let it be busy in its own way. I saw a little fellow, one day, intently occupied for a whole breakfast-time, and some time afterwards, in trying to put the key of the house-door into the key-hole of the tea-caddy. When he gave the matter up, and not before, his mother helped him to see why he could not do it. If she had taken the door-key from him at first, he would have missed a valuable lesson. At this period of existence, the children of rich and poor have, or may have, about equal advantages, under the care of sensible parents. They can be busy about anything. There is nothing that cannot be made a plaything of, and a certain means of knowledge, if the faculties be awake. If the child be dull, it must, of course, be tempted to play. If the faculties be in their natural state of liveliness, the mother has only to be aware that the little creature must be busy while it is awake, and to see that it has variety enough of things (the simpler the better) to handle, and look at, and listen to, and experiment upon."

2. Children should be Instructed in Learning to Talk.—Children are characterized by talkativeness. They possess a wonderful capacity to learn words and to form them into sentences. When five years of age, children have been known to speak with considerable fluency five different languages.

The use of language renders the acquirement of knowledge more easy and rapid, if it is not essential to it; and in this, probably, may be found the reason why children are endowed with the remarkable power just referred to. A child likes to know the names of all he sees, and is constantly asking, "What's this?" and "What's that?" He prattles all day with father, mother, brother, sister, servant, playmate; and, when no one will listen, he talks to his cat, bird, dog, toys, or to himself. It is just as natural for him to do this as it is for a plant to grow, or a bird to sing; and his nature could not indicate more clearly that it is the duty of parents or teachers to instruct him in learning to talk.

A child in learning to talk performs two distinct operations: the first, one of association; the second, one of imitation. He first associates certain verbal utterances with particular things or thoughts, and afterwards learns to imitate them. In learning a word, therefore, a child must hear it correctly uttered, and then learn to utter it correctly himself.

Instruction in learning to talk can be given to a child in two ways: first, indirectly, by good example; second, directly, by correcting his errors and presenting him proper models for imitation.

Parents should be careful, as far as practicable, to suffer their children to listen to none but pure and proper language, for they will imitate the language to which they listen. If the words they hear spoken are bad words, or the sentences uttered in their presence are inelegant or ungrammatical, no care in after life can completely correct the improper habits of speech thus formed. In order to prevent their children from forming such habits, parents should use good language in talking with them or in their presence, and be careful in the selection of servants, governesses, and others with whom they come in contact. Especially should this care be exercised in the choice of companions and playmates. A single afternoon spent in play with those who use them, will serve to introduce into a child's vocabulary quite a list of bad words and uncouth expressions. His taste is thus blunted, and his heart may be poisoned. The Gracchi, it is said, were indebted to their mother's conversation for their eloquence; and Alexander could never get rid of the defects of manner, gait, and speech which he contracted in his infancy from his instructor, Leonidas. Every one, indeed, must have noticed the difference in the language of children whose parents and associates exhibited good taste in their speech, and that of those who did not possess this characteristic. The scanty vocabulary and the rough forms of speech which characterize the poor peasant-child, whose parents are ignorant, contrast strongly with the full flow of words and finely formed sentences which distinguish the child whose parents are educated and refined.

In addition to this indirect but most effective teaching by example, parents should take advantage of their capability of learning words so readily to impart to their children more directly certain kinds of instruction in language. It may be done by attentively noticing their articulation and their improper forms of expression, and carefully correcting them. For this time and patience will be required. The corrections should be made more in the manner of play than of formal instruction. The child could not appreciate reasons if given. The parent, noticing the fault, should present the correct model, and playfully induce the child to imitate it, once, twice, or as many times as may be necessary, until the difficulty shall be overcome.

At two years of age, a child will understand little stories, if related or read to him in simple language, and such exercises furnish valuable lessons. After receiving them, children immediately exhibit in their conversation the forms of expression thus acquired. I cannot recommend these exercises of conversing and reading with children too highly. They should be engaged in every day. Those mispronunciations and misconstructions, called "baby-talk," however, are generally both hurtful to the child and unbecoming to the parent.

Children can be taught to speak in learning to sing or in hearing others sing. They are nearly always fond of music, and will gladly commit little songs and hymns, and thus improve their speech while they cheer the household with their joyful melodies.

3. Children should have their Appetite for Knowledge gratified. — It has already been shown that children should be allowed to exercise their senses, and it will now be made equally evident that their appetite for knowledge should be gratified. They should not only be encouraged to use their senses for the purpose of using them, but for the purpose of gaining knowledge. With very young children the discipline of the senses is the principal end aimed at, but in a short time the attainment of knowledge assumes greater importance.

Children exhibit great curiosity. They like to see things, to handle and examine them. They stand in raptures when papa opens his watch, or mamma her drawers, for them. All their waking hours are devoted to looking at things, playing with them, or tearing them to pieces. These restless inner promptings are natural to children, and indicate an educational want which ought not to be overlooked. The searching curiosity goes out through the active senses and returns laden with rich stores for the capacious memory. A beautiful correlation exists between the functions of the curiosity which prompts, the senses which are the instruments, and the memory which receives and retains, and the order of their development. This whole mental apparatus seems nicely adjusted to bring about the end of collecting multitudes of facts, and storing them away in the memory to be eventually classified, and made to constitute the data for scientific generalizations.

The appetite children have for knowledge can be gratified by conversing with them. The names and qualities of things can be talked about—their color, size, form, weight, number, uses. Children ask many questions, and these, whenever possible, should be answered. Parents often rebuke their children for asking them questions, but this is to do them great wrong, since it serves to check the growth of the intellect, and may stop it altogether. If parents would spend a short time each day in conversation with their children much valuable information could be imparted to them. The best method of presenting knowledge on such occasions is that of relating incidents, describing objects, or telling stories. Children will listen to such narrations with breathless attention, and receive from them lasting impressions. Quite similar to conversations of this kind is the practice of reading suitable books to children. This practice may commence some time before the children themselves can read. Parents may read, and afterwards make what they have read a topic of conversation. If the selections be appropriate, and the conversations be judiciously conducted, parents can have the satisfaction of seeing the minds of their children expand like opening buds. Not the least important good derived from such exercises is their influence upon the character and opinions of children.

The appetite children have for knowledge can be gratified by showing them interesting objects in nature and art. They may be made familiar with many minerals, flowers, trees, birds, reptiles, insects. What valuable lessons they could learn about bees, ants, spiders, beetles, frogs! With what interest they would examine an ant-hill, an old hornet's nest, a spider's web, or the chrysalis of a butterfly! How much knowledge they could gather in walks over fields, through woods, along streams! Let there be pointed out to them, growing plants and ripening fruit, birds building their nests, fishes sporting in the water, animals caring for their young, the shifting clouds, the many-colored rainbow, the dew-drops as they glisten upon leaves and flowers in the morning sunlight. No suitable opportunity should be lost of taking them to mills, factories, workshops, menageries, and museums. The Stereoscope and the Magic Lantern may be used with much profit in exhibiting to them the scenery of distant countries, their cities, buildings, manners, and customs. Engravings, too, may be made a most valuable means of instruction. Children love pictures, and nothing pleases them better than to be allowed the privilege of examining a picture-book. There is no mode probably in which a child can be taught so much in the same time as by means of pictures. The best pictures for the purpose are those which represent animated nature—scenes of life among animals or among men. Opportunities of pointing out the form, number, color, and other properties of the things they see should not be overlooked. Much valuable instruction of this kind can be imparted incidentally.

The appetite children have for knowledge can be gratified by furnishing them with proper toys and playthings. A child needs play as much as he needs food. He must have it, and this disposition can be turned to good account mentally as well as physically. Whenever possible, a suitable apartment should be arranged in every house in which there are children, for a play-room where they might be allowed to run, jump, and play without danger to themselves or disturbance to others. This play-room ought to be provided with swings, hobby-horses, little wagons, jumping-ropes, balls, blocks of many shapes and sizes, and some with prints of animals, letters, &c., upon them, wheels, beads of different colors arranged on strings, blackboards and chalk—anything indeed of which an interesting play can be made. To make these plays most valuable, some older person must assist in planning the plays and superintend the children in playing. In fine weather the plays may take place in the open air. A yard with a sward of grass is the best place for them. The Infant Schools of Europe have gardens or yards attached to them in which the children sing, and dance, and play, under the constant care and direction of teachers whose presence is no restraint upon the fun, but who seize the fit opportunity to intermingle instruction with it. In writing what has just been said, I have had in mind quite young children. Some additional playthings may be provided for those who are older. Among these toy-towns with different kinds of buildings, people and animals walking in the streets, vehicles passing along, &c.; slates and pencils; cup-and-ball; paper for cutting pictures out of; clay for modeling figures; tea-sets and house-furniture in miniature; letters and maps cut into sections; the Chinese puzzle; blocks of great variety and shape, with which stools, chairs, tables, houses, monuments, towers, castles, churches, bridges, &c., could be made. For amusement out-of-doors, balls, kites, hoops, bows and arrows, carts, wheelbarrows, garden tools, quoits, and other things of the same kind are proper. It must not be supposed that it is expected that any one family will procure all the articles mentioned, the design is only to name those out of which selections may be made. Toys and playthings should be kept under lock and key, and children be allowed at one time only those articles which they may choose or which may be considered proper for them. Frequent changes will keep them ever new. Besides, children should be allowed to exercise their own ingenuity in inventing means of enjoyment. It will be observed that our list of toys and playthings includes only those which may be made use of for the purposes of instruction and discipline, and these are the only kinds I would permit children to handle. Space need not be taken up in describing in detail the manner of mingling instruction with play, for after what has already been said the instincts of those who sympathize with children will guide them correctly.

4. CHILDREN SHOULD BE FURNISHED OCCASIONS FOR APPLYING THEIR POWERS OF KNOWING WHAT IS TRUE, BEAUTIFUL, AND GOOD.—Truth has been defined as the correspondence between thought and its objects. There are different kinds of truth, but no classification of them is needed here. The truths with which a child becomes first familiar may be called truths of perception. He learns by means of his senses that iron is hard, that ice is cold, that roses are red, that birds sing, that plants grow green in the sunshine, that animals need food, that water seeks a level, that the whole is equal to all its parts; and every effort should be made to widen his experience, for this will fix in his mind the correspondence between thought and thing. The stories children are so apt to tell arise mainly from defective observation or from the mistake they sometimes make of supposing that the pictures of their fancy are the perceptions of their senses. A child that comes to his mother and says that he saw a cow in the field that has five legs, or that he talked with his grandfather who is a hundred miles away, does nothing at which a parent should be alarmed. Habits of correct ob-

servation will make it all right. A judicious mother would take her child by the hand and go and look at the cow, or ask him to find the place where he met his grandfather, and a good lesson would be taught him. Always set a child right when he says a thing that is wrong, and never fail to give him every chance of learning what is true. A very young child can recognize the difference between truth and falsehood. If his brother tell him that his ball has rolled behind the door and he does not find it there, or that a bright penny is in one hand when he finds it in the other, he shows by his looks that he understands the deception that has been practiced upon him. I am firmly convinced that it is in great measure owing to the deceptions of which he is the witness on the part of servants, playmates, brothers and sisters, and even parents, that a child learns to tell falsehoods. How can he remain pure and innocent while he beholds constantly about him those who practice exaggeration, deception, and falsehood? Let all conduct in the presence of a child be open and sincere, let all words spoken before him be honest and truthful; and, furnished with such occasions, he will not only learn what is true but be truthful. One who is himself truthful will trust others, and this is the ground upon which rests our earliest and purest faith.

Children appreciate the beautiful in objects at a much earlier age than is generally supposed. I have noticed well-marked evidences of such appreciation at the age of two years. This taste for the beautiful, like the early buddings of a tender plant, requires careful culture. The attention of children may be easily called to beautiful flowers, trees and buds; to the rippling brook, the towering mountain, the rising or the setting sun; to pattering rain-drops, falling snow-flakes, and drifting clouds. Nature is everywhere full of beauty, and it may be used with an unsparing hand to make glad the hearts of children. Art, too, has beauties which are attractive to the young. Of course, they cannot appreciate a fine painting or piece of statuary; but they are keenly alive to what might be called surface beauty—that which depends upon color, form, proportion, motion, and like qualities. Let their thirsty spirit drink at these fountains until they come to find purer draughts deeper down. If every child could have a bed of flowers to plant and cultivate, or a pet bird or rabbit to care for, it would do much to improve his taste and awaken feelings of tenderness and love.

Clearly there is a power within us which God designed to enable us to distinguish between right and wrong. We may not make good use of it and accept error for truth, but that does not invalidate the certainty of the great fact that the faculty exists. Young children can discriminate between good acts and bad acts, and this power they seem ready to apply when proper occasions are presented. If the good is constantly exemplified in the conduct of those who surround a child and whom he loves, his sense of right and wrong must be quickened by the exercise it would receive. Would that all parents felt the great importance of this fact! Besides, pains can be taken to point out good acts to a child—acts of honesty, justice, kindness, mercy, gratitude, patriotism. Life in every neighborhood has incidents of this kind, and history is full of them. Let his conscience be kept active by frequent appeals to it, and the child will grow daily in virtue.

What is said in the preceding paragraphs is predicated upon the assumption that the human mind has the power in itself to determine what is true, beautiful, and good, and that the duty of the instructor consists only in multiplying occasions for its exercise. But to arrange these occasions so as to answer their end is a work so delicate and difficult that none but the most accomplished teachers can perform it skilfully. Something, however, may be done by all who love children and sincerely desire to have them become virtuous and happy themselves and a blessing to mankind.

5. Children should be allowed facilities for practice in the Elements of the Arts.—The mental nature of children is characterized by vigorous imitative powers and a lively fancy. This leads them to imitate and contrive things, and gives zest to many kinds of play in which they delight.

A slate and pencil or blackboard and chalk may be made very useful for the purpose of preparing children to write and draw. At first, a child might be allowed to make such marks as his fancy prompted or he might be encouraged to imitate simple figures of various shapes and sizes. If any one desires to see how much a child is interested in this kind of work, let him draw while the child looks on, the picture of a cat, a dog, a house, a stage-coach, and witness the effort he will make to imitate it. If a little judicious help be given, a child will spend willingly an hour or more every day at such exercises.

Like instruction may be derived from other employments in which children greatly delight, such as coloring pictures or cutting them from paper or pasteboard; moulding various kinds of objects from terra cotta, such as animals, flowers, fruit, dishes, boats, &c.; building with suitable blocks, houses, castles, bridges, &c., or making of them tables, chairs, bedsteads, &c.; dressing dolls and arranging doll-houses; imitating the several varieties of work which they see going on in the kitchen, in the shop, and on the farm; and I recommend them all as means of instruction which may be made very valuable by judicious management. Much information can be furnished children likewise, by allowing them to visit shops and manufactories and to see machinery in operation.

Every father who has young sons would find it much to their advantage to provide a shop in which they could work, and supply it with suitable tools. Sets of children's tools can be bought for a few dollars, and their value in making boys more ingenious and active can scarcely be calculated. Girls can derive similar benefit from needle-work, crochet-work, and embroidery. Whatever may be their circumstances, children should learn to work. Ability to handle tools will not prove amiss in any sphere of life.

Without such instruction as that now indicated, the productive powers of children would remain undeveloped, and all thinking persons must acknowledge that this would be a grave educational error.

II. Formal Instruction in the Elements of Knowledge.—The preceding section has given hints as to the kind of instruction children ought to receive in their younger years, and as to the methods by which it should be imparted. This informal or incidental instruction must be continued as the child advances in years and acquirements, but in addition he must receive other instruction more formal and systematic. He must be trained to more regular habits of study. He must learn to work as well as play. Knowledge should not merely be presented to him in disconnected fragments but in regular lessons.

Thinking men accustomed to observe tne mental nature of children were long ago convinced that the dry and tedious methods of hearing them give the names of letters, and spell and pronounce words, as usually practiced in Primary Schools, could not be the best to awaken interest in study or develop the powers of the mind. Children have a natural appetite for knowledge, but it must be presented in such a form as adapts it to the condition of their mental digestive-apparatus, or it will cloy that appetite instead of satisfying it.

As we have seen, a child's first intellectual lessons are learned wholly in connection with objects. When older, if allowed to follow his instinctive promptings, objects will still engage his attention and supply the object-matter about which he thinks; and it is obviously unwise to divert his intellectual faculties from their natural course in obtaining knowledge. The lessons constructed in view of this theory are generally known by the name of

Object Lessons; and Object Lessons may be defined as *lessons designed to teach the Elements of Knowledge by the use of objects.*

It is proposed to consider:

1. The Design of Object Lessons.
2. The Matter of Object Lessons.
3. The Preparation for imparting Object Lessons.
4. The Method of conducting Object Lessons.
5. The Dangers to which the Object-Lesson System is exposed.

1. The Design of Object Lessons.—The general design of Object Lessons is made sufficiently plain in the definition just given, but it may be well to state it a little more in detail.

Object Lessons supply a want in elementary instruction. No one can be mistaken as to the lessons of which children are most fond. Their intense curiosity, their active senses, their capacious memories, and their great loquacity indicate very clearly the direction in which they can be best educated. Little is done, however, in most schools to take advantage of these vigorous manifestations of certain mental faculties. Pupils in our Primary Schools are made to sit down, shut themselves away from the world of objects in which they might find so much to interest and delight them, and engage in the dull work of learning to read, write, and cipher —dull, because abstract. Reading, writing, and arithmetic must be learned, and may be learned to some extent in the Primary School; but neither of these branches, nor others like them, can meet the pressing educational wants of children. The true philosophy of education teaches that advantage should be taken of all mental capabilities at the time, in the manner, and with respect to the degree, in which they manifest themselves. This wise mental economy is much disregarded in the common methods of teaching; and the quick perceptive powers of children, their strong memory, and their lively fancy are made much less use of than they might be in imparting knowledge, and are suffered to remain almost altogether without systematic discipline. Children might learn much more and learn it in a much more grateful manner, they might receive much more mental discipline and receive it much more in accordance with the nature of their minds, if a well-devised system of Object Lessons were substituted for the usual course of elementary instruction. A child is a germ put into the hands of the educator, and it is his duty to supply the conditions necessary to its full development. No potentiality of its nature should be allowed to lie dormant, no talent should be buried, and unjust will be the steward who violates his trust.

Object Lessons impart valuable knowledge in a form best suited to the capacity of children. Object Lessons teach things, facts, phenomena, words, in short, the elements of knowledge — the foundation upon which the whole superstructure of learning must rest. Children have strong impulses prompting them to learn. They are constantly obtaining knowledge without a teacher. Nature teaches them, and they enjoy her teachings. Object Lessons are intended to lead the child methodically in the way nature indicates that he should be taught. At first, they present to him things which are simple, and afterwards those which are less easily discerned or less easily comprehended.

A characteristic feature of the object method of teaching is that the matter presented to the pupil may be greatly varied. It is a common practice in our schools to confine young children to one or two special branches of study; and of these they soon grow weary, and consequently misspend much of their time. A variety of objects must be presented to children in order to enlist their attention, and gratify their appetite for knowledge. A child may learn lessons in the elements of all the sciences as he walks through field or meadow. Nature has not separated one class of things from another, but presents all in rich profusion. The teacher should learn from her.

Object Lessons furnish the best discipline for the young mind. By the ordinary methods of teaching a child his letters, to spell, and to read, he receives very little mental discipline. The same is true of the process of committing to memory and repeating forms of words which are not understood and are soon forgotten. But let a child use his senses in observing and noting the qualities of interesting objects, and it will soon be perceived that his whole intellectual nature is developing itself. One might as well deprive a plant of light or heat, and expect it to grow, as to endeavor to impart healthy mental discipline to a child without the presence of objects.

The concrete should precede the abstract in the work of education.

2. The Matter of Object Lessons. — The field from which the objects themselves may be chosen is as boundless as nature. It may embrace multitudes of things in the mineral, vegetable, and animal worlds, and multitudes of events in the history of mankind. Writers upon Object Lessons have given long lists of such objects, and it is quite unnecessary to repeat them here. It is of much more importance to determine the principles which ought to guide the teacher, not merely in the selection of proper objects for his lessons, but in the disposition of the matter connected with those objects with which he would make his pupils acquainted. The principles about to be stated will be better appreciated if the reader will keep in view the fact that Object Lessons are designed to teach the elements of knowledge, and that the expression, elements of knowledge, is here intended to comprehend the elements of all the sciences and arts.

The matter of Object Lessons must be adapted to give exercise in their early growth to all the mental faculties. In the simple perception of an object and its discrimination from other objects, a child, probably, calls into requisition every faculty of his mental nature. It is a psychological error to suppose that any of his mental powers are dormant. Some manifest themselves more actively or more obviously than others, but all act, and all should be furnished an opportunity of gaining strength. Teachers have been accustomed to consider Object

Lessons simply as designed to give culture to the perceptive powers; but this is a very narrow view of the subject. As the perceptive powers are more active in youth than any others of our mental faculties, they are more capable of receiving culture, and Object Lessons are peculiarly adapted to impart it; but it should not be imparted to them to the neglect of any other faculty of the mind. The matter of an Object Lesson, in addition to what it contains that can be known by the senses, may present something to be retained in the memory, something to excite the imagination, something to start a train of reasoning, or something to call into play one of those ideas of the reason which, whether consciously or unconsciously, condition all our thinking. Take, for example, such a simple object as a piece of bread. The teacher may call the attention of his class to the sowing of the seed, the gathering of the harvest, the threshing of the grain, the grinding of the flour, the baking of the bread — all of which furnish exercise to the perceptive powers and the memory. The imagination is exercised as well in conceiving the ripening wheat, harvest-time, the threshers at their work, the mill, the bakery. A very little child can answer such questions as—Why is the ground ploughed and harrowed when it is desired to sow it with wheat? Why is the ripe wheat gathered and put in barns? Why is it threshed out and taken to mills?—and thus learn to use his judgment or learn to think. So, too, it would be proper in giving such a lesson, for the teacher to say that God gave us the grains of wheat; He causes it to grow; He ripens it and makes it fit for food;

and He is good. Such instruction will find a lodgement in children's minds, because it is adapted to their mental nature, thus showing that the noblest faculty of our minds, the reason, is active in early youth.

The matter of Object Lessons must be adapted to increase the pupil's facility in the use of language. Thoughts are helpless without words. But words are best learned in connection with things. With fit opportunity, it is surprising how rapidly a child becomes acquainted with language, but the ordinary instruction of our primary schools does not furnish this opportunity. If the system of object teaching is not diverted from its true function, it will give prominence to linguistic culture. According to this system, the names of things, and the names of qualities of things are constantly pressed upon the attention of the pupils. They are taught, not only to make observations, but to tell what they know, to repeat what they have learned; and every lesson acquaints them with new words. A constant succession of interesting objects is made to pass before them, and they are taught to give them names. An Object Lesson is, in part, an exhibition of objects, and, in part, an application of words, and the two processes should be inseparable.

The matter of Object Lessons must be adapted to communicate the elementary facts which constitute the foundation of knowledge. It was previously shown that all the sciences took their rise from the common experience of men. A child can be made to experience by design what men at first experienced incidentally or by accident, and this is one of the principal ends proposed by the object system of teaching. A child can be made acquainted with an immense number of facts, which are not only valuable in themselves, but form the basis of further knowledge. Almost every common object may be made the subject of interesting lessons. Many of the objects technically belonging to the various branches of Natural History, many of the simpler phenomena of experimental science, certain national peculiarities of customs and manners, and large numbers of historical incidents, when properly presented to children, are well calculated to instruct and delight them. The experience of children can thus be made broader, and a great number of valuable facts and useful words be stored away in the memory.

The matter of Object Lessons must be adapted to expand the elementary ideas which furnish the conditions and measure of our knowing. That there are such ideas has been already shown, and no student of the human mind can doubt it. No exhaustive enumeration of them will be attempted here, as this is properly the work of the mental philosopher. It may be said, however, that they can be divided into two great classes: *Empirical* ideas, or those which are derived from experience, and are limited by it; and *Rational* ideas, or those of which experience is simply the occasion, and which transcend experience. These form respectively the bases of the Empirical and the Rational sciences. Among the ideas which I would denominate empirical, are those of *form*, *number*, *relation*, *size*, *weight*, *color*, *consistency*, *locality*, *&c*, which relate to material things; and those of *duty, right, truth, beauty, goodness, &c.*, which are moral qualities. Among the ideas which I would call rational ideas, are those of *space, time, order* or *harmony, identity* and *difference, the infinite, the absolute, the true, the beautiful,* and *the good.* Chronologically the former class of ideas precede the latter in consciousness, but logically they are evolved from them. For example, a child realizes the idea of form before the idea of space, but the idea of space contains all possible forms. So the idea of number is involved in the idea of time, the idea of relation in the idea of order or harmony, the ideas of particular truth, beauty, or goodness in the all-comprehending ideas of the true, the beautiful, and the good; but in all these cases, and in all others, the mind passes from that which can be presented in a concrete form to that which can only be conceived abstractly. Hence lessons in form, number, relation, &c., are valuable in themselves, and more valuable for furnishing the occasions of the realization in consciousness of the all-comprehending ideas which involve them.

If the ideas now designated do furnish the conditions and measure of our knowing (and no thinking man can doubt it), it should be one of the principal aims of those who instruct the young, to expand them, or to increase the knowledge which is based upon them. Their ideas of form can be expanded by having children notice, describe, and name objects of various forms; draw these forms upon slates, paper, or blackboards; or imitate them in wood, stone, or clay. Their ideas of number can be expanded by counting objects, as beans, pebbles, or grains of corn ; and adding, subtracting, multiplying, and dividing them. No object exists in nature that has not its relations—its relations to other objects, and the relations of its parts to one another; and many of these are so simple that children of five years of age, and even younger, can understand them. Other ideas relating to material things may be expanded in the same way. Moral ideas must be expanded by acquainting children with the acts which exemplify or illustrate them. History, biography, personal experience, must be made to contribute stores of incidents that can be made to do much to enlarge the conception children have of right and wrong, and to form their character to virtue.

The matter of Object Lessons must be adapted to improve the artistic taste and talent of the young. Children have productive as well as receptive powers. These productive powers can be stimulated to activity by the exhibition of objects of art. The teacher can call their attention to the structure of houses, bridges, mills, vehicles, articles of furniture, and machinery in great variety. Such lessons are lessons on objects, and so are those which relate to the mechanism of plants, animals, and the human frame-work. They can also receive exercise in practicing the elements of writing, drawing, painting, and making things of wood, and stone, and clay, or of any other suitable materials. Fathers and mothers could attend to this duty better than teachers, but teachers can do much. Our schools cannot have shops connected with them, as had those of Pestalozzi and De Fellenberg, but still such instruction can be given in them as greatly to improve the taste and talent of the young. Nor need this instruction be wholly confined to what are called the useful arts, for it happens that many children can appreciate some of the artistic qualities which distinguish the grander works of nature, and the finer creations of man.

It need scarcely be added that the matter of Object Lessons must be selected and arranged with reference to the age and acquirements of pupils. Some objects may furnish matter more appropriate as lessons for young pupils, and other objects be better suited for the study of those who are older; but it will often happen that the same object may be used in teaching both classes, provided due regard is paid to their intellectual differences. Objects generally have some qualities, resemblances and differences, relations, and uses which are easily discerned and open to the observation of children ; and others which being more hidden require close inspection, or careful experiment to reveal them. Sheldon's work on Object Lessons makes five series of lessons each more difficult than the preceding. This is an excellent arrangement.

3. The Preparation for imparting Object Lessons.—An important part of the preparation for imparting Object Lessons consists in procuring suitable objects. Knowledge is most effectually conveyed to children through the medium of the eye. Whenever it is possible, therefore, the teacher should present to his class the object upon which he desires to give a lesson. For this purpose primary

schools should be furnished with cabinets of Things. These should contain many common objects; collections from the mineral, animal, and vegetable kingdoms; tools used by different tradesmen, and, if possible, specimens of manufactured articles; models of machinery; curiosities exhibiting the manners, customs, and degree of civilization among tribes and nations; coins; sets of weights and measures; blocks of various forms; in short, any object about which a useful lesson may be given. Sometimes, it is more convenient for a teacher to take his class to see an object than to bring the object into the presence of the class. Children are greatly profited by visits to a museum, a menagerie, a gallery of pictures; by rambles down a valley, through a wood, or along the ocean shore, and they should frequently be indulged in them.

When the object itself cannot be exhibited to a class, the best substitute is a picture of it. A vast amount of useful knowledge might be pleasantly imparted to the young by means of pictorial illustrations. At present such illustrations are mainly used incidentally; I would make a systematic use of them. There have been prepared in Europe, and some of them in this country, Charts of Lines and Forms, Charts of Colors and Colored Cards, Charts of Natural History, Charts of Common Things, Moral Prints, Scripture Prints, and Prints illustrative of the History and Peculiarities of Nations. It would not be very difficult to prepare a set of engravings which might be used to great advantage in elementary instruction. If a teacher can draw, the blackboard is a never-failing resource.

In addition to objects and pictures of objects, there are certain kinds of apparatus that seem indispensable in the work of primary schools. Children will watch with intense interest the revelations of the Microscope. A Stereoscope can be used with great advantage, as can also a Magic Lantern. A teacher can procure, with trifling expense, the means of making many simple philosophical and chemical experiments, and his pupils will be delighted with them.

But with all it is necessary sometimes to rely upon descriptions. When this is the case, the descriptions, whether given by the teacher or presented in a book, must be of the most lively character. The story must be well told, and calculated to awaken in the most vivid manner the imagination of children. Most children are fond of the novel, the marvelous, and the witty, and this fondness must be turned to good account.

A teacher of Object Lessons must prepare himself both in respect to the matter and the method of the lesson. A text-book may enable a teacher ignorant of the subject of the lesson to ask questions of his pupils and know whether their answers are correct or otherwise; but all such botchwork as this is out of the question in object-teaching. In giving an Object Lesson, a teacher must collect and arrange his own materials. His knowledge of the matter he would present must be full, precise, and ready, or a failure is inevitable. No proper inquiry from a pupil should take him by surprise or make him hesitate for on answer.

No small degree of skill is required to adopt a

proper method of imparting a lesson on an object The matter must be arranged with reference to its own logical relations, and also with reference to its adaptation to the mental capacities of the class. This work requires skilful handling, and cannot be done without careful consideration. The difficulty is increased when a general subject is intended to be developed by a series of lessons, which is always best except with the youngest pupils. It is a good plan for a teacher first to fill his mind with the details of the subject, and then arrange them under prominent headings, calculated to present the parts of the lesson in their proper relations, and to make an impression upon the minds of his pupils. He may write out a full sketch of the lesson for his own convenience, but a well-planned outline of it is indispensable. Such an outline should not be referred to at the recitation, but it should be strictly followed. Without such adherence to a method, the desultory modes of thinking which characterize children will make the lesson fruitless of good in effecting that mental discipline which is its main object. Still the outline should only guide, not cramp, the recitation. An Object Lesson should not consist merely of a number of questions asked and a number of answers given; the teacher should propose to himself in every lesson certain points to be presented, certain ends to be attained, and then strive to accomplish what he purposes. It is more a training than a teaching exercise; and each question should be put with a well-defined object, and other questions should follow until that object be attained.

Something will be gained in all cases if the teacher would announce the object about which a lesson is to be given some time before the recitation takes place. When this is done, the pupils can make some preparation for the lesson. They can observe, make inquiries, and, instructed to that extent, can increase their information by reading. It does not follow that because the kind of instruction now contemplated is called Object Lessons that pupils are precluded from increasing their knowledge from books, and it is well to have suitable books, books of reference, books containing pictures of objects and descriptions of them, provided in every primary school. A lesson about an object of which the pupils know nothing will always be dull, and is likely to be profitless. Teachers sometimes furnish an outline of the proposed lesson to their pupils before the recitation, and this practice, it is thought, guides them in their search for information, and enables them to make a more systematic arrangement of it.

4. THE METHOD OF CONDUCTING OBJECT LESSONS. — A school-room presents no more delicate or difficult work than the recitation. Nothing else tests more severely the teacher's skill. This is especially the case with lessons on objects. In most other recitations, the text-book furnishes some help, but in giving an Object Lesson a teacher is thrown mainly upon his own resources.

The teacher is supposed to have in his mind the point which he wishes brought out in the lesson. This may be the communication of a knowledge of important facts, the pointing out of a quality, the development of a principle, the expansion of an idea, the exhibition of a relation; but whatever it is, it must be allowed to give direction to the recitation. Going forward with a well-defined aim, the recitation has three stages which should be severally noticed:

First, it is the teacher's duty to obtain all the information concerning the matter of the lesson which may be in the possession of the class. He may ask questions or make suggestions, but before giving any information himself he must be sure that no member of the class could give it. Pupils will not exert themselves to prepare a lesson unless they think they will have permission to show what they have learned. A lesson about an object is not intended to be a lecture upon it. Besides, if the teacher does the observing and thinking for his class, the disciplinary purposes of the Object Lesson are in great measure defeated.

Second, it is the teacher's duty to give his pupils the opportunity of finding out all they can. Skill in teaching does not so much consist in what a teacher imparts to a class as in what he leads them to find out for themselves. In object-teaching especially pupils should be constantly prompted to observe new facts, explain new phenomena, and perform new mental operations. Each lesson is a voyage of discovery in which the teacher acts as captain and pilot, but in which the pupils make, record, and elaborate the observations. When pupils hesitate for an answer, they should not be told it directly unless hints will not suggest it to them, or they cannot be brought to infer it from what they have previously learned. To lead a pupil from what he knows to find out what he does not know requires the highest order of teaching talent, and to attain this ability should be the constant aim of the teacher. Without it, no successful object-teaching is possible.

Third, when pupils have exhausted all their knowledge acquired before the recitation and all their ingenuity in adding to it during the recitation, the teacher may impart any further information he deems proper.

The three stages of a recitation now named are sufficiently well marked, but of course it is not meant that any one of these stages can be completed in all the particulars of a lesson, until the others are entered upon. The teacher must not wait to give hints or impart knowledge in regard to one point, because the pupils have not exhausted their information in regard to others.

5. THE DANGERS TO WHICH THE OBJECT LESSON SYSTEM IS EXPOSED.—Doubtless the greatest danger to which the Object Lesson system is exposed arises from the want of a proper appreciation of it on the part of teachers. Many teachers even who profess to use the system, entertain extremely narrow views respecting it. They do not apprehend the great educational truth that *all the sciences rest upon certain elements as bases, and that these elements are only known by means of our experience with objects.* The system of object-teaching well understood is broad enough to embrace all the elements which constitute the

foundation of knowledge, and that system is much disgraced by those who allow it to degenerate into loose lessons on pieces of paper, bits of glass, lumps of sugar, or stalks of grain. Besides, those who would fully comprehend the system of object-teaching must study its adaptation as a means of developing the mental faculties of children as well as of its capability, when well administered, of imparting instruction in the elements of knowledge. With an inadequate conception of the function of Object Lessons it is no wonder that many teachers fail in securing any advantage from them. No one who has been accustomed to a slavish dependence upon text-books can succeed. But success is possible to all who possess teaching talent and strive to make themselves acquainted with the nature and design of Object Lessons.

In addition to the danger to the Object Lesson system which arises from ignorant teachers, several special dangers to which it is exposed may be briefly referred to. They all arise from a misconception as to the true nature of Object Lessons, or are faults in the methods of imparting such lessons.

The Object Lesson system is apt to become an exercise in learning words without ideas. Children are capable of making great progress in the use of language, and they should be instructed with reference to this end. In giving a lesson upon an object, it does not seem objectionable to allow children to name every quality they can readily discern, nor do I see any serious objection to the use of scientific names; but it is objectionable and quite contrary to the spirit of the Object Lesson system, for children to commit to memory the names of the qualities of things which they cannot be made to perceive without great difficulty, if at all. The lists of the names of the qualities of certain objects, as they appear in some of our works on Object Lessons, ought to be much shortened.

The Object Lesson system is apt to tempt the teacher to introduce matter into the lesson which the pupils cannot comprehend. This is a temptation to which all teaching is liable, but it seems to be stronger when the teacher makes his own selection of matter for a lesson than when that matter is arranged in a text-book. At any rate, the fact is certain that many who impart instruction in Object Lessons err in this particular. The desire is so great to communicate to others what seems most important or is most interesting to ourselves, that if such teachers could sit in judgment upon their own work they would find it to consist, not wholly in an effort to impart the simple elements of knowledge adapted to the capacity of children, but in an effort to expound principles of science quite beyond their comprehension.

The Object Lesson system is apt to continue instruction in the *concrete* after pupils can appreciate the *abstract.* All instruction should commence with the concrete. The elements of all kinds of knowledge must be taught in connection with objects, but an acquaintance with material things is far from being the highest end of study; and object-teaching pushed too far tends to degrade education. Back of all there are principles, ideas, controlling things, which are the soul's most nourishing pabulum

Soon after a child has learned to count with objects, he may begin to count without them; soon after he has become acqainted with real forms, he may begin to deal with ideal ones. Through facts and phenomena he should be led to apprehend the laws that control them and the Lawgiver. The contemplation of truths should bring into clear consciousness the idea of truth, and of virtues, virtue.

The tendency of the times is towards materialism in education. It manifests itself in the oft-repeated objections which are made to the study of the Ancient languages, to the study of higher Mathematics, and especially to the study of Metaphysics. In this spirit some have favored Object Lessons, because it was thought the system tended to cultivate in the young a taste for concrete rather than abstract science, to teach them to handle substantial realities rather than airy nothings. Blind guides these; all earthly phenomena are fleeting, while the powers that cause and govern them are eternal. Herbert Spencer, in his inquiry as to "What knowledge is of most worth?" arranges education with reference to its relative degree of worth into the following classes: 1st. That education which prepares for direct self-preservation; 2d. That which prepares for indirect self-preservation; 3d. That which prepares for parenthood; 4th. That which prepares for citizenship; 5th. That which prepares for the miscellaneous refinements of life. All this looks like an implied denial of man's immortality—as if the interest of self was man's only interest. But is that education of highest worth which prepares for direct self-preservation? I am not unmindful of the value of life, but surely there are many things for which it is well to sacrifice it. The preservation of life is not to be compared in importance to the preservation of the soul's integrity. Let education be guarded from the influence of a low materialism. Concrete science is worth much, but abstract science is worth more. The former is but a means of reaching the latter. Let us devoutly study the works of the creation, but let us not forget that God made them.

The Object Lesson system is apt to cramp the imagination, and weaken the trustfulness, of children. Every one has noticed the lively imagination of children. They gild the narrow horizon of their vision with dreams. Elysian fields cover all their future. Unless this characteristic indicates an abnormal condition of the youthful mind (and no one can believe that it does), it is wrong to limit their education to the acquirement of dry, hard facts. Facts must be learned, true enough, but we must allow some room for the play of the imagination. It is a great mistake to suppose "That facts alone are wanted in life." The sunlight plays about the rugged mountain heights, and silver lakes nestle down below frowning crags and cliffs. I would but chasten his imagination, I would not destroy a single air-castle of a child.

God made children trustful. No scheme of education could be worse than one which proposes never to describe anything to a child which he cannot see, never to tell a child anything which he cannot understand, for this would be to weaken the power which was given him to be developed into that faith which lays hold of things unseen—immortality, God. Doubts will come soon enough, and strong enough; childhood is the time for trust.

CHAPTER II.

INSTRUCTION IN LANGUAGE.

"MAN, in fact," says Sir William Hamilton, "only obtains the use of his faculties in obtaining the use of speech; for language is the indispensable means of the development of his natural powers, whether intellectual or moral." The truth of this statement is unquestionable, and it shows at once the deservedly high place Language holds in a course of study. For its beauty as a science, for its usefulness as an art, for its disciplinary advantages as a study, Language can scarcely be outranked in excellence by any other subject open to the contemplation of finite minds.

The following divisions are deemed proper:

I. Instruction in our Mother-Tongue.
II. Instruction in the Dead Languages.
III. Instruction in Living Foreign Languages.

I. Instruction in our Mother-Tongue.

Nobody will deny that to be able to read and write our Mother-Tongue with accuracy and facility is a valuable acquirement, but even some teachers hold that its further study is of little use. In these circumstances it may be worth while to make a few statements intended to favor the study of the English Language as a science.

A knowledge of the English Language, as a science, is necessary to a nice appreciation of it. One who is accustomed to hear well-spoken discourses, or to read well-written books, may be able in good degree to understand the meaning and perceive the beauty of what he hears or reads; but to enable an individual to appreciate those more delicate shades of thought, or those finer touches of beauty, which may be expressed in words, careful study is necessary. If any doubt it, let them test the matter. Take a poem of Milton's, or an oration of Webster's, and enter upon a critical examination of it with a well-read man who has never studied Grammar or Rhetoric, and you will most likely find that many things relating to its arrangement, its choice of words, its introduction of figures, its construction of sentences, its order of paragraphs, have almost altogether escaped his attention; and that even many things which he has noticed he cannot express in appropriate words. No art, indeed, can be fully appreciated without a knowledge of the science or sciences upon which it is based, and language is no exception.

A knowledge of the English Language, as a science, is necessary to its skilful use. With suitable models for imitation, a child may learn to speak and write correctly. A favored son of genius may be so gifted with speech that without the preparation of study he can lead men captive by the charms of his poetry or the power of his eloquence. But these facts do not invalidate the proposition which heads this paragraph. Suitable models for imitation may, indeed, enable a child to speak and write his Mother Tongue with as much accuracy as is generally required by the common usages of society, but the degree of skill thus acquired would be entirely inadequate to the higher purposes of Literature. If the gift of genius in the use of language, on the part of the one who has it, be taken as a fact indicating that no necessity exists for study on the part of the thousands who have it not, there is no reason why the same principle might not be applied to all human efforts, for in each of these, at some time, genius has enjoyed triumphs. It is not possible for ordinary men to use language with skill who have not closely studied the signification of words, the structure of sentences, the characteristics of style, and the composition of discourse. The Greeks made their language a prominent object of study, and the classic elegance of their writings is the delight of all readers. The Parisians, by the same means, are fast making the French the language of refined society throughout Europe. Demosthenes prepared his unequalled orations with immense labor, and the same is true, with fewer exceptions than is generally supposed, of all great speakers and writers.

A knowledge of the science of the English Language is valuable for its own sake. We study not merely to use, but to know. Knowledge is of much worth in itself. Language is subject to laws which control its growth, its changes, its constructions. If it is worth while to study the laws which relate to the mineral masses of the earth, to plants, to animals, to stars, it cannot be less worth while to study the laws which relate to human speech. The science of the English Language contains as much worth knowing as any other science, the study of it is as valuable for discipline, and as well calculated to lift the mind up to the contemplation of what is most noble in human life and human thought. Indeed, it would seem that our Mother-Tongue ought to have more interest for us than almost any other thing. It is by means of our powers of speech that we hold converse with our friends, in words we embalm our thoughts, in words our heart's highest aspirations are expressed. Except the soul itself, earth can present nothing more wonderful or more clearly evincing Divine wisdom and goodness than Language.

A knowledge of the science of the English Language is valuable to us on account of the relations of the science of language to other sciences. Language must be used to record all the observations and discoveries which are made in any department of science, and the scientific man feels the constant want of words adapted to express his meaning. He sees things which he cannot describe; he feels thoughts stir within him which he cannot express. Suffering from such a disability, he says what he does not mean, and is misunderstood, perhaps maligned. The history of science records many "wars of words." Bacon, Locke, and many other writers lament the errors in science which arise from a misuse of language. While language has thus an intimate general relation to all the sciences, its relations are particularly close to History and the

Philosophy of the Mind. The language of a people reveals their inmost life. Not only what they did, but what they were, becomes fossilized in words, and men can read the record after the lapse of centuries. So the mind reflects itself in speech as in a mirror. The laws of thought are found expressed in the laws of speech, and hence the sciences of Logic and Grammar have much in common.

The preceding statements, showing the value of a knowedge of our Mother-Tongue, prepare the way for a detailed discussion of the methods of instruction adapted to the various branches which relate to it. Generally stated they are as follows:

I. Learning to Read our Mother-Tongue.
II. Learning to Understand our Mother-Tongue.
III. Learning to Compose in our Mother Tongue.

I. Learning to Read our Mother-Tongue.

Under the head of Learning to Read our Mother-Tongue, we will discuss methods of imparting instruction in the *Alphabet*, *Pronunciation*, *Spelling*, and *Reading*.

The Alphabet.

Already something has been said concerning methods of teaching children to speak correctly, hereafter something further will be presented on the subject; here some degree of familiarity with spoken words on the part of the pupil is taken for granted.

Reasons have been given also why the instruction of a child should commence with things rather than with words; but, since there will come a time when he must be made acquainted with written language, we will now consider methods of teaching the Alphabet.

There are twenty-six letters in the Alphabet of the English Language. In order that children be made acquainted with these characters, they must learn: first, to know their forms; second, to associate their names with their forms. That will be the best method of teaching the Alphabet which impresses the forms of letters most deeply upon the memories of learners, and succeeds in making the most lasting associations between these forms and their names.

In teaching the forms of letters, the sense of sight is addressed; and in teaching their names, the sense of hearing. To the blind, a knowledge of the forms of the letters is communicated through the sense of feeling. The deaf and dumb cannot learn the names of the letters—they can learn to write but not to read.

It is possible that our English letters are the changed forms of symbols used by the ancient Phœnicians or Egyptians, and they may once have represented real objects; but now they are wholly arbitrary. Many other forms might be adopted that would answer the purpose just as well. The names of the letters, too, are arbitrary; at least so far as a child can understand. The names of some of them do possess an analogy to the sounds they are intended to represent; but there are so many departures from this principle that little practical advantage can be derived from it in teaching. A child cannot see why *de* is a more appropriate name for the letter *d*, than *ge* would be; why *z* should be called *ze*, instead of *zed*, *izzurd*, or any other name; nor why the twenty-six names in use have been chosen in preference to as many others.

To learn our Alphabet, then, a child must become acquainted with twenty-six arbitrary forms, and associate with them twenty-six arbitrary names.

Infants first notice objects, as cat, dog, clock; next, they learn to associate certain verbal utterances with these objects, and always look for the thing when its name is mentioned; and, finally, they attain the power of imitating these utterances, or they learn to talk. Objects familiar to a child may be represented by pictures, and he may be exercised in naming the objects thus represented. Such exercises upon the pictures of familiar objects may be followed by others upon the pictures of unfamiliar objects, and the child may be taught to call the pictures of a lion, a tiger, a camel, an ostrich, &c., by their right names. Other lessons might acquaint the child with the forms and names of some of the simpler diagrams used in Mathematics, such as squares, triangles, circles, and rectangles. These exercises seem to present a series of easily followed progressive steps from the first attempts at talking to the task of learning the Alphabet. They follow essentially the steps which preceded the invention of the Alphabet. The principle is the same in all, that of learning forms and their names. The

Alpnabet is more difficult to learn, because its forms and names are arbitrary.

The Alphabet may be taught in two ways: first, by commencing with letters; second, by commencing with words. The first may be called the *A B C Method*, and the second the *Word Method*.

1. The A B C Method.—The A B C Method commences with letters. As the manner of conducting a recitation in the Alphabet, according to this method, depends somewhat upon the kind of apparatus used, a convenient classification may be based upon it.

1st. *The Manner of teaching the Alphabet from a Book.*—As the Alphabet was taught some years ago, and as it is taught now to a more limited extent, each pupil was provided with a book, called a Primer, or an A B C Book, from which he recited his lesson. Teachers generally called their pupils up singly, and, with pen, pencil, or pen-knife, pointed to the letters, from *a* to *z*, or from *z* to *a*, and asked their names, or told what they should be called. The whole twenty-six letters were named in quick succession, little effort was made to impress their forms or names upon the pupils' memories, no questions were asked or instruction given apart from the lesson which might be calculated to add interest to it, and the work of recitation was a short process, but a very dull and dry one.

More skilful teachers may use books in teaching the Alphabet to better advantage. Instead of pursuing a fixed order in their teaching, and invariably passing from the first letter of the Alphabet to the last, or from the last to the first, they may select at the commencement a few of those letters which possess the most easily remembered forms, describe them, ask questions about them, and engage their pupils in searching for them among other letters. Used in this manner, the Alphabet may be taught from a book quite readily; but as only one at a time can be heard conveniently, this manner of conducting a recitation loses the advantages of classification; and, besides, looking at and talking about forms are not the best conditions for remembering them.

2d. *The Manner of teaching the Alphabet with Cards.* —Cards used for giving instruction in the Alphabet should be large, and the letters should be printed upon them in large type. The first Card might have a few of the letters most easily learned, as *O*, *X*, and *S*, placed prominently in the centre, and the same arranged promiscuously with a few other letters about the margin. The second Card might have a few additional letters placed in the centre, and these, with those first learned, and a few others, might be made to occupy the margin, as in the first Card. This arrangement of the letters should be continued upon other Cards until the whole Alphabet was presented.

Imagine such a set of Cards, a suitable frame upon which to place them, the teacher with pointer in hand, and a class of pupils, and you will be ready to appreciate the lesson which is about to be described.

The teacher first calls the attention of his class

to the large letters in the centre of the Card. He speaks of their forms, peculiarities, and resemblances; gives their names, repeats them, and asks appropriate questions about them. Then, the interesting search for the letters, as they are arranged about the margin of the Card, commences. Mary finds six *e's*, but John detects another one. James counts four *b's*, but the rest insist that one of them is a *d*. Sarah finds out three *r's*, and no one can find another. Emma names a letter, and the rest are requested to look for it. It is *p*. The eager search begins, and it is eager, for Emma well knows that *p* is a hard letter to remember, and there is but one on the Card. James calls out, "I have it." Other letters are named and found; and when the recitation has ended, the pupils take their seats reluctantly, and wait impatiently till the time again arrives when they can have another game of "hide and seek" with letters. It cannot be doubted that, with Cards skilfully used, a knowledge of the Alphabet can be quickly and pleasantly imparted.

3d. *The Manner of teaching the Alphabet on the Slate or Blackboard.*—The best way of impressing forms upon the memory is to make them. In drawing an object, one is compelled to look at it closely, and follow out all its details, and this is well calculated to deepen the impression it leaves upon the mind. For this reason, the slate and blackboard, upon which letters may be copied, are considered useful articles of apparatus in teaching the Alphabet.

If the teacher can draw skilfully, he may place letters for imitation upon the slate or blackboard;

but if not, he must have suitable printed letters for models.

In conducting a recitation, the teacher may first require his pupils to imitate the forms of several letters which he has placed upon the blackboard. Next, he may engage them in criticising their own work, and comparing it with the models. All the peculiarities in the forms of the letters must be commented upon. If deemed expedient, the letters may be redrawn. The teacher may draw the letters awkwardly on purpose, in order to excite interest, and induce criticism. Finally, the names of letters, thus drawn, may be given, pointed out by the children, and repeated in various ways.

One of the advantages of using the slate and blackboard, in teaching the Alphabet, is that the teacher can furnish pleasant employment for the class when not engaged in reciting. Lessons which have been recited may be repeated upon the pupils' slates at their seats, or upon blackboards suitably located for the purpose; or new lessons can be prepared in the same manner. Children are very fond of work of this kind, and it will be found greatly to facilitate their progress.

There are certain letters in the English Alphabet which, from the similarity of their forms, are more difficult to distinguish than others, such as A and V, M and N, and E and F, among capital letters; and *b* and *d*, *p* and *q*, *c* and *e*, and *u* and *n*, among small letters. The distinctions between such letters can be more prominently brought before the learner's mind when exhibited upon the blackboard than in any other way, and if he be required to draw them repeatedly himself he cannot easily forget them. For the purpose of illustration, we will take the letters, *b*, *d*, *p*, and *q*, and describe a lesson upon them. Having drawn the letters conspicuously upon the black-board, the teacher may call the attention of the class to their forms, leading them to see that these are composed mainly of two parts. He may then draw these parts separately, and give them names. I call them *stem* and *curve*. Afterwards, it will be well to draw a stem, and by placing the curve, first at the top, and then at the bottom of the stem, and upon both sides, it will be shown that all the letters can be made. Let the teacher now satisfy himself that his pupils know their right hand from the left, and he may send them to the black-board, with the direction to draw a stem, and place the curve at the bottom, at the top, on the left side, on the right side, until they are quite familiar with all the forms, and can draw them readily. The names of the letters may now be given, and the teacher will ask such questions as these: If I place the curve at the top of the stem on the right-hand side, what letter do I make? If I place it on the left-hand side at the bottom, what letter do I make? On the left-hand side at the top? On the right-hand side at the bottom? Which letter is *p?* Which is *d?* Which is *b?* Which is *q?* How is *d* made? How is *q* made? Where do you put the curve in making *b?* Where do you put it in making *p?* The lesson may conclude by requiring the pupils to make each of the letters upon the blackboard when its name is given.

4th. *The Manner of teaching the Alphabet with Letter-Blocks.* — It is easy to obtain small blocks with letters painted or pasted upon them, and these may be made to answer a good purpose in teaching the Alphabet. To make the lesson most interesting and profitable, each pupil should possess a set of the blocks.

At recitation, the pupils should be stationed around a table or desk, each with his blocks before him. The teacher may first require the pupils to separate all the letters they think they know from those they do not, and have mistakes corrected by the class. He may then take up a block upon which is the letter he designs to teach, and make them acquainted with its form and name, and request each pupil to select a similar letter from among those before him. If any make mistakes, the class should correct them. When several letters have been selected in this way, the remaining time of the recitation may be devoted to teaching those selected. Suppose *c*, *e*, *h*, and *k* to be the letters selected. Each pupil will push aside all his other blocks, and with these only before him, the recitation is ready to proceed. The teacher may hold up each letter in succession, and inquire its name; a pupil may be appointed to hold up the letters, while the others name them; or all may be required to select the letters when the teacher gives their names. The teacher may make words with the letter-blocks, and ask the pupils to imitate them, both when they have the privilege of looking at them, and from memory; or words, as models, may be given in books, or placed on a blackboard.

Letter-blocks may be cut into sections; and pupils can be amused and instructed in putting the sections together so as to form letters. The differences between letters which are nearly alike can be strikingly exhibited in this way. If, for example, one block represented the stem of the letters *b*, *d*, *p*, and *q*, and another the curve, it would be easy to show their relative position in the formation of these letters.

The letter-blocks can be used most conveniently with a frame. Such a frame is called a Reading-Frame. The body of the frame may be made somewhat like a common blackboard, about three feet wide, and long enough to allow two feet to each member of a class. At convenient distances apart, horizontal grooves should be placed along the face of the frame in such a manner that the letter-blocks would stand upright when placed in them. At the base of the frame, and extending out a foot or more in front, there should be boxes appropriately divided into apartments for the blocks. All the Alphabetical exercises which can be performed with letter-blocks, can be better performed with a frame constructed in this manner. It is used somewhat as type are set; and words and sentences can be built up and taken apart by children with as much interest as they would take in a puzzle. With the "Education Tables," manufactured at Windham, Connecticut, and consisting of block-letters moving in grooves, I have seen children teach themselves to spell words and to read short sentences with very little assistance, and that given in answer to their questions.

It has now been shown how books, cards, slates

and blackboards, and letter-blocks may be used in teaching the Alphabet. All that remains to be said is that all these articles of apparatus may be used by the teacher at his pleasure, or they may be combined in teaching. A teacher violates no principle if he use book, cards, blackboard, and blocks at the same recitation. Children are fond of variety, and it can hardly be doubted that a teacher who varies his methods and means of teaching will cause his pupils to make more progress than one who confines himself to a single method or to the same means, even though he may choose the best.

2. THE WORD METHOD. — The A B C method of teaching the Alphabet commences with letters, and when the pupil is sufficiently acquainted with these, he proceeds to learn words by a process of synthesis. The method of teaching the Alphabet about to be described commences with words, and proceeds by a process of analysis to resolve them into their component letters.

The first step in a linguistic course of study is to become acquainted with oral words. Children learn the names of things. They learn to talk. Starting here, there may be found a series of nice gradations, which, if followed in teaching, will lead naturally to a knowledge of the Alphabet.

1st. *Lessons upon the Names of Pictures.* — The pupil has learned the names of objects. By pictures he will learn that objects can be represented, and he will acquire the power also of looking closely at the details of different forms in order that he may distinguish one from another. These picture-lessons may be given from books or cards prepared for the purpose.

2d. *Lessons upon the Names of Words.*—These lessons may at first embrace only the words which stand for the objects represented in the pictures. They should be printed near the pictures in order that an intimate association may be formed between the picture, its name, and the word which stands for the name. In asylums for the blind, labels with raised letters cut upon them, are sometimes attached to familiar objects, in order that an easy connection can be formed between the object and the word which symbolizes it. After such an introduction, the pupil should be exercised upon the names of words, disconnected from pictures or objects. A set of cards could be easily contrived presenting, first, pictures without words; second, pictures with words, and, last, words without pictures.

3d. *Lessons upon the Names of Letters.*—Having learned to use spoken words, and to distinguish some written words, pupils would seem to be prepared to analyze these words and ascertain the parts of which they are composed, or to learn their letters. The words first selected for analysis should be short, should represent some familiar object, and should be composed of letters which are easily learned; such as *ox*, *cow*, *cat*, *boy*, *hen*, &c. In analyzing words into letters, books, cards, slates, blackboards, and letter-blocks may be used as described when speaking of the A B C method. Pupils, having been made familiar with the letters composing certain words, can make the words on slates and blackboards, or form them with letter-blocks.

Several reasons may be given in favor of the Word method of teaching the Alphabet.

It is the natural method. Children use words in speaking, and the transition seems natural from spoken words to written words, and then to the letters of which words are composed. If we commence with letters, there can be no immediate connection between that knowledge of language which the pupil has and that which he is expected to acquire. Besides, the Word method follows the order in which written language was invented. Characters were first used for objects, next for words, and last for letters.

It possesses more interest for children. A child cannot be made to take much interest in abstract, arbitrary forms like *a*, *b*, *c*; while all children delight in talking about a *bird*, a *dog*, a *bell*, a *coach*, and consequently may be pleased to learn the words for such objects, and the letters composing such words. Teachers unconsciously show the truth of what is here said, when they tell their pupils that *a* stands for apple, *b* for boy, and *d* for dog, &c.

It aids pupils in learning to pronounce. The pupil necessarily learns the pronunciation of some words in learning the Alphabet, but the benefit claimed has reference to the habit he acquires of associating the names of words with their forms; and it will be shown in the article on methods of teaching pronunciation that the learner is more dependent for his skill in pronuciation upon such associations than upon the names or the sounds of the letters.

Two additional suggestions will close the discussion:

The names and the sounds of the letters should be taught cotemporaneously. If the A B C method be adopted, the powers of the letters should be taught before attempting to teach pronunciation, for the names of the letters are of little use in pronouncing. Practice will prove moreover that both the names and sounds of letters can be taught in nearly the same time that either can be, and hence dictates the policy of teaching them together. If the Word method be adopted, the analysis of words into the letters of which they are composed, and into their component sounds, will prove each an advantage to the other. The variety this double analysis will furnish will add interest to the lesson, and since the eye is engaged in one, and the ear in the other, the process cannot be wearisome. Nothing need be said specially in regard to the methods of teaching the sounds of the letters, as their names and sounds must be taught substantially in the same manner. The sounds of letters, however, are more difficult to utter than their names, and the teacher must train his pupils to utter them after him, and carefully guide them in placing their organs of speech in the proper position to do so.

The capital and small letters should be taught at the same time. Those letters which are alike will be remembered from their resemblance; and those that differ, from contrast; and one class of letters will be needed by pupils about as soon as the other.

Pronunciation.

Pronunciation consists in naming words upon seeing the characters which compose them, or hearing uttered the names of these characters or the sounds represented by them. In reading, words are usually pronounced upon seeing the characters which compose them. A familiar word can be pronounced without seeing it, if some one name the letters of which it is composed; and the pronunciation of all words is but the combination of their elementary sounds.

The orthographical peculiarities of the English language render the work of acquiring its pronunciation exceedingly difficult. If there was a single character to represent every elementary sound in the language, the name and sound of the letters would be identical, and the pronunciation of a word would merely consist in a synthesis of its elementary sounds and could present no serious impediment to the progress of a learner. But we are to speak of methods of teaching the Pronunciation of the English Language, and must therefore accept it as it is.

Pronunciation may be taught in two ways; first, by causing the pupil to name or notice the characters composing words, and utter in combination the sounds they are intended to represent. This may be called the *Synthetic method.* Second, by causing the pupil to associate the names of words with their forms. This may be called the *Associative method.*

1. The Synthetic Method.—The names of all words are syntheses of their elementary sounds. If each linguistic sound was represented by a single

letter, and the name and sound of the letter were the same, the teaching of Pronunciation would consist: first, in acquainting the pupil with the elementary sounds; second, in impressing upon his memory the characters by which these sounds are represented; and, third, in teaching him to pronounce words by uttering the sounds in combination. This is strictly a process of synthesis.

With respect to the English language, each sound is not represented by a single letter, and the names and sounds of the letters are seldom identical. Our present task is to show how the Pronunciation of such a language can be taught synthetically. As might be supposed, the Synthetic method has assumed several forms, each of which will be discussed in its order.

1st. *The Alphabetic Method.*—To commence properly the work of teaching Pronunciation according to this method, the pupils must know the names of the letters of the Alphabet. When able to point out and name all the letters presented individually, they are required to point them out and name them as they occur in words, and then to pronounce the words. At first, monosyllabic words which contain no silent letters are selected, and afterwards the pupils are gradually introduced to more difficult monosyllabic, dissyllabic, and polysyllabic words.

This is the method generally practiced in our schools; but it will require little argument to show that it cannot be the best that might be adopted. The radical error underlying it is the assumption that the *name* of a word is a synthesis of the *names* of the letters composing it — a thing which is not true of a single word in the English language. A child cannot know upon merely naming the letters in a word, what sounds they represent, whether other letters may not represent the same sounds, or whether they represent any sounds at all. Take such simple words as *at*, *go*, *me;* name the letters, and then combine the sounds uttered; and there will be formed a result wholly unlike the names of these words. If the simplest words cannot be pronounced by combining the names of their component letters, still less can words like *leisure*, *victuals*, *phthisic*, *knife*, *yacht*, *ycleped*, and thousands of others whose pronunciation could hardly be guessed from a knowledge of their orthography.

It must be admitted, however, that pupils do learn to pronounce in schools where no other method of teaching Pronunciation than the Alphabetic is used. The proper explanation of this fact is that the teacher supposes he is teaching according to one method when he is actually teaching according to another. The child is not guided to the pronunciation of a word by naming its letters, as many teachers seem to think, but he learns to associate the name of the word which the teacher gives him with its form, the parts of which he has named. Every teacher who has used this method will testify that after pupils had named the letters composing a word, he had to give them its pronunciation, and sometimes to repeat it again and again, before it became fixed in their minds. In stating this, it is not intended to be denied that naming the letters may sometimes aid the pupil in pronouncing

The names of letters may do something to suggest their power, when practice has made these powers partially familiar; and so far as this can be the case, some advantage in pronouncing may be derived from the Alphabetic method.

2nd. *The Phonic Method.*—According to the Phonic method, the teacher first imparts to his pupils a knowledge of the sounds of the language. His next object is to teach them to combine sounds. This he may do by uttering individual sounds, and then showing how they can be combined; and afterwards requiring his pupils to utter sounds and make combinations of them. Such lessons are valuable, and children may be taught in this way a correct oral pronunciation.

The point of difficulty with the Phonic method is to apply it to written words. As applied in teaching the pronunciation of the German language (and this method comes to us from Germany), it answers a good purpose, because nearly all the German letters have but a single sound, and where this is not the case, the power of the letter can generally be determined by the notation. The peculiarities of the Orthography of the English language, with the same characters representing several sounds, and the same sounds represented by different characters, its silent letters, and its double consonants, must render the application of the Phonic method to the teaching of the pronunciation of our language a work of much difficulty. Indeed, it is scarcely possible to do it to any useful extent, without employing the aid of orthographical rules, classifications of words, and systems of notation; but with these auxiliaries many teachers esteem it the most philosophical and practical of the methods now in use. The leading features of the method when thus used must be described.

As already stated, the first step in the Phonic method is to impart a knowledge of the elementary sounds of the language and the characters by which they are represented; and as there are more than twenty-six of these sounds, and some of the letters of the Alphabet have several sounds, some system of notation must be adopted.

The second step in this method is to teach pupils to combine these elementary sounds so as to form words. The work of combining sounds may commence as soon as pupils become acquainted with a sufficient number of them to form combinations.

It is evident that these two steps constitute the whole work of teaching Pronunciation, but in practice many difficulties will be encountered of which something must be said.

It is best to teach first the short sounds of the vowels: as *a* in *at*, *e* in *en*, *i* in *it*, *o* in *ox*, *u* in *us*. Next should be taught the sounds of the simple consonants: as *b*, *d*, *f*, *l*, *m*, *n*, *p*, &c. Then come words of two letters; as *an*, *at*, *in*, *ox*, &c.; or combinations that form parts of words: as *ad*, *et*, *in*, *ol*, *up*, &c.; and afterwards words composed in the same way of three or four letters may be given. The word-tables composed of such monosyllables as *ba*, *ma*, *le*, *he*, *si*, *no*, *tu*, *bla*, *ble*, *bad*, *mad*, &c., as found in our old-fasnioned spelling-books, could be made very useful as exercises in phonic synthesis.

The preceding paragraph points out what is appropriate in lessons for beginners. In advancing further, it will be best to choose a spelling-book in which words are arranged according to their analogies in respect to some peculiarity in sound, and presented in an order progressing from the easy to the difficult. Interest may be added to first lessons by introducing words that represent objects and actions familiar to children.

In giving first lessons in Pronunciation according to this method, cards, letter-blocks, and blackboards may be advantageously used. As an example of the mode of teaching such lessons, an exercise upon a blackboard will be described. Let the teacher draw a letter, say *a*, upon the blackboard, and require the pupils to give its sound; then *t* may be placed on the right side of it, its sound given, and the two sounds combined; and, afterwards, *r* may be placed upon the left side of it, its sound given also, and the whole word, *rat*, pronounced. Erasing *r*, *b*, *f*, *m*, *n*, *s*, or *v* may be substituted, and the pupils required to pronounce the new combinations. The other letters composing the word can be changed in a similar way, and other words can be chosen and built up or taken apart in a manner, when performed by an ingenious teacher, that never fails to engage the attention of pupils. At times, it may be well for pupils to point out or draw in their order the characters which represent particular sounds, uttered by the teacher, and then combine them into words; or the combinations may be made without the characters. As soon as pupils are made thoroughly acquainted with the elementary sounds of the language, and the characters used to represent them, and have attained some facility in combining them into syllables and monosyllabic words by practicing a series of exercises designed to accomplish that end, they may take up the more formal lessons of a well-arranged spelling-book. In such a book the words are carefully classed according to their analogies of sound, and the character or combination of characters which is used to represent the sound, common to the whole, is placed prominently at the head of the lesson, and serves as a key to the pronunciation. For example *a*, as in *fate*, might be the key, and then the lesson would contain such words as *aid*, *gay*, *they*, *veil*, *break*, *guage*, *&c.*; or the sound of *sh* in *ship*, might be made to indicate the pronunciation of a large class of words in which that sound is represented by *ti*, *si*, *ci*, *ch*, *s*, *ce*, *se*, and *sch*.

After pupils have learned the pronunciation of the words of a lesson by making a synthesis of their elementary sounds, they must have much practice in naming words without uttering the individual sounds of which they are composed. The division of words of more than one syllable into syllables is proper for children in their first efforts to pronounce; but the same words should be immediately pronounced without such division. A Spelling-Book, arranged in conformity with the method of teaching Pronunciation now indicated, should contain many miscellaneous exercises, in which all classification and all notation should be discarded.

From what has been said, it is evident that the Phonic method of teaching Pronunciation is more philosophical than the Alphabetic method. It presents the subject in a series of well-graded exercises. It is consistent with itself, systematic, and logical. There are, however, some objections to it which must be noticed.

It is objected that the classes of words required by this method, if made according to their analogous sounds, would be so numerous that few children could remember them. Besides, if all the words belonging to a particular class were to be always arranged in a single lesson, it would bring together both easy and difficult words in a manner that could not fail to perplex the learner. The authors of Spelling-Books, it would seem, might easily obviate this objection.

It is objected further that pupils taught to rely upon analogy of sounds or a system of notation for the pronunciation of words, would find themselves greatly perplexed in dispensing with these helps when it became necessary in general reading The miscellaneous exercises in pronouncing referred to on a preceding page would remove this objection.

It is objected finally that there are many words in the English language that do not admit of classification with other words in any way that would be useful to a learner, and whose Orthography is so peculiar that a synthesis of their elementary sounds would scarcely aid him in remembering their Pronunciation. This is the most serious objection that can be brought against the Phonic method of teaching Pronunciation, and I see no way of answering it. It would seem that the Pronunciation of such words can be best learned by a different method.

3d. *The Phonetic Method.*—It is generally agreed that there are over forty elementary sounds in the English language. Our Alphabet contains but twenty-six letters. The advocates of the Phonetic method of teaching Pronunciation generally use the letters of our present Alphabet, each to represent one sound, and invent others as signs for the sounds unrepresented.

The first step in the application of this method is to teach the elementary sounds and the characters which have been agreed upon to represent them.

The second step is to teach pupils to combine sounds when uttered by the teacher or suggested by their appropriate symbols. These combinations consist at first of two sounds, then of three, and thus on, until they include all of those found in the longest words. Spelling-books and spelling-cards suited to this method have been prepared and can be used as in the other methods. The same advantage, too, may be derived from the use of blackboards and letter-blocks.

The third step consists in having pupils make the transition from the pronunciation of words spelled phonetically to those spelled in the common way. This transition may be made by placing the same words spelled in both ways in parallel columns or in alternate lines. There is so strong a resemblance or so great a contrast between the two modes of spelling that pupils do not find much difficulty, it is claimed, in passing from the phonetic word-symbols to the common word-symbols.

It is but just to say that experiments have been made, and apparently with fairness, designed to test the relative advantages of the Phonetic and other methods of teaching Pronunciation; and results have been reported decidedly favorable to the former.

Upon the other hand, other experiments have failed to yield the same results and some very strong objections have been urged against the Phonetic method.

It is alleged that a pupil taught to pronounce upon the principle that every letter is sounded and that every sound is represented by a single character, would be completely bewildered in attempting to dispose of the silent letters, and the numerous characters used to represent the same sound, and numerous sounds represented by the same characters, which are incident to our English Orthography. In consequence, it is denied that the transition from the pronunciation of words spelled Phonetically to the pronunciation of those spelled in the ordinary manner can be easily made, or made at all without a departure from the principle of the Phonetic method.

It is maintained, too, that pupils taught according to the Phonetic method, will experience great difficulty in learning to spell. Practicing phonic analysis exclusively, they would be apt to make the number of letters in a word equal to the number of its elementary sounds, and this would tend to introduce errors into their Orthography.

2. The Associative Method. — According to the Associative Method, Pronunciation is learned by associating the names of words with their forms. No conscious synthesis of the names of letters or of sounds represented by them is made, but the pupil is taught at once the written signs for oral words.

Children can be taught to pronounce by this method. Oral language exists. Children can talk. They use words. Written language was designed to be the medium of communication between the ear and the eye — to convert the products of the former sense into forms recognizable by the latter. It is a matter of history that various forms of writing have prevailed at different periods, and it is well known that in Stenography and Telegraphing the common word-signs are not used. Besides, it is plain that any arbitrary symbol may be agreed upon to represent a word, and by familiar association be made to suggest it. It is upon this principle that the Associative Method of teaching Pronunciation is based, and it has no reference to the component letters, or the component sounds of words.

Since the association between the names of words and their forms is arbitrary, the irregularities of the Orthography of the English language present no difficulties in the way of acquiring its pronunciation that would not be presented in a language strictly phonetic.

Teaching, according to this method, will be successful in proportion as it succeeds in making a lasting association between the names of words and their forms. Much skill will be required on the part of the teacher to attain this end.

It is best to select for first lessons words which stand for things in which children are most interested, as *boy*, *girl*, *dog*, *cat*, *whip*, *tree*, &c. These may be given first in connection with pictures, but afterwards without the pictures.

The second class of lessons should contain such words as *of*, *in*, *a*, *to*, *an*, *the*, *and*, *is*, *are*, *has*, *have*, &c.

The third class of lessons may embody the same words in short sentences. These should be so constructed as to interest children.

In all these lessons, books and cards suitably prepared, letter-blocks, and blackboards may be advantageously used. The forms of words must be impressed upon the pupils' memories by describing and analyzing them, talking about the objects they represent, and making their names familiar by frequent repetition.

The lessons which succeed these, containing more difficult words, should be arranged upon the same principle, and instruction given in them in the same manner. Each lesson should consist of a proper number of words, and when the pupil is familiar with their pronunciation individually presented, he can be taught to pronounce them in sentences intermixed with words learned in preceding lessons.

In estimating the value of this method, it must be admitted that no one can pronounce words with facility who has not formed a familiar association between their names and their forms. The attempt to do this directly, in the manner proposed by the Associative Method encounters some difficulties.

It would be a task of great difficulty to acquaint pupils with the immense vocabulary of the English language without the aid of phonic synthesis or the analogies of the language. It would be subject to the same objections as the Verbal System of writing practiced by the Ancients, or the clumsy word-signs of the Chinese.

It would also involve the additional labor upon

the teacher of pronouncing every word for the pupil. In strict accordance with the method, the pupil could not aid himself in pronouncing by naming letters, giving sounds, seeking out analogies, or searching Dictionaries.

Sufficient has been said of each of the methods of teaching Pronunciation when applied independently. It has been seen that difficulties lie in the path of all of them, and it remains to be ascertained whether some of these may not be removed by a judicious union of methods. The method thus formed may be called the *Eclectic Method.* Some repetition may be necessary in describing it.

A word is the simplest subdivision of discourse. A child uses words when he begins to talk, not sentences on the one hand, or letters or elementary sounds on the other. It is most natural, in learning written language, that the pupil should also commence with words—that he should translate words he can understand by sound into words he can understand by sight. So far as the first lessons in Pronunciation are concerned, then, I would follow the Associative Method. It may be followed to the extent of teaching pupils to read short sentences.

As soon as pupils are able to pronounce a certain number of words at sight, or while they are learning to do it, they should be required to analyze them into their component letters and sounds, and, afterwards, be instructed as to the manner in which elementary sounds are combined to form words, and as to the fact that letters are used to represent sounds, and that their names and their sounds are different.

All this should be abundantly illustrated. As some of the letters of the Alphabet have several sounds, it will be necessary to adopt a system of notation.

From this point on through the Spelling-Book, I would adopt the arrangement of words and exercises previously described as appropriate to the Phonic method; but I would not adhere to that method in conducting the recitations. I would conduct recitations in the following manner, which, I think, enables pupils to profit by what is good in all methods. First, let the teacher pronounce the words and the pupils imitate him. Second, let the pupils name the elementary sounds in a word, and then pronounce it. Third, let the pupils name the letters composing a word, and then pronounce it. Fourth, let the pupils pronounce the word without giving the elementary sounds or naming the letters. Of course, the words should be disposed of in this way one at a time. The first step enables the pupil to obtain a correct pronunciation of a word, and to initiate an association between its name and its form. The second is an exercise in phonic synthesis. The third is an application of the Alphabetic method and has advantages in itself, and in the preparation for learning to spell which it affords. The fourth is the consummation of the end aimed at—the pronunciation of a word at sight. Thus, as I conceive, the strong points of one method may be made to supply the weak points of another, and each deriving help from the others, an Eclectic method can be formed that is at once philosophical and practical.

Pupils must not only be taught to pronounce words, but they ought to be taught to pronounce them correctly; and it is requisite that something be said in this connection regarding the method of attaining this desirable end. Contrary to the common practice, great care should be taken to have the pupil acquire a correct pronunciation to the greatest extent possible, before he begins to read—pronouncing words in sentences is not reading.

In teaching pupils to pronounce correctly, two things must be attended to: first, *Enunciation;* second, *Accent.* Enunciation relates to the manner of uttering sounds. Accent is stress of voice placed upon particular syllables in words.

Certain impediments frequently lie in the way of pupils' acquiring a good Enunciation. Among them are imperfect vocal organs, timidity, and bad habits.

When pupils are unable to utter certain sounds on account of imperfect vocal organs, the teacher may, in some cases aid in removing the difficulty by training them to speak with due deliberation, with an expiring breath, and with the mouth open, so as to allow the weak organs freedom of movement; but a want of time in school will generally prevent that prolonged application of remedies deemed essential to effect a cure. Lisping, stammering, stuttering, and like vocal defects, can often be cured; but special schools are wanted to apply properly the means. If the teacher find the impediment to arise from inability to utter a certain sound, he can often remove it by securing practice upon the most nearly related sounds. He can do something, too, by showing the position of the organs in uttering the sounds with which difficulty is experienced. He can always do much by patiently giving general vocal culture.

If pupils mispronounce words in consequence of their timidity, the teacher must endeavor to gain their confidence by speaking words of encouragement and showing an interest in their work. He must also lead them step by step to have confidence in themselves.

Bad habits are the most common source of mispronunciations. Children listen to words incorrectly pronounced, and, of course, imitate what they hear. The spoken language of few neighborhoods is free from errors; and that of many is full of them. Children learn to utter certain vocal elements erroneously, to omit them when they ought not to be omitted, and to use them when they ought not to be used. These bad habits can only be corrected by long and patient training in phonic analysis and phonic synthesis. Pupils must be made familiar with all the elementary sounds of the language. They must be taught to make words by combining sounds, and to distinguish the simple sounds contained in words. They should be allowed much practice upon combinations of sounds of difficult utterance, and words and classes of words which they are liable to mispronounce. Great difficulty will be experienced with the vocal sounds in unaccented syllables, but the teacher must make his practice conform to the best authorities he can find upon the subject. Beginners may derive advantage from a division of words into syllables.

All words in the English language of more than one syllable have one accented syllable. Polysyllabic words have generally both a primary and a secondary accent. The placing of the accent is an important matter in pronouncing words, and teachers should carefully train their pupils to do it properly. Their own pronunciation should be a correct model for imitation. Patient attention must be paid to the accentuation of words new to pupils, and frequent repetition is necessary to break up habits of mispronouncing words with respect to which they have been accustomed to place the accent upon the wrong syllable. Much advantage may be had from the practice of having pupils write on slates or black-boards columns of words, and then mark the accented syllables. Lessons of the same kind may be made with the words as arranged in Spelling-Books. As soon as pupils can use a Dictionary, they should have access to one. It will only be added that more attention to the principles of Orthoepy in Primary schools would save much labor in higher schools and many foolish blunders in society.

ORTHOGRAPHY.

Spelling consists in expressing the characters composing words upon hearing or conceiving those words. In pronouncing, the forms of letters are presented to the eye, or their names or sounds to the ear, and the pupils are expected to name the words thus constituted. Spelling is this process reversed. More concisely, it may be said that in pronouncing, we have given letters or letter-sounds to find words; and in spelling, we have given words to find letters or letter-sounds. Pronunciation is essentially a synthetic process; but Spelling is an analytic process. Logically, Pronunciation must precede Spelling in a course of study, because children must be acquainted with words as wholes before they can reproduce their component parts. Practically, however, it may be convenient to include exercises in both in the same lesson.

Words may be analyzed in two ways; and consequently there are two methods of teaching Orthography. The first method consists in resolving the words into their elementary sounds, and in expressing the characters which represent these sounds. This method is founded upon an analysis of sound, and depends upon the sense of hearing. It may be called the *Auricular method.*

The second method consists in resolving words into their several parts, and in expressing these parts. This method is founded upon an analysis of form, and depends upon the sense of seeing. It may be called the *Ocular method*

Both methods are dependant upon the memory.

1. The Auricular Method.—If the English was strictly a phonetic language, the Auricular method of teaching spelling would have advantages over any other method. In that case, spelling would consist in the analysis of words into the simple sounds which compose them, and the representation of these sounds by their appropriate characters. Children could be readily taught to do this, and thus escape the heavy task of memorizing spelling-lessons. The English language, however, does not conform its Orthography to the Phonetic principle. Many of the letters composing words are silent. Many letters represent more than one sound, and many sounds are represented by more than one letter.

Even with words of the simplest Orthography, an analysis of their sound never gives the names of the letters.

Orthography is the reverse of Pronunciation. The Auricular method of teaching Orthography is the reverse of the Synthetic method of teaching Pronunciation, and might be divided into the same number of special methods. As letters can be named and the Pronunciation of words suggested by them, so the names of words may suggest their component letters. As elementary linguistic sounds can be combined to form words; so words can be analyzed into their simplest sounds. As a classification of words according to their analogies aids in learning Pronunciation working forwards, so may such a classification be made to aid in the work of learning Orthography working backwards. As separate characters may be used to represent all the elements employed in phonic synthesis, so may they be used to represent the results of phonic analysis. Thus methods of teaching Orthography might be arranged to correspond to the Alphabetical, the Phonic, and the Phonetic methods of teaching Pronunciation. This detail is deemed unnecessary here, however, since whatever merits or demerits these methods have with respect to Pronunciation they must have with respect to Orthography.

2. The Ocular Method.—We spell more by form than by sound. We are more apt to remember letters as parts of whole words, than we are to remember them as characters representing sounds.

We use the sense of seeing in spelling more than that of hearing. In proof of this position, it might be stated that most persons are accustomed to write words with respect to the Orthography of which they are in doubt, or to conceive their form, thus judging whether words are spelled correctly by their *looks*.

Proof-readers, whom I have consulted, allege that they seldom consider what elementary sounds compose words, and then what characters represent them; but they think of words as pictures which are marred by bad spelling.

It is the general experience, too, that the blind spell with more difficulty than the deaf.

The Ocular method of teaching Orthography is founded upon the same principle as the Associative method of teaching Pronunciation, and corresponds to it. By this method, the problem of Pronunciation is: given the form of a word to determine its name; and that of Orthography is: given the name of a word to find its form. Pronunciation is the translation of eye-language into ear-language, and Orthography is the translation of ear-language into eye-language. It need scarcely be added that the advantages and disadvantages of teaching Pronunciation by the Associative method belong equally to the Ocular method of teaching Orthography.

In the preceding Article it was stated that the different methods of teaching Pronunciation might be combined, and that an Eclectic method might be formed that would avoid many of the objections which could be made to each of these methods when used by itself, and embrace the certain advantages derived from all of them. The same may be said in reference to methods of teaching Orthography. Pronunciation and Orthography should be taught together, and both require the same arrangement of subject-matter; and as this arrangement has already been indicated, a repetition is now uncalled for.

As the most important thing to be attended to in teaching Orthography is to impress the form of words upon the memory of pupils, some suggestions may be made with reference to this end. The correct forms of words may be impressed upon the memory of a child by selecting words that he understands, and that represent something in which he is interested. It may be done by calling attention to the peculiar forms of words, their analogies, and by requiring pupils to draw or write their spelling-lessons before reciting them. If pupils be taught to spell immediately the same words that have furnished their pronouncing or reading lesson, it will be found to be of great advantage. One exercise may contain words correctly spelled with which pupils may be made familiar, and then pass on to another in which the same words are used with letters omitted, added, or misplaced, that they are required to correct. Words of like Pronunciation but unlike Orthography can be most easily spelled when their meaning is known and contrasted. Pupils should be made familiar with the various methods of spelling words of doubtful Orthography, and for this purpose lists of such words should be frequently spelled. There are a few Orthographical rules, such as those with respect to changing *y* into *i*, and doubling the final consonant, a knowledge of which may be profitable to pupils. Each rule should be fixed in the mind by numerous examples.

After this statement of principles, it is deemed proper that a more detailed description should be given of methods of conducting recitations in Orthography.

1st. *Spelling Exercises for Beginners.*—Much attention should be paid to Orthography in our Primary schools. Those who do not learn to spell well when young, seldom acquire the ability to do so. Each lesson should be pronounced and then spelled. Pupils may repeat the names of words uttered by the teacher and associate them with their proper word-signs. They may name the letters or sounds composing words and again pronounce them. They may pronounce the words, and then give the letters or sounds. They may pronounce the words without giving either the letters or sounds. Finally, they should spell the words both by giving the names of the letters and the elementary sounds of the words. Each of these exercises will aid the others, and all ought to be embraced in the same lesson. The words contained in every primary reading lesson should be spelled, and the words used in a spelling lesson should be embraced in sentences and read.

A Reading-Frame with block-letters can be used very advantageously in teaching young children to spell. Words made of these letters can be imitated, taken apart, and put together in a manner well calculated to impress their forms upon the pupil's memory. The *handling* of the letters tends to fix the attention upon their relative locations in words.

Before children can write, they may draw or print words upon their slates or upon the blackboard. They can copy in this way their reading and pronouncing lessons.

2d. *An oral Exercise in Spelling.*—The common mode of managing an exercise in oral Spelling is to require pupils to prepare several columns of words from a Spelling-Book. A class is then formed, and the words are given out to each pupil, commencing at the head of the class and proceeding toward the foot. If a pupil misspell his word, the next below him may spell it and take his place; if two misspell a word, a third may try it, and so on to the end, unless some one spell it correctly.

It may be objected to this method that, by collusion among one another, each pupil knowing the order in which the words will be given out, may prepare only those words which he calculates will be assigned to him. This objection, however, can be easily obviated by the teacher's changing the order of assigning the words.

It is also objected to this method that, while pupils are spelling at one end of the class, they may be inattentive at the other end. This result does not occur unfrequently, but it may be prevented by the teacher's assigning words miscellaneously. If it be desirable to retain positions of honor and dishonor in the class, at the end of a recitation, those who have misspelled the fewest words can pass to the head of the class; those who have misspelled the next to the fewest words can occupy the next place, and thus on until all are located, such as misspelled the same number of words retaining the same relative position as when the recitation began. This changing of position need occupy but a moment, and necessitates no confusion. Each pupil can be readily accustomed to recollect the number of words he misspelled, and honestly to report it, or some one can be appointed to keep the account.

A more serious objection to the method of oral spelling is that by this mode of reciting each pupil can receive but a small portion of the words of the lesson, and the teacher does not know whether the whole lesson has been prepared or otherwise. In other studies the teacher may nearly always judge how well a pupil knows the whole lesson by the manner in which he recites a part of it, but this is obviously not the case with Orthography. Though this is a strong objection to oral spelling, yet the practice of it ought not to be wholly discarded. It sometimes happens that pupils cannot write, and sometimes it is inconvenient for them to do so; and if neither was the case, variety of method in reciting gives zest to study. Now and then, indeed, I do not think it out of place for the teacher to indulge his pupils in an old-fashioned spelling-match. The interest they will take in preparing for the contest will acquaint them with the Orthography of many words.

3d. *Method of using Slates in a Spelling Recitation.*—Those who spell well orally do not always write words correctly. Every teacher has witnessed and wondered at this fact. It may be that, in oral spelling, we rely more upon the sense of hearing than upon that of seeing, and that in written spelling the reverse is true. Whatever may be the cause, the fact is as stated, and hence the necessity that pupils should have ample practice in spelling words by writing them. This exercise may be conducted by using slates. The pupils having made the necessary preparation by looking closely at the words of the lesson, writing them, and naming the letters composing them, are supposed to be conveniently seated, each with a slate and pencil. The teacher now pronounces the words of the lesson, or such of them as he may select, and all the pupils write them. When the words have all been written, the teacher must ascertain how many of them have been spelled correctly. For this purpose, I have found the best plan to be for the teacher to spell the words in the order he gave them out, and require each pupil to mark such of them as he may have misspelled. Pupils may, however, spell the words by turns, or as called upon, and correct one another, marking misspelled words as before. How to dispose of the misspelled words is an interesting question. It would be a great mistake merely to have them marked, and then allow them to pass without further notice. It is an excellect plan to require each pupil to write upon paper lists of all the words he misspelled, and then to make special preparation to spell them at certain fixed times, once a week, or more frequently, in a review lesson. At such a recitation, all the lists must be handed to the teacher, and he can assign the words in the usual manner; and as each pupil has only the words misspelled by himself to prepare, it can justly be expected that no mistakes will be made.

In addition to the attainment of the ability to write words correctly, some of the advantages of this method are that each pupil has the opportunity of spelling all the words of the lesson, all the members of the class are constantly employed during the recitation, no one who does not know his lesson can escape detection, and misspelled words can be restudied and recited a second time.

4th. *Method of using the Blackboard in a Spelling Recitation.*—In order to conduct a spelling recitation upon a blackboard, there must be sufficient surface to allow to each pupil the requisite amount of space upon which to write his lesson. When ready to recite, each pupil takes his place in front of the space upon which his lesson is intended to be written; and with a piece of crayon in one hand and a suitable rubber in the other, prepares himself to write. The lesson is then given out, written, corrected, and reviewed, as when slates are used. Instead of each pupil's correcting his own work, all may change places, and each correct the work of another. Slates can be exchanged in the same manner; but in both cases, there is always some loss of time, and there may be ill feeling.

I prefer slates to the blackboard in conducting a spelling lesson, for the reason that while the general advantages are the same, pupils cannot so readily copy from a blackboard their misspelled words after the recitation, and during the recitation there is a strong temptation to watch each other's work and profit by it. This latter objection can be partially removed by dividing the whole class into two sub-classes, placing the members of each alternately, and giving out the words of the lesson to each sub-class in a different order; but this arrangement is itself not free from objections.

5th. *False Orthography as an Exercise in Spelling.*—Proof-readers become very expert spellers. They detect instantly by its *look* every misspelled word. An exercise something like proof-reading might be profitably introduced into our schools. Pupils could be made to notice carefully the correct spelling of certain collections of words, and afterwards these words might be embraced in miscellaneous exercises systematically misspelled. Reading lessons might be followed by exercises in False Orthography, or misspelled words might be introduced into sentences and the pupils be engaged in correcting them. Examples of False Orthography might be placed under each of the Orthographical rules, and pupils could thus become familiar with the rules in applying them. A book containing matter suitably arranged can easily be conceived. In preparing such lessons, pupils ought to have loose slips of paper upon which they could make their corrections for the teacher's inspection.

6th. *Dictation Exercises.*—All exercises that require pupils to write words when given out by the teacher may be called Dictation Exercises; but by such exercises in this connection are meant sentences, paragraphs, or short pieces of composition read by the teacher and written by the pupils. The meaning of words contained in sentences is more readily discerned than when they are arranged in columns, and consequently children take more interest in spelling them. Besides, the spelling of sentences seems to them to be working to more purpose than spelling the words of dry spelling-book columns.

Dictation exercises should be first written upon slates, but when they have been corrected they may be transferred to paper. The manner of correcting the exercises may be the same as in the ordinary spelling upon slates. With advanced classes, the teacher will do well to make such selections for dictation as are worth preserving on account of their literary merit; and something may be done in this way to cultivate the taste even of beginners.

It is considered proper to append a few additional suggestions. They have a general application.

Some attention should be paid to Orthography in all branches. It is not amiss to ask pupils to spell the new words with which they meet in Arithmetic, Geography, Grammar, or any higher study. Especially is it proper that pupils be required to spell the new words which occur in their reading lessons. I have noticed pupils increase their skill in spelling English words by practice in spelling the words of other languages.

A wonderful degree of interest can be created among children by giving them lessons in which they are required to spell common things, such as the things about the school-room, articles of furniture, articles of wearing apparel, kinds of food, things bought at stores, things taken to market, names of trees, flowers, vessels, vehicles, men, women, &c., &c.

In giving out a spelling lesson or dictation exercise, the teacher should always pronounce the words correctly, and in a clear, audible voice.

The teacher should never mispronounce a word in order to aid the pupil in spelling it.

A word or sentence should be repeated but once, and in oral spelling but one trial should be allowed the pupil. In written spelling, since the pupil cannot know immediately whether his work is correct or not, he will not often desire to change what he first writes.

It is well for pupils to pronounce the words in oral spelling after the teacher has done so, and before spelling them; and also to give the pronunciation of each syllable as spelled by itself, and in combination with the preceding syllable or syllables, if there are such.

What has been said on the subject of methods of teaching Orthography has reference only to acquiring skill in spelling words as authorized by good authorities. There are Etymological and other reasons why words are spelled as we see them. Orthographical peculiarities have not been produced by mere chance or caprice. They are often the result of linguistic laws, which can be investigated. When pupils have made that degree of advancement necessary to prosecute these philosophical inquiries, teachers will find any effort they may make to encourage them amply repaid. In no department of science can there be opened a richer field than that which embraces the origin, nature, and changes of written language. While we are careful to investigate the Orthographic laws relating to foreign languages, let us not forget what is due from us to our Mother-Tongue.

Reading.

Reading, as a branch of instruction, is the art of giving proper oral expression to written or printed composition. Taken in this sense, the words Reading and Elocution are synonymous, although the latter term is generally applied to the higher departments of Reading. Skill in Reading may be desired for the purpose of understanding written or printed language, and without any intention of reading for the benefit of others; but it is evident that a teacher can only judge of such skill by an oral exhibition of it. What is said of Reading in the following discussion will apply almost equally well to Declamation and the different forms of Public Speaking.

Methods of teaching Reading are readily divisible into three classes: first, those which relate to *Reading as a Vocal Art;* second, those which relate to *Reading as a Mental Operation;* third, those which relate to *Delivery.*

1. Method of teaching Reading as a Vocal Art. — In reading we use the vocal organs as instruments; and, if these instruments are defective, it will be impossible to acquire the ability to read

well. As well might it be expected that a musician could make good music upon an instrument broken or out of tune, as to expect a person to read well with an uncultivated voice. Good reading depends as much upon the voice as good singing; and yet the systematic culture of the voice for purposes of reading is little attended to in educational institutions, and that is one great cause why there are so few good readers. The human voice is a wonderful instrument, and greatly susceptible of culture. No one can doubt who has heard a great vocalist sing, or seen a great actor play, that much of our singing, speaking, and reading might be better done. The Creator evidently intended that the voice should express all kinds of truth and all forms of sentiment that can originate in the soul.

Vocal culture in reading may either relate to the simple utterance of linguistic sounds, as they occur in words; or to the utterance of such sounds with respect to their Elocutionary qualities. The first division has already been called *Pronunciation;* the second may be called *Modulation.*

As methods of teaching Pronunciation were treated of in a preceding Article, it seems only necessary to say here that no one can read well who is unable to pronounce correctly and fluently. Exercises upon the Enunciation of sounds and the Pronunciation of words may, therefore, appropriately introduce a lesson in Reading. These exercises should be based upon the reading-lesson, and adapted in kind and extent to the acquirements of the class. Pupils just beginning to read should be taught to pronounce the words of the lesson before reading it, either as arranged in sentences (in which case they should be named in a reversed order from that in which they are read), or as arranged in columns. Some of the worst habits of bad reading arise from permitting children to attempt to read a lesson before they can pronounce the words contained in it. Even those counted good readers sometimes spoil the delivery of a sentence by a failure to articulate correctly a sound or a combination of sounds, or by the inability to pronounce readily a word or a succession of words.

Modulation, in the sense here used, includes the *Quantity*, *Compass*, *Movement*, and *Quality* of the voice.

Quantity.—By Quantity, in an Elocutionary sense, is meant the volume of voice that can be used—the power with which sounds can be uttered. Force, Emphasis, Slur, Stress, and Accent all relate to Quantity of voice. Force is the volume of voice applied in reading. Emphasis is the manner of applying more Force to certain words in a sentence, or sentences in a paragraph, than to others with which they are connected. Less Force, thus applied, produces the Slur. Stress is the manner of applying Force in uttering single sounds, syllables, or monosyllabic words. Accent is the greater Force with which certain syllables in pollysyllabic words are uttered than others in the same words.

Quantity of voice depends upon the power of the lungs, and a good reader must be able to control this power so as to utter loud or soft sounds at pleasure. A feeble voice may arise from general ill-health, or from weak lungs, or from a want of exercise of the pulmonary organs. It is the teacher's special duty to supply the want of exercise to these organs; but as the general culture of the voice can only be attained by particular applications of vocal power, the methods of doing so will be detailed in speaking of Force.

Some sentiments require to be given with a low, soft voice; and others with a voice loud and strong. Hence the necessity for vocal training in respect to Force. A reader should always make himself distinctly heard by those who listen to him; but weak voices, bad habits, timidity, and affectation stand in the way of securing this end in our schools. Not unfrequently, classes composed of girls read in a tone so soft as scarcely to be audible. It is not uncommon at Young Ladies' Seminaries for the pupils to undertake to entertain an audience by reading compositions of which scarcely a word can be heard; and the listeners are compelled to be content, if they can notice a slight motion of the reader's lips, and, now and then, a change of position. Strength can be given to the voice by judicious breathing exercises, and by oft-repeated lessons in uttering letters, letter-sounds, syllables, words, and sentences, with different degrees of loudness. The teacher should illustrate these lessons, by first making the sounds himself, and afterwards aid his pupils by accompanying them with his voice in their efforts to imitate him. I have succeeded best in this kind of training by using sentences selected in reference to the degree of Force in utterance required by the sentiment. It is an easy matter for a teacher to collect a great variety of such sentences. It is an advantage to place reading classes at some distance from the teacher, and to classify the voices of those who read in the same class and hear them in sections. Special care must be taken with those whose voices are naturally weak, and kind encouragement must inspire the timid with confidence. It is an easy matter to train children to read with sufficient Force. Nothing will please them better than exercises in "loud reading." It is not so easy to succeed with older pupils, but the methods proposed will be found the most effectual. Loud reading, must not be suffered to become a habit or the voice will be rendered incapable of uttering sounds with that variety of Force which the expression of different kinds of sentiment requires.

The masters of English speaking and English reading make very great use of Emphasis. In no other language, probably, is its use so common or so effective. Without it, not only would the sense of discourse be frequently ambiguous, but reading would be extremely monotonous. No better test of good reading can be found than a skilful use of Emphasis. Teachers should, therefore, train the vocal organs of their pupils so that they could apply Emphasis whenever and in whatever degree the sense requires it. Drill exercises in Emphasis might consist in uttering the sound of some letter or word a number of times with the same degree of Force; and, at certain intervals, or at a given signal, increasing the Force. In pronouncing a series of letters, figures, or words, some of them might be designated to receive Emphasis. Practice may be had with sentences in which the emphatic words are indicated to the eye. These may be either selected from a book, or written on the blackboard. It is in favor of such training that, while pupils are receiving this kind of vocal culture, they can, at the same time, learn the use of Emphasis, and the different methods of giving it. The Slur, in an Elocutionary sense, is directly opposed to Emphasis. If some sentences and parts of sentences are uttered with much Force, it necessitates the utterance of others with little Force. When a sentence or a part of a sentence is read more rapidly and less forcibly than others, it is said to be slurred. Examples of the Slur may be shown by reading parenthetical clauses, or side remarks in dialogues. The drill exercises are necessarily similar to those for Emphasis.

Emphasis and Slur have reference to the comparative Force with which sentences and parts of sentences are uttered; but if close observation be made, it will be found that the Force used in the utterance of single sounds is not equally distributed throughout the vocal movement. This modification of Force is called Stress. All the different kinds of Stress may be applied in the utterance of any simple sound or single syllable; but I have succeeded best in training the voices of pupils to utter sounds, with regard to Stress, by requiring them to imitate the pronunciation of words in which these different kinds of Stress are exemplified. Such words as *ring* and *ears*, might serve for Radical Stress; *bell* and *low*, for Vanishing Stress; *strike* and *sad* for Median Stress; and so of the other kinds.

Of Accent something was said in another connection, and it need only be added here that the best training exercises are those in which pupils imitate the teacher as he changes the Accent in pronouncing words, or follow him when he designates where the Accent should be placed. It increases interest when words are selected in respect to which a change of Accent brings about a change of meaning.

Compass.—In speaking or singing, the human voice moves between certain limits, above or below which it cannot utter sounds. The space included between these limits is called the Compass of the voice. The Compass of the voice is a limitation in extent of height or lowness, while the Quantity of the voice is a limitation in degree of power. The Compass of the voice may be marked by a regular series of gradations of sounds. Such a series is called a Scale, and the general name for its different degrees is Pitch. In other words, Pitch in reading denotes the point of elevation or depression of the voice. These points are called notes in Music. They are placed at considerable intervals, and the voice generally passes between them by leaps; while in Reading the intervals are mostly crossed by sliding the voice from one note to another. This sliding the voice from one degree of Pitch to another is Inflection, and it seems proper to consider it in connection with Pitch.

There may obviously be as many degrees of Pitch in Reading as there are notes in Music, but Elocutionists have not deemed it necessary to distinguish all of them. For all practical purposes five degrees of Pitch are sufficient, viz.: Very Low, Low, Middle, High, and Very High. The teacher will not find it a very difficult thing to train children to pitch their voices upon any key within their Compass. For this purpose he may select vowel sounds as *a*, *o;* syllables as *do*, *ra;* words as *on*, *one*, *book;* or suitable sentences. In exercises like these the teacher must first utter the sounds, that the pupils may imitate him as he passes from one degree of Pitch to another; but in the end the pupils must be able to give sounds or read sentences with any degree of Pitch required without such aid. It is an easy matter to arrange a list of sentences which would be good examples for the kind of practice here insisted upon. The list should not only contain sentences the sense of which would require them to be read with different degrees of Pitch; but some in which a change of Pitch is required in reading the same sentence.

Skill in reading depends greatly upon ability to manage the Inflections of the voice, and nothing but careful training can impart it. As in Pitch, the teacher may use for his training exercises the elementary vocal sounds, letters, figures, words, the syllables of the Diatonic Scale, or sentences adapted to the purpose. An interesting mode of recitation consists in arranging a series of sounds, letters, figures, or words, in the form of questions and answers, and allowing one portion of the class to put the questions, and the other to give the answers. The different kinds of Inflection are best illustrated by means of sentences; and these, too, furnish the most effective drill. Some Elocutionists have arranged bars, like those used in Music, and placed upon them certain marks indicating to the eye the upward and downward slides of the voice. By taking a simple sound or syllable, practice can be had in inflecting the voice as readily as in running up and down the Diatonic Scale.

Movement.—By the Movement of the voice is meant the degree of rapidity with which sounds can be uttered. It is a limitation in time. The degree of rapidity with which sounds are uttered in reading is called Rate. Closely connected with the Movement of the voice is Pause. Pauses in reading are suspensions of the voice for the purpose of giving rest to the reader, or effect to the reading.

Words or syllables should not be uttered in that stated measure which is heard in Music; but it is very evident that solemn discourse requires a Slow Rate; simple narrative, a Moderate Rate; gay, glad description, a Brisk Rate; and wild passion, a Rapid Rate; and it would be very much amiss to overlook these facts in reading. The voice, then, should be so trained as to be able to utter sounds rapidly or slowly at pleasure. Like a good musician, it should be able to keep time whether it be quick or slow. For the purpose of training his pupils to keep time in reading, the teacher will find the drill exercises used in Vocal Music to effect the same end, to be very valuable. Pupils can be made to give the Elementary Vocal Sounds, to count, to name the letters of the Alphabet, or repeat series of words in quick or slow time, as the teacher may direct.

Numerous sentences can be selected which require to be read with the different degrees of Rate, and should be made the subjects of frequent lessons. With a class in which some pupils read too fast or too slow, it is well occasionally to practice reading in concert. If the teacher observe the proper rate in leading the concert, the pupils will soon accustom themselves to follow.

Two kinds of Pauses are to be noted in reading. The first are those indicated by the marks of Punctuation; the second are those required by the sense but not indicated by the marks of Punctuation. The latter are called Rhetorical Pauses. Both require the same kind of vocal training. Pauses enable the reader to supply himself with breath, to rest his organs of speech, to make his delivery more effective. The Pauses which are indicated by the common marks of Punctuation must not be disregarded; but all rules which direct pupils to pause long enough at a Comma to count a certain number, a certain additional number at a Semicolon, and twice as many, perhaps, at a Period, are wholly arbitrary and serve only to confuse the pupil. Counting may be done rapidly or slowly; and, besides, since the place and length of the Pauses depend altogether upon the sense, a longer pause may be required at a Comma in one place, than at a Period in another. About the only successful mode in which a teacher can train his pupils to make proper Pauses in reading, is to present them correct models for imitation. He may either select sentences or take the ordinary reading-lessons, and then read each sentence slowly and with due regard to all the Pauses, requiring the pupils to follow, both singly and in concert, until his end is gained. The melody of verse requires certain Pauses in reading not used in prose. To train his pupils to properly regard these in blank verse as well as in that which is rhymed, and at the same time to have them avoid all appearance of sing-song tone, will demand great care on the part of the teacher.

Quality.—The Quality of the voice is its capability of uttering varied sounds. It is a limitation in kind, and includes the manner of uttering all varieties of vocal sounds. The particular Qualities of the voice applied in reading, are called Tones. The Tones are the language of the heart, and no department of Modulation requires more delicate management. It is by means of Tones in great part that Reading and Speaking are made lively and interesting. The sense of discourse can be conveyed by words, but the feelings of an author can only be expressed in the natural language of Tones. A reader or speaker who would interest an audience must not utter words coldly like a talking machine, but his manner of utterance must indicate his personal sentiments. His individuality must appear in what he says, and this is impossible without the use of Tones. There is a very great number of different Tones used in reading, many of which can only be appreciated by the ear, and cannot be expressed in words. Elocutionists, however, have formed the following general classes, viz.: Pure, Orotund, Aspirated, Guttural, and Tremulous. Pure Tone is clear and smooth, Orotund, deep, energetic, dignified; Aspirated, whispered; Guttural, harsh, growling, throat-formed; Tremulous, irregular, plaintive. Ability to use any one of these Tones at pleasure, or to change readily from one to another is to some a gift of nature; but there are few, whatever faults of Tone they may have either natural or acquired, whose voices do not admit of great improvement by judicious culture. Since the vocal organs are more flexible in youth, than when older, teachers who commence a course of training with their pupils, at an early age, will find their efforts productive of most fruit. Indeed, almost all that is then required is to preserve their natural purity and sweetness of Tone. No teacher who cannot himself utter sounds in the different Tones must expect his pupils to learn to do so. Children are generally apt imitators of sounds; but they cannot imitate what they do not hear. If a teacher be able to use correctly the different Tones in reading, he can readily find means of imparting the same power to his pupils. Any sound, syllable, or word can be uttered in various Tones. It is said that certain Elocutionists could make an audience laugh or weep, awaken their pity or their indignation, by the mere recitation of the letters of the Alphabet. In addition to this, every teacher of Reading should collect numerous prose sentences and stanzas of poetry, requiring a variety of Tones in the reading, and adapted to the capacities of the pupils, and use them for purposes of drill. Both teacher and pupils should have them committed to memory. The teacher should first utter the sentence in the required Tone; and then patiently aid the pupils in doing so. Much effort will be required to remove faults of Tone which have become habitual. Examples of Pure Tone should first be practiced upon; and, afterward, examples of the other Tones. The exercises must be continued, until the pupils shall have acquired the power of uttering sounds in any Tone when so directed.

2. METHOD OF TEACHING READING AS A MENTAL OPERATION. — Skill in reading does not depend wholly, or, perhaps, mainly, upon vocal culture. It matters not how well the voice is trained, unless there are intellects to think and hearts to feel, there can be no good reading. The best instrument will make poor music, if the performer be unskilful. If ability to make and vary sounds constitute all the requirements of good reading, a machine might possibly be made to read.

As a mental operation, Reading may either relate to the intellectual part of the mind or to the emotive part of it. Our discussion must, therefore, embrace: 1st, *Reading as related to the Intellect;* and, 2d, *Reading as related to the Emotions.*

1st. *Reading as related to the Intellect.*—No one can read well what he does not understand. Great powers of imitation and a well-cultivated voice would be quite as likely to make worse his reading who attempted to read what he did not understand, as to make it better. A parrot could never be taught to read. School boys make sad work reading Latin, until they come to appreciate the meaning of the words they use and the sentiments they utter. A person can read that which he has written himself better than that which others have written, because he more fully comprehends it. No one can read a passage well who is not able to place himself in the position of its author, enter into his spirit, see as he saw, and understand as he understood.

In view of the fact above stated, a teacher should never assign a reading-lesson to his pupils that they are not able to comprehend. Sufficient attention is not paid to this principle with any class of pupils; but no where is it so palpably violated as in the case of children just learning to read. Reading-books are frequently placed in their hands which contain matter entirely beyond their comprehension. In the great majority of our schools, the pupils are using reading-books which are too difficult for them. Many teachers, from a desire to gratify patrons, a misdirected ambition, or a false standard of excellence, advance their pupils into the higher numbers of their series of reading-books at much too early an age. The consequence is not only that they learn little in reading that is of value, but they acquire bad habits which it is scarcely possible to correct. Reading-books for beginners should contain little else than simple narrations and lively conversations concerning objects in which they feel an interest. Starting here, such books might so increase their range of subjects and so add to the variety of their style, as to adapt themselves to the pupils of any age or degree of acquirement in learning. At present, however, it must be confessed that reading-books are not so much in fault as reading-teachers.

Teachers should make careful inquiry concerning

their pupils' knowledge of the subject-matter of the reading-lesson. Pupils should be accustomed to study the lesson with this prospect, and the inquiries should, in general, be made before they are permitted to read. Teachers must be careful in the reading, as in other lessons, to adapt their questions to the capacities of the pupils to whom they are addressed. The matter of reading-lessons is so varied that it is difficult to designate in detail the questions that may be asked concerning it. In general, it may be said, that they should be such as to call forth the pupil's knowledge of the subject presented in the lesson, and to extend, consolidate, and impress that knowledge. Pupils may be required to give the sense of the selection or passage to be read in their own language, and those who have minds sufficiently mature, may show the relation of the sentences in a paragraph to one another, and the relation of each paragraph to the whole composition. Questions addressed to young learners must be calculated to give exercise to their perceptive powers and their memories; but those asked of advanced pupils should call into requisition the faculties of judgment, reason, and imagination. Incidentally, in reading-lessons, allusions are often made to distinguished persons, to noted places, to the principles of science, to works of art, to certain books, to the customs of antiquity, to human duties, and to many other things that cannot be here enumerated; and as these give life and beauty to discourse, as well as reveal the under-currents of the author's thought, no teacher can fully discharge his trust who does not make them the subject of study and explanation. It thus appears that, while all reading-books should be arranged primarily with reference to Elocutionary ends, they may be made the means of imparting very important information, and inducing highly beneficial culture.

It is the duty of a teacher of reading to see that his class fully understand the language of the author read, and appreciate his style. For this purpose, he must call their attention to the definition of the words, the form and construction of the sentences, the marks of punctuation, and the various kinds of figures used in the composition. He must make language transparent, in order that thought may be revealed. Let the idea be hereafter wholly discarded that flippant pronunciation is good reading. Better that the whole time of a recitation be spent upon a single paragraph, or even a single sentence, than to suffer pupils merely to utter sounds without perceiving the sense they represent. If teachers would make good readers of their pupils, they must teach them to weigh every word, phrase, and sentence of the lesson. The reading-lesson prepared and recited in this manner becomes a fine intellectual exercise, and furnishes good opportunities of imparting valuable instruction in practical Grammar and practical Rhetoric. To those pupils who are properly prepared, many questions relating to the language used in the lesson to be read, need not be put at any one recitation, but enough should be asked to keep the attention of the class constantly alive to the importance of understanding it.

Skilful reading is hardly possible for one who is not a good general scholar. A person who has been accustomed to study, to think, who has read good authors, and heard intelligent conversation, will readily see the meaning of a word, the drift of a sentence, the aptness of a figure, the propriety of an illustration, the point of a witticism, the significance of an allusion, the force of an argument, or the scope of a discourse, which would be wholly obscure to another, less gifted by nature, or less favored by education. The whole work of the teacher is, therefore, a preparation for the reading-lesson, and much benefit may result from so regarding it.

2d. *Reading as related to the Emotions.* — Something more is necessary, in order to read well, than to understand the meaning of what is read. There is, probably, no literary production that is the cold work of the intellect alone. In all that has been written of prose or of poetry, the emotions play an important part. The plainest composer does not write wholly without feeling, and the heart-beats of the true poet stir in his every line. No one can read skilfully who does not appreciate the sentiment expressed in what he reads, or who does not feel for the time being as its author felt when he wrote it. He cannot read well of beauty who never saw anything beautiful, nor he of gayety, who never felt gay, nor he of sorrow who never evinced pity, nor he of wit who never enjoyed a joke.

Our school classes seldom seem to feel what they undertake to read. It is not uncommon to hear passages, as unlike in sentiment as possible, read without variation of Force, Pitch, Rate, or Tone. It is uncommon to hear reading done with that regard to the feeling expressed in the composition which at once evinces good taste and careful culture. Something may be done to improve this bad reading.

Such reading-lessons should be assigned as are calculated to interest the classes of pupils who are to learn them. If the feelings of children do not respond to the sentiments expressed in the lessons they read, it is not because their hearts are cold. Let the feelings be such as their child-nature can appreciate, and they will evince no want of sympathy with them. It is not difficult to make an application of this principle to all classes of those who are learning to read.

The teacher should lose no opportunity of impressing upon his pupils the ennobling sentiments which he may find in the reading lesson. Many occasions will present themselves to the watchful teacher of awakening in their minds a greater love for the beautiful, the true, and the good. There are beauty, truth, and goodness in the works of nature, in art and science, in human life, in the Bible, in God, the Fountain of all; and, now and then, they are caught up by some master hand, and, ever after, like the pearly drops that hang upon the flowers, like the beaded bubbles that break upon the stream, grace our literature. These the teacher can hold before the gaze of admiring pupils, until their hearts respond in answering sympathy. Sentiments of an opposite character may be found in reading-lessons, for literature is but a reflection of human nature, and has its dark side; but right teaching will do much to guard against their influence. Bad sentiments will not be more loved because well read.

One of the highest aims of composition is to adapt the linguistic expression of thought and feeling to their nature. Without a close analysis of the language used by an author, it is scarcely possible to feel as he felt. The heart of an author and the heart of a reader hold communion through the medium of words. It is the teacher's duty to remove all obscurity from this medium, not only by explaining their meaning, but by exhibiting the music and the poetry of words. I have marked the pleasure expressed on the countenances of pupils when they first began to appreciate the beauty of a Metaphor, or the force of an Antithesis, and was not disappointed in judging that such appreciation would improve their reading.

All education that tends to improve the taste and to give proper direction to the emotive nature, will be valuable preparation for the reading lesson. Among means of this kind, may be mentioned extensive and varied reading, intelligent travel, familiarity with the beauties of nature and art, and sympathy with the comforts and pleasures, the wants and woes, the fond aspirations and the proud successes, the blasted hopes and the fruitless enterprises, which so strangely checker human life. The Elocutionist must be a student of man's mental nature, learn to analyze the mingled emotions that agitate his bosom, and observe and imitate the most effective manner in which they express themselves in posture, in gesture, and in words.

3. Method of Teaching Delivery.

Delivery is the manner of reading. Success in Delivery depends upon observing the relation between thought and feeling and their expression. The practical end for which skill in reading may be desired, is to give full force to the meaning, and full effect to the sentiment of an author. A person may possess a well-trained voice, and may have both the head and the heart to appreciate what he reads, and, still, for want of power to adapt the one to the other in practical use, fail to read well. In other words, his reading machinery can be quite perfect, and yet he may not succeed in putting its several parts in working order.

What is designed to be said of Delivery can be embraced under three heads: *Expression*, *Posture*, and *Gesture*.

Expression.—Expression is vocal Delivery. The great principle to be observed in vocal Delivery is that all the mechanical modifications of the voice should be governed by the nature of the thought and feeling to be expressed, and the construction of the sentence in which they are embodied. This principle may be applied in teaching reading in two ways: first, the teacher may read correctly and require his pupils to imitate him; and, second, the relations existing between thought and feeling and their utterance in words, may be generalized into rules which can be learned and followed in reading.

With children just beginning to read, the teacher must instruct them mainly by using their powers of imitation. His voice must be their constant model. Rules can be but of little service to them. A large number of suitable sentences for practice may be prepared; and these the teacher should continue to utter, until the pupils can deliver them in the proper manner. Faults of reading should be prevented by showing what is right, and similar faults should be corrected by showing in what they consist. All descriptions of the variations of the voice in Quantity, Compass, Movement, or Tone, will be unmeaning, unless the sound described be itself exhibited. This method of teaching Reading by imitation is not only applicable to young learners, but must be used throughout the whole course of instruction. In advanced classes, however, it is to be employed in connection with the second method above indicated. It follows from all this that the teacher should be a good reader. Reading can no more easily be taught by one who is not an Elocutionist than Vocal Music can be taught by one who is not a Musician.

Books which treat of Elocution contain many rules that relate to Delivery. There are rules designed to aid the student in the use of Force, Emphasis, Slur and Stress, Pitch and Inflection, Rate and Pause, and Tone. The manner in which sentences of different forms should be delivered is pointed out; and, in order to leave no doubt in the pupil's mind concerning the application of the rules, certain reading lessons are arranged with a notation indicating the Quantity, Compass, Movement, and Quality of voice required. Of course, rules relating to Posture and Gesture, are also given. That some advantage may be gained from the study of these rules by learners who are able to understand and apply them, can hardly be questioned; but that harm may be done likewise is to be greatly feared. If pupils can be made to see that conformity to the requirements of Elocutionary rules in their reading enables them better to present the thought and feeling of an author, and adds more force and gracefulness to their Delivery, these rules may be profitably studied and applied; but if such rules are themselves arbitrary, imperfectly understood, or have been derived by a wrong method, the more effort that is made to apply them, the more stiff and formal will the Reading become. These remarks appropriately introduce the question: What constitutes good Delivery? The teacher must have some standard of excellence to which he aspires to elevate his class, and by which he criticises their Elocutionary performances — What is that standard? It is an easy matter to require pupils to commit and mechanically apply the ordinary rules for reading found in the works on Elocution; but upon what foundation do the rules themselves rest? Some say, "Nature is the Standard." It is admitted that if we read as we speak, we would read much better than we do; but it is still true that much of our reading would not then be in accordance with good taste. There are very few persons whose vocal organs do not need culture; and, even of those who have received it, scarcely any two have the same natural style of speaking. Whose style is to be taken as a standard? Others maintain that Delivery is to be measured by its effects upon an audience — if it please, it is good, but if it displease, it is imperfect. A reader may learn much respecting his improprieties of Delivery by watching its effect upon his hearers; but he will find such a standard very unreliable, as what some count excellences others will consider defects. The truth is that Reading is a Fine Art, and like Painting, Sculpture, Architecture, and other such Arts, no rules of criticism derived empirically are as an ultimate measure of beauty applicable to it. Every man is endowed directly by his Maker with the power of judging between beauty and deformity, and he uses this power in criticising nature herself. Given suitable occasions for its exercise, and this taste is capable of improvement, and detects beauty with more certainty. Delivery in Reading, as well as style in the other Fine Arts, is wholly a matter of taste; and Elocutionary rules made by others than those who are capable of judging what is most fit and beautiful in Expression, or most graceful in Posture or Gesture, are entirely unworthy of confidence. Such rules as express the laws of taste, however, the teacher is at liberty to impress upon the minds of his pupils. He must always exemplify them by his own reading. Thus learned, they will serve as models. Properly presented, they do not destroy the learner's individuality, they do not convert him into a mere machine, but they leave room for the display of the peculiarities of his own genius, and tend only to promote the normal growth of that noble part of his nature which directs him where to find the beautiful and how to appreciate it.

Supposing that pupils have received proper vocal training and that intellectual and moral instruction which fits them to read well, the teacher's further duty consists in cultivating their taste in Delivery by furnishing occasions for its exercise, in presenting them a chaste model for imitation in his own Delivery, in guiding them by such rules as express the generalized results of the masters of the art, and in providing for them those opportunities of practice which are necessary to make the required modes of Expression and Action habitual. Skill in Reading, thus attained, will be a growth of that which is within the learner, and not an imposition upon him from without — it will be the realization in Expression of his own ideals of beauty.

Posture. — The position which the body assumes in Reading or Speaking is called Posture. Posture relates simply to the disposition of the different members of the body before or during Delivery, while Gesture is applied to such of the motions of these members as indicate or enforce thought or feeling.

It will be necessary upon this subject to do little more than to announce the general principles which have reference to it.

1st. *The Posture of the Reader should be one of ease to himself.* — To secure an easy Posture, the reader must violate no Physiological law. He must stand firmly, but not stiffly, on his feet; change his weight frequently from one foot to the other; keep his body erect; project his chest forward and throw his shoulders back; and allow his arms to hang naturally by his side. If a book is used, it should be held in the left hand, in order that the right may be readily employed in turning the leaves, or in Gesticulating

In short, the easiest Posture should be sought and maintained for all the members of the body.

2d. *The Posture of a Reader should be graceful.* — If a reader stand perfectly at ease, his Posture will exhibit a good degree of gracefulness. In addition to this, however, a reader should rise gracefully; walk forward gracefully; take his position, and change it, when necessary, gracefully; make all the members of the body retain their place, and perform their part gracefully; and, when done, gracefully take his seat.

All Postures must be practiced until they become habitual. The pupil's taste, as to what is graceful, must be chastened by an exhibition of the best models the teacher can furnish.

Gesture. — Gestures are the actions of the various members of the body, which indicate and enforce thought and feeling. Reading and Speaking in the English language are characterized by less Gesticulation than was used by the nations of antiquity, with which we are best acquainted, or than is now used among many modern nations; but still the subject deserves more attention than is generally accorded to it. There can be no doubt that Reading, Declamation, and Oratory are all much more effective when Expression in Delivery is accompanied by appropriate Gestures.

In speaking of methods of teaching Gesture, all that was said of Expression might be repeated, with little modification. Gesture can be taught by imitation, and, also, by learning and applying the rules which express the relations between sentiment and Action. Young beginners can be taught only by requiring them to imitate the models the teacher may exhibit to them. He must *show* them what is right, and patiently train them to do it. Elocutionists profess to have analyzed the bodily actions which indicate and enforce thought and feeling, and to be able to frame rules that will serve to guide pupils in Gesticulating. Each thought and each feeling in these systems is indicated and enforced by certain motions of the hands, the arms, the feet, the head, the mouth, the eyes, or some other member or members of the body; and pupils are expected to learn and apply them in reading. Reading-lessons, too, are sometimes notated in such a manner as to indicate what Gestures are deemed appropriate. Rules for Gestures, thus formed, are advantageous to pupils, under the same conditions as those for Expression, and open to the same objections. Gestures should express some meaning, or else not be used. The same standard, that of cultivated taste, by which Delivery in sound may be criticised, is equally applicable to Delivery in action. And, finally, as in Expression, the teacher must multiply occasions for the exercise of the taste of his pupils in Gesticulation, he must give them in his own Delivery a fit model for imitation, he must teach them to conform to rules which good taste has everywhere sanctioned, and he must provide them that practice which is necessary to prompt the ready Gesture, even while the words leap from the tongue.

It is proper to close this discussion with a summary of topics which may profitably be considered in conducting a recitation in Reading. They may aid pupils in preparing lessons, as well as guide teachers in hearing recitations. Many or few questions may be asked under each head according to the circumstances of the class; or, in particular cases, some of the topics may be altogether omitted. A perfect recitation would require a perfect knowledge of all that is embraced in the list. It may be added that passages should be daily committed to memory, and declaimed. All Delivery is much crippled by the use of a book.

List of Topics for a Recitation in Reading.— Before reading a passage, pupils should be able—

1. To pronounce the words.
2. To define the words.
3. To understand the subject-matter.
4. To explain the language.
5. To account for the marks of Punctuation.
6. To point out what is true, beautiful, and good in the sentiment.
7. To show the manner of Delivery, and give reasons for it.

II. Learning to Understand our Mother-Tongue.

In learning to understand our Mother-Tongue, it is necessary to acquaint ourselves with four distinct branches of study, viz.: *Lexicology*, or the science which treats of words; *Grammar*, or the science which treats of sentences; *Rhetoric*, or the science which treats of discourse; and *Philology*, or the science of the origin and growth of Language.

Lexicology.

I use the term Lexicology to denote the science which treats of the meaning of words; and methods of teaching the meaning of words is the subject intended for discussion in the present Article.

There can be no conscious thinking without the use of symbols. The most convenient of all thought-signs are words. Words, indeed, are the wheels by which the thinking process goes on.

Words are the vehicles of social intercourse. Without them, the fountains of the soul would be almost sealed up.

Words are the repositories of science and art. The dead past lies buried, but living words commemorate it and transmit its mighty deeds to the far future. Words are the caskets in which are preserved forever the jeweled thoughts of the good and great. How much feeling, thought, or power may be concentrated in a single word: as *love, truth, will!*

Words are the medals of the mind. All our mental energies impress themselves upon words. A nation's character can be best read in its language. "Language is concrete Metaphysics."

Words are the media of instruction. A knowledge of the simplest facts as well as the deepest philosophy is almost helpless without the motive-power of words. Words are the winged messengers that convey information from one mind and heart to another. All knowledge must be labeled with words or it can find no place in the cabinet of the memory.

Such is the worth of words. It is surely worth while to study their meaning.

There are many ways by which the young may learn the meaning of words. They may learn it by *direct intuition;* by *concrete explanations;* by *the use of simplified expressions;* by *observing their signification as used in sentences;* by *the study of foreign languages;* by *an acquaintance with Etymology;* and by *scientific definitions.*

The meaning of words may be learned by direct intuition.—Children learn the first elements of language by hearing persons speak, and noticing the association made between certain verbal utterances and sensible objects. When a little older, they seem to increase their vocabulary by catching the meaning of words from the connections in which they are used. In all nature there is nothing more wonderful than the process by which children learn to talk. They seem to possess a language-forming instinct. They have thoughts and feelings imprisoned within them, and instinctively seek to set them free. If they had no opportunity of hearing words they would invent them. As it is, they add to their stock of word-knowledge every day, their memories clinging tenaciously to all the words they listen to. They catch up words from parents, brothers and sisters, companions, servants, visitors, and often, indeed, coin new ones. In all this, there is no conscious reasoning, no formal instruction, and I call the process intuition.

In view of the power children possess of learning

the meaning of words by intuition, it becomes the teacher's duty to allow them an opportunity to exercise this power. He may talk to them of things in which they feel an interest, tell them stories, or read suitable selections to them. If he adapts his matter and style to their mental condition, he will not want attentive listeners, and he will enjoy the satisfaction of seeing them acquire the use of new words and new forms of expression every day. A teacher must not only talk to his pupils, but he must listen to their talk. Children are great talkers. There is within them an impulse strongly and constantly impelling them to hear, to see, to examine things, and then to tell about them. Prevent a child from talking, force him to perpetual silence, and you will make him an idiot. Besides, a child loves to use the new words he has acquired, and the watchful teacher can readily detect the reproduction of his own expressions in the language of his pupils. As soon as children are able to read they will have opened up a new source from which to enlarge their knowledge of words.

The meaning of words may be learned by concrete explanations. — By concrete explanations of words are meant such explanations as may be given by means of an exhibition of the objects, actions, or qualities for which the words stand. For example, the word *pistil* could be explained by pointing to that part of a flower, the word *decrepitate* by throwing a little salt into the fire, and the word *transparent* by holding up a piece of glass. In the absence of an object, the well-remembered experience of a child may be used instead of it.

No one can doubt that if proper skill was used, the pupils in our schools might be made acquainted with a large number of words in the way just named. Lessons on objects are well calculated to impart this kind of instruction, but a teacher who sees the importance of it can find opportunity to impart it in giving a lesson on any subject. Special lessons planned with reference to this end, might be made very profitable as well as very interesting.

The meaning of words may be learned by the use of simplified expressions.—If the meaning of a word is not understood, it may be explained by using less obscure synonymous words or forms of words—that is by the use of simplified expressions. A very large proportion of the words in a Dictionary are defined, if the process is properly called defining, in this manner. The "definition" of the word *abandon* is *to give up, to forsake ;* of the word *abbreviate,* to *shorten ;* of the word *abrogate,* to *repeal ;* of the word *absurdity, the quality of being inconsistent with obvious truth ;* and so on for thousands of words. It is evident in all these cases that if a pupil comprehends the "definition" he can comprehend the word defined.

How can a teacher make use of simplified expressions in teaching the meaning of words? In the first place, no words must be used in the explanations which the pupils do not understand. The unknown can be understood only from its connections with the known. Many school dictionaries err gravely on this point and thus defeat their whol object. Moreover, a School Dictionary ought to illustrate the meaning of every word by appropriate sentences in which the word is used. It would be much better, too, for the purposes of teaching, if the words were arranged in lessons according to the subjects or things to which they relate, and not Alphabetically.

The common school-exercise of "learning definitions" is open to serious objections. It requires pupils to commit the explanations of words to memory and recite them, but presents no test to ascertain whether they are understood or otherwise. A new word is valuable only when accompanied by a new thought, or when it furnishes a better expression for an old one. Words simply memorized are dead, mere skeleton-words, without life or soul in them. They lie in the memory a confused mass, of which no use can be made. If text-books on Lexicology were arranged as indicated in the preceding paragraph, they might be used in classes, to the great advantage of the pupils. If, in addition to the usual synonymes and synonymous expressions, sentences embodying each word were presented, its meaning would become apparent. Besides, pupils should be required to compose original sentences containing the words of the lesson, and this they could not do without understanding them. Words having some relation to one another form a much more interesting lesson than dry lists of disconnected words.

The meaning of words may be learned by observing their Signification as used in Sentences.—It has already been intimated that the meaning of words can be more readily discerned in sentences than in the columns of Spelling-Books or Dictionaries. Children especially are apt in learning the meaning of words in this way. They rise from the perusal of every good book with a rich accession of new words; and a person can often tell the volume a child has been engaged in reading by his language. Moreover, the finer shades of meaning, which distinguish individual words, the innermost thought embodied in a word, cannot be learned from a Dictionary. Lexicographers explain each word by the use of other words or forms of expression, but, since these cannot mean exactly the same thing, every scholar has felt the deficiencies of Dictionaries, and is aware that they cannot be supplied. Those who desire to realize the deepest meaning of words must study them in discourse.

Teachers can do much to inculcate a taste for reading among their pupils, and in this way, among other good results, enable them to increase their facility in the use of language. The reading-lesson furnishes a good opportunity for calling the attention of pupils to the meaning of words, as used singly, or in phrases, clauses, or whole sentences, or whether in a plain or a figurative sense. Something may be done, too, to impart similar instruction in hearing recitations in any branch of knowledge. If new or uncommon words occur in a lesson, it is well for the teacher to require an explanation of them. The attention of pupils can thus be kept directed upon the words they meet with in their studies, and every day some addition will be made to their practical vocabulary.

The meaning of words may be learned by the study of Foreign Languages.—In the study of foreign languages, we necessarily use our Mother-Tongue. No practice can be better calculated to familiarize us with the meaning of words than that of translating the words of our own into another language, or the reverse. It is hardly possible otherwise to develop that fine sense by which the nicer distinctions among words and forms of expression can be perceived. Nothing further need be stated here, as elsewhere there will be found a discussion of methods of teaching these languages.

The meaning of words may be learned by an acquaintance with Etymology.—The English is a composite language. Its ground-work is the Anglo-Saxon element, but it has been enriched by the introduction of multitudes of words from the Latin, Greek, French, German, Danish, and other languages. Anglo-Saxon words mainly compose the language of common life, and their meaning is generally learned without study. Those words for whose meaning we search Dictionaries are mostly derivative words; and in order to understand them fully it is almost necessary to study their Etymology. It is not going too far to say that without performing an Etymological analysis of words, no student can use them with nice discrimination and full effect.

Etymologists have made three classes of the elements of words, as follows: Prefixes, Suffixes, and Root-Words. With respect to methods of teaching, the first two classes may be placed together.

A method of teaching Prefixes and Suffixes may

be readily indicated. A well-arranged text-book on Etymology should contain lists of Prefixes and Suffixes, their signification, and numerous examples, in which the meaning of each is plainly illustrated. Lessons may be assigned and prepared, as in other studies. At the recitation, pupils may be required to write on the blackboard lists of the elements embraced in the lesson, together with their significations. They may point out the Prefixes and Suffixes in the words presented as examples in the book, and write words containing any given element. Teachers ought to prepare themselves with a number of miscellaneous words as tests of their pupils' skill.

When pupils have been made thoroughly acquainted with the Prefixes and Suffixes, the work of teaching them the Root-Words of the language should commence. Almost the only Root-Words whose meaning is not known without study are those which have come into our language from the Latin and Greek, and the signification of these must be learned from text-book or teacher. Text-Books on Etymology generally present a Root-Word, explain its meaning, and then give lists of words derived from it. For example, the Latin word *traho* is presented; its primary meaning is stated to be *to draw*, and then follow words like *attraction*, *subtraction*, *detraction*, *protraction*, *contraction*, *retraction*, *traceable*, *trackless;* and others more obscure in their derivation, as *contractability*, *subtrahend*, *drag*, *portrait*, *track*, *trade*, *tract*, &c. In reciting, pupils should be required to give the Root-Words and their meaning, and then to analyze the derivative words presented as examples, pointing out the force of the elements composing them, and the laws of their union, and, finally, explaining the meaning of the whole word. The mode of Etymological analysis may be illustrated by an example. Take the word, attraction: ATTRACTION. PREFIX, *at-*, signifying *to*, changed from *ad* on account of euphony; SUFFIX, *-ion*, signifying *the act of* or *process;* ROOT-WORD, *-tract-*, derived from the Latin, *traho* or *tractum*, which signifies *to draw;* MEANING OF THE WORD, *the act* or *the process of drawing to*, or *the tendency of bodies to approach one another and adhere together.* After analyzing a word, pupils may embody it in sentences. A text-book ought not to contain full lists of derivative words, as pupils are much profited by searching for them. Miscellaneous exercises in the analysis of words must be furnished either by the text-book or the teacher. It may be remarked further that instead of committing to memory the meaning of Prefixes, Suffixes, and Root-Words, and analyzing words by the aid of this knowledge, lists of words which contain some common element may first be given to the pupil, the meaning of that element be ascertained and traced in other words, and, finally, syntheses of such elements be formed. This method, however, will not be found to differ materially in practice from the preceding.

In conducting exercises in Etymological analysis, the teacher can deepen his pupil's interest in the study of words by imparting information, now and then, in regard to the origin and history of words. He might introduce into almost every lesson a few words whose primitive meaning would attract special attention, or whose history would excite peculiar curiosity. It might be explained how new words come into a language, how old ones become obsolete, and why some languages contain words for which no expressions are found in others. This is, indeed, a rich field, and it can be worked by a skilful teacher so as to yield fruit a hundredfold.

The meaning of words may be learned by scientific definitions.—A definition is a connected statement of the essential properties or qualities of a name or a thing. These properties or qualities may be the results of experience or they may be the pure products of the Reason. The definitions peculiar to the Empirical Sciences are of the former class, and those which belong to the Formal and Rational Sciences are of the latter class. Compare, for example, the definitions of a mountain, a leaf, a bone, on the one hand, with those of a circle, order, truth, beauty, goodness, considered abstractly, on the other.

It is to be remarked that the construction of scientific definitions requires very accurate knowledge both of things and words. A good definition is always a scientific triumph. It indicates that the thing defined has been thoroughly investigated; that all that is essential to it has been connected in thought and expressed in words. Such definitions make plain the meaning of words to those who will take pains to study them.

In regard to teaching scientific definitions, it is scarcely necessary to say that little advantage is derived from simply committing them to memory. If not understood, they are mere empty words that but cumber the mind without strengthening it. The kind of definitions now referred to can only be learned by learning the elements, real or ideal, of which they are made up. The teacher must carry his pupil back from the forms of words to the relations of things, and then no school-exercise can be more useful than that of learning definitions.

GRAMMAR.

Few branches of study have been taught less skilfully than Grammar. This bad teaching is owing to both text-book and teacher.

There is no text-book on English Grammar that is a strictly scientific exposition of the principles of the English language. Treatises upon this subject may be found which contain a great deal that is valuable; but, in all of them, there is too much effort made to fit the peculiar constructions of our Anglo-Saxon speech to the forms of the ancient languages. More independence of thought is wanted in treating of the English language. Not till some scholar is strong enough and bold enough to strip the subject of its superfluous forms and rid it of its incorrect definitions, and present its laws in a concise, consistent, and logical manner, will we have, what can be truly called, an *English* Grammar. Besides, the arrangement of most of our Grammar books is the worst possible for the purpose of teaching beginners. They commence by giving a definition of Grammar, by stating its great general divisions, by fixing the number of Parts of Speech, &c. --none of which generalizations can possibly be understood without at least some knowledge of the language. They would be more appropriate at the end of the book than at the beginning of it. In teaching, definitions should be accompanied with an exposition of their contents; and generalizations, with a statement of the facts on which they are founded; but these principles are constantly violated by our authors of Grammars.

Good teaching may neutralize the bad results which are apt to follow from the use of imperfect text-books; but it is to be feared that in the case of Grammar many of the commonly practiced methods of teaching tend rather to increase these bad results than to diminish them. A majority of teachers to-day in teaching Grammar blindly follow the order of the text-book; and though every recitation should furnish evidence that this is an error, they fail to appreciate it. Grammar, as generally taught, consists in memorizing definitions, declensions, conjugations, and rules, and in applying them in parsing and in the correction of examples in False Syntax. Pursued in this manner, it is an artificial and arbitrary system built up apart from the ground upon which as a science it must rest. Definitions, rules, and forms, in Grammar are merely words and mean nothing disconnected from the facts and principles which underlie them.

Grammar is the science of sentences. English Grammar is the science of the English sentence. There are certain general principles which are applicable to the sentences of all languages, and there are other principles which belong only to those of particular languages. The division just made is therefore a proper one. Grammar is not an art. Composition treats of the art of speaking and writing.

Sentences are composed of words, and these words may be classified according to their individual meaning or office; the modifications, properties, and relations of each class may be determined; and the whole be made to constitute a system of English Grammar. This method of studying the sentence may be called *Etymological* inasmuch as it deals with words as the best defined, integral parts of which sentences are composed.

Sentences are composed of elements, some of them essential and others non-essential, at some times consisting of a single word and at other times of several words combined, and these elements may be classified according to their sentential relations, each class become the subject of scientific investigation, and the result be made to constitute another system of English Grammar. This method of studying the sentence may de called *Logical* inasmuch as it is based upon the mutual relations of the elements of sentences.

These two methods are both essentially analytical, and are not at all antagonistic. Both ought to be combined in practical teaching. The Logical method might first consider sentences as wholes and then find and dispose of their elements; after which the Etymological method might treat of the individual words of which they are composed. Neither can be dispensed with in the construction of a system of Grammatical science.

To commence the study of the science of Grammar proper, with the prospect of much profit, pupils ought to possess considerable general knowledge, and be from twelve to fifteen years of age. The first steps may be easy, but it requires some maturity of thought to comprehend the principles which are soon involved. Previous to the time of their commencing the study of the science of Grammar, pupils should have much practice in elementary Composition, of which it is intended to speak hereafter, and it would be greatly to their advantage to be taught the exercises now about to be described. I call them *Etymological Exercises*, and desire that they should be considered as an introduction to the study of Grammar

Etymological Exercises.

Exercise First.—*Nouns.*—The class may be required to write on slates or blackboard the names of the objects in the school-room. This work having been criticised by one another and corrected by the teacher in respect to spelling, punctuation, neatness, &c., they may be required to write further the names of things seen in coming to school, those which stand for kinds of trees, flowers, the organs of the body, the parts of a house, the tools used by farmers or mechanics, the articles purchased at stores, &c.; and submit their work for correction as before. They may now be told that the names of objects are called Nouns; and much further practice should be allowed them in selecting the Nouns in sentences and framing sentences containing Nouns.

Exercise Second.—*Kinds of Nouns.*—The teacher may name the boys in the class, and ask for the name common to all. The girls may be named in the same way, and also particular cities, rivers, mountains, &c., and like inquiries be made concerning them. Some common name can then be assigned as horse, book, man, and the pupils required to write all the particular names that they can think of which are comprehended in the general name. This done, the terms Common and Proper, as applied to Nouns, can be defined, and pupils be profitably engaged in classing them accordingly, in pointing them out in sentences, and in constructing sentences containing them.

EXERCISE THIRD.—*The Properties of Nouns.*—Gender, Number, and Person are the only Properties of Nouns that can be taught intelligently without an analysis of sentences. Case, therefore, except the Possessive, cannot be treated of in this connection.

The teacher need not point out many examples to enable pupils to understand the distinctions of Gender and Number. They can readily see, too, that some objects speak, some are spoken to, and others are spoken of. They should be required, however, to write lists of words denoting objects in each Gender, Number, and Person; and point them out as they occur in sentences. Sentences may be written containing such words.

EXERCISE FOURTH.—*Verbs.*—The method of teaching Verbs will be understood by the following illustration: What does the fire do? *Class.* "It burns." Write the word "burns" on your slates. What does the wind do? *Class.* "It blows." Write "blows," also. What does the rain do? *Class.* "It falls."

What are the birds doing in yonder grove? *Class.* "They sing." What can you say of plants? *Class.* "They grow." Write the words "falls," sing," and "grow" under the others. Now each take a place at the blackboard, and write the names of all the acts you can think of that boys do. The class write—"boys play," "boys read," "boys write," "boys run," "boys eat," "boys laugh," &c., &c. The actions that girls, horses, dogs, birds, &c., perform may then be written, if time permit, or assigned for future lessons; and, when pupils are fully prepared to understand it, they may be told that all the names of actions are called verbs. In further lessons, they may be required to form sentences containing particular verbs and to point out the verbs in sentences.

Exercise Fifth.—*Kinds of Verbs.*—Adopting the common classification of Verbs, lists of them may be written upon the blackboard as follows:—

FIRST LIST.	SECOND LIST.	THIRD LIST.
Boys play.	The table stands.	The boy was whipped.
Birds fly.	The book lies.	The soldier is wounded.
Men work.	The curtains hang.	The horses were sold.
Dogs bark.	The teacher sits.	The pitcher was broken.

Pupils having learned that the names of actions are Verbs, can readily point out the Verbs in the first list. They may then be asked to point out the words that most resemble Verbs in the second and third lists. This done, they may be shown the differences in the meaning of the three kinds of Verbs, and learn to call them by their names—Active, Neuter, and Passive. A great deal of practice must be allowed pupils in naming the different kinds of

Verbs as they occur in sentences, and in composing sentences containing them.

Exercise Sixth. — *The Properties of Verbs.* — Whether Verbs are the names of actions which are perceptible, or of those which are imperceptible; whether they denote actions performed or actions endured, they must have reference to *time* and *manner.* Pupils can readily give orally or write the names of actions which are taking place at the present time; and it is not much more difficult to suppose that the same actions took place yesterday, or will take place to-morrow, and to express them accordingly. After full practice upon the Present, Past, and Future Tenses, the pupils may be made acquainted with those subdivisions of them thought to be necessary by Grammarians.

The teacher can write lists of sentences containing Verbs in the different Modes, and instruct his pupils in those peculiarities of expression upon which distinctions of Mode are founded.

Many examples of Verbs should then be given, and the pupils be required to state their Tense and Mode. Sentences can also be constructed containing Verbs of certain given Tenses and Modes.

Verbs denote by their form whether actions are performed or received by one person or more, or by a speaker, a person or thing spoken to, or a person or thing spoken of. This can be readily exemplified in the manner previously described.

Pupils should not only be required to commit the Conjugation of verbs, in a certain order, but they should be expected to answer questions asked miscellaneously upon it. The teacher may name Modes, Tenses, Numbers, and Persons, and demand of the pupils forms of Verbs that answer the conditions, he may require such Verbs to be embodied in sentences, or he may assign the sentences and engage the pupils in distinguishing and classifying the Verbs.

Exercises similar to those now described should be given in respect to Pronouns, Adjectives, Adverbs, Prepositions, Conjunctions, and Interjections; but any teacher who has appreciated the spirit of the method indicated can do it for himself. The spirit and form of these Exercises are identical with those recommended in giving lessons on objects. The more obscure distinctions in Etymological Grammar can be presented in the same way to pupils prepared to understand them. It must be remembered, however, that these exercises do not contemplate an exhaustive discussion of the Parts of Speech.

Grammar as a Science.

An effort will now be made to point out the proper method of teaching Grammar as a science.

Our thinking is regulated by laws. The science which treats of these laws is Logic. Language is the verbal expression of thought, and therefore there must be a close analogy between the laws of thought and the laws of speech. Hence the relationship which exists between Grammar and Logic.

We think, talk, and write in sentences. Discourse is made up of sentences. A sentence in Grammar corresponds to the unit in Mathematics. It is the least integral part of discourse, as words are but fractional parts of sentences. The first step in teaching Grammar therefore is to communicate to pupils an idea of a sentence. To do this a teacher may ask his class to say something about a *book*, a *horse*, a *bird;* and what they say he may write on the blackboard. These expressions and others like them they may be told are called sentences. The division of their reading lessons into sentences may be pointed out. In this manner children can learn to know simple sentences. Further practice should be given them in writing sentences about particular things, and in detecting combinations of words that do not form sentences. A sentence is a form of words containing a proposition; but such a definition would be quite out of place at this stage of progress.

When pupils have learned to know simple sentences, they may begin the work of analyzing them, and the elements thus found must be classified and investigated. The system thus built up should present the principles of the language in a clear and logical manner. A sufficient number of steps in this analysis will be presented to indicate to the thoughtful teacher the method by which the whole may be taught.

The Subject.—The teacher may write such sentences upon the blackboard as *birds fly*, *men work*, *fire burns*, *rain falls*, &c.; and call the attention of his class to the fact that in each of these sentences there is a word which represents a thing of which something is said. The pupils may then point out such words or forms of words in these and numerous other sentences, and learn that they are called subjects. They may be asked to name things of which something may be said, and to tell what can be said to *run*, *fly*, *eat*, *work*, &c.

The Predicate. — In the same manner, it can be shown that sentences like those named in the preceding examples contain words or forms of words that are used to say something of the subject. These are called Predicates. Pupils can be led to point them out in such sentences and in others. It is well also to give them practice in naming words which are used to say something of things, and to write on slate or blackboard what can be said of *boys*, *girls*, *horses*, *fishes*, *birds*, &c.

In miscellaneous exercises upon Subjects and Predicates, a Subject can be given and the pupils required to find suitable Predicates, or a Predicate can be given and the pupils required to supply suitable Subjects, thus:

Given, *Boys.* Required,	Required, — Given, *Walk.*
Play,	*Boys,*
Run,	*Girls,*
Walk,	*Horses,*
Eat,	*Dogs,*
Write,	*Birds,*
Read,	*Cattle,*
Talk,	*Men,*
Laugh, &c.	*Women,* &c.

When able to point out the Subject and Predicate in sentences, pupils may be told that the two taken together constitute a Proposition, and then be allowed to point out and to construct Propositions.

Kinds of Subjects. — The attention of the pupil should be called to lists of sentences printed in his Grammar-book or written on the blackboard like the following: *John studies*; *he studies; to study is right; that he studies is certain.* When fully comprehending the different kinds of Subjects, he may be told that the name of the first kind of Subject is Noun; of the second, Pronoun; of the third, Phrase; and of the fourth, Clause. Finally, he must be allowed to point out the different kinds of Subjects in numerous examples, and to construct sentences containing any required form of Subject.

If the teacher deem it proper, his pupils may now learn the nature of the Noun and Pronoun, their kinds and their properties. The manner of doing this has already been explained. The Phrase and Clause must be treated of when the pupil is prepared to understand them.

Kinds of Predicates. — The kinds of Predicates can be taught in essentially the same manner as kinds of Subjects. The teacher must first present such sentences as: *boys learn; they are to learn; Spring is pleasant; it is as I told him.* It is unnecessary to make more than two kinds of Predicates: first, the Verb simply; and, second, the Verb with some added word, phrase or clause. The nature of the Copula may be explained. Much practice in pointing out and classifying Predicates, in sentences, and in constructing sentences to contain Predicates of a particular kind cannot be dispensed with.

If not done before, the teacher may now make

his pupils acquainted with the nature of the Verb, its kinds, and the properties which belong to it.

To the extent of the knowledge now acquired, pupils may engage with great profit in the exercises, beautiful when combined, of Analysis and Parsing. Numerous miscellaneous sentences must be provided for the purpose.

Pupils may be taught also that Pronouns, when used as Subjects, are in the Nominative Case, and have a particular form, and that Nouns are said to be in the same Case when used in the same way. Verbs also agree with their subjects in Number and Person. Many sentences violating these principles may be submitted to the pupils for correction.

Adjective Elements.—A word or a form of words used to modify the meaning of the Subject is called an Adjective Element. The same name is applied to the words, phrases, and clauses which modify Nouns and Pronouns in whatever relation they may be placed. The teacher should begin his instruction by calling the attention of his class to sentences in which the Subject is modified by simple Adjectives, as: *good boys study; pretty flowers grow,* &c. When they fully understand the nature of the Adjective Modification, it will not be very difficult to lead them to see the words and forms of words that perform similar offices in such sentences as follow: *his book is lost; James, the carpenter, built the house; John's finger is hurt; a book of poems is on the table; the boy who did not know his lesson is detained after school.* This done, and all that remains necessary is to allow full opportunity for practice in pointing out these elements in sentences and constructing sentences containing them. Adjective elements admit division into classes; but it requires the application of no special methods to teach them. Rules of Syntax relating to the correct use of the Adjective and Adjective element may now be given, and examples of sentences in which this part of speech is incorrectly used, may be assigned for correction.

Adverbial Elements.—A word or a form of words used to modify the meaning of the Predicate may be called an Adverbial Element. Adverbial Elements should be classified and taught in the same manner as the Adjective Element; and repetition is deemed unnecessary. Rules for the construction of Adverbial Elements must not be overlooked.

Nothing special need be said in reference to teaching the *Preposition*, *Conjunction*, and *Interjection*, as the offices they severally perform in sentences are easily detected, and readily illustrated.

All that has been said is intended to apply to simple Declarative sentences. At the proper time, other forms of sentences must be presented to the pupil, and he must be taught to trace their relations to the Declarative form. Phrases and Clauses must be carefully studied. The close analysis of Complex and Compound Sentences, and the classification of the elements thus found, the discussion of the idioms of our language, the changes in construction it has undergone, the relationship of thought and its expression in words, general and special Philological laws, must complete a full course of instruction in Grammar.

This discussion will be concluded with a summary of the general principles by which the teaching of Grammar should be governed, and which has guided the preceding discussion.

1st. All Grammatical principles or rules should be deduced directly from sentences, or proven by reference to them.

2d. The pupil should begin the study of Grammar by analyzing the simplest forms of simple sentences, and then proceed by safe gradations from the easy to the difficult. A sentence admits of a logical discussion only by descending from the general to the particular. A classification of sentences ascends from species to genera.

3d. No definition or rule should be given that presupposes knowledge that the pupil does not possess. The whole system should be logically connected, and introduce the pupil to new principles just at the time he needs, and is prepared to understand them.

4th. Rules of construction and government, with examples in False Syntax, should be taught in connection with the sentences or elements of sentences to which they relate. This principle, logically necessary, will be found of considerable practical advantage.

5th. The Analysis of a sentence consists in finding its elements, or in reducing it to the Parts of Speech, of which it is composed. Parsing consists in finding out these Parts of Speech and determining their properties and relations. Both should be combined, as is the case in similar operations in other sciences. The Botanist analyzes a plant, and then names and describes its several parts. The Anatomist dissects a subject, and then characterizes the organs thus brought to his notice. Grammar can be studied successfully in no other way. Parsing, without a preceding analysis, can lead but to a very imperfect knowledge of the organic structure of sentences.

6th. Grammatical knowledge should be applied throughout the whole course in the construction of sentences. Pupils should be allowed ample opportunity of framing all the different kinds and varieties of sentences, and of embodying in them, all the elements of sentences, words, phrases, and clauses, in all their forms, and with all their modifications.

7th. The study of the English language may be made to yield the same kind of culture that is derived from the study of the classical languages of Greece and Rome. To do this, several standard authors, or selections from many such authors, must be subjected to a critical examination as to the forms of sentences; the location of the elements in sentences, their relations, and their fitness to express the thought intended; and the origin, history, and meaning of words.

Rhetoric.

It is by no means easy to define the limits of the study of Rhetoric, or to fix its position among the sciences. There seems to be no general agreement among writers respecting the ground which it should occupy.

Logic treats of the laws of thought. These laws necessarily condition language. Grammar investigates them as they occur in sentences. But as all discourse is subject to logical conditions, there is room for a science which may be called the Science of discourse. Rhetoric, however, not only treats of the laws of thought as they appear in discourse, but likewise includes an application of the laws of taste. It is based upon the science of Logic, on the one hand, and Æsthetics, on the other. It is also closely related to Grammar.

Some writers deny to Rhetoric the rank of a science; but since, in addition to the principles it embodies, that are found to grow out of the relations which the different parts of discourse sustain to one another, its rules are the generalizations of what experience has shown to be most effective and pleasing in speaking and writing, it may, at least, as justly claim that rank as any Inductive Science.

It would not be proper in this connection to speak of methods of teaching either Logic or Æsthetics, notwithstanding they constitute the foundation upon which the superstructure of Rhetoric is erected. Rhetoric, as presented in our books, treats of the several kinds of discourse, the qualities which experience shows to be necessary in good writing and speaking, and the manner of arranging ideas and expressing them in language. Of methods of teaching Rhetoric, when thus considered, it is my purpose to speak.

1. Kinds of Discourse.—It will be convenient to

consider first, *discourse as classed with regard to form;* and, second, as *classed with regard to matter.*

Classed with regard to form, discourse presents two great divisions, viz.: *Prose* and *Poetry.* A difference in form may not be the only difference between prose and poetic composition; but it is the most prominent.

The leading divisions of prose composition are *Orations, Lectures, Essays, Theses, Fictions, Narratives,* and *Letters.* Several of these classes of composition admit of subdivisions.

The leading divisions of poetic composition are *Epic, Lyric, Pastoral, Dramatic, Didactic,* and *Satiric* Poetry. The form of Poetry differs also according to the versification.

Classed with regard to matter, discourse may be *Novel, Witty, Humorous, Satirical, Sublime,* and *Beautiful.* Or from another point of view, discourse is *Explanatory, Argumentative, Pathetic,* or *Persuasive,* according as it narrates or describes, argues, appeals to the feelings, or attempts to move the will.

The teacher's whole duty to his pupils, in acquainting them with the different kinds of discourse, may be expressed in three words, *describe, define,* and *illustrate.* Each kind of discourse must be carefully described, the general terms made use of must be defined, and the whole must be impressed upon the pupil's mind by numerous, appropriate illustrations.

2. QUALITIES WHICH CHARACTERIZE WELL CONSTRUCTED DISCOURSE.—All well constructed discourse must be characterized by *Purity, Propriety, Precision, Perspicuity, Strength, Euphony, Harmony,* and *Unity.*

In teaching, pupils must first be led to see what is meant by these qualities. Many examples of each should be exhibited to them. It will be greatly to their advantage if extracts from authors, faulty in respect to these qualities, be presented to them for correction.

3. Arrangement and Style of Discourse. — The invention of ideas, or, more properly, the obtaining of ideas, does not properly belong to the Science of Rhetoric. Ideas are furnished by investigations concerning the subject-matter of other sciences. Rhetoric treats only of the arrangement of these ideas, and the style in which they should be expressed.

By the arrangement of discourse is meant the selection of suitable matter, and its proper distribution. Out of the multitude of facts, arguments, incidents, illustrations, which may be presented on a particular subject, it is important to be able to judge what should be chosen, and in what order the selected matter should be arranged. Orations, according to the method of the ancients, and the practice is quite similar now, were divided, into the *Exordium*, *Narration*, *Proposition*, *Discussion*, and *Peroration*.

In other kinds of discourse, little more has been done by Rhetoricians than to name the principal parts, viz.: the *Introduction*, *Body*, and *Conclusion*. Pupils, however, must not be allowed to conclude from this that the matter of books, lectures, poems, dramas, fictions, any kind of composition, indeed, can be thrown together in confused fragments. Nothing can be more important than the arrangement of the matter of discourse, and the teacher should submit many well-written compositions of different kinds to his pupils that they may carefully analyze them in this respect. Not that pupils should be trained to a slavish imitation of any author; but that they may see in a concrete form what has proved itself pleasing and effective, and profit by this experience.

By style is meant the manner of expression in language. The style of an author or speaker must vary according to his individual peculiarities, and the circumstances which surround him; but Rhetoricians have made several divisions, according to the degree of ornament used, as follows: the *Dry*, *Plain*, *Neat*, *Elegant*, and *Florid;* according to the structure of the sentences, the *Simple* and *Labored*, and the *Concise* and *Diffuse;* and, according to the effect produced upon the hearer, the *Nervous* and *Feeble*. Under the head of Style, too, may be discussed the various kinds of Figures used in discourse. The teacher will find this a pleasant department of the subject to present to his pupils; but will have no need to depart from the method of teaching indicated in the preceding divisions of the subject.

The discussion of the subject will be concluded by presenting a few additional observations.

A course of study in English Literature should follow one in Rhetoric. Selections from different authors may be arranged chronologically; but all should be closely analyzed with reference to kind, qualities, arrangement, and style. Such an exercise might be called Rhetorical Parsing, and its value if well conducted would be very great.

Pupils should be expected to observe the principles of Rhetoric in all their writing and speaking. It is taken for granted that Rhetoric is studied not only to be known but to be used. Indeed, it can scarcely be fully known without being used. Hence, in all recitations, the attention of pupils should be called to faults in Rhetoric. A good recitation consists not alone in giving correctly all the facts and principles of the lesson, but in making the most appropriate arrangement of them and expressing them in the best language.

In learning Rhetoric, it is not enough for pupils to study the compositions of others; they must compose themselves. They must be patiently trained to exemplify in their own writing and speaking all that has given value to the writing and speaking of others. The end of the study of Rhetoric is not chiefly to acquire the power of describing how skilful authors write and speak, but to be able to write and speak well ourselves; and no effective teaching of this science is possible without allowing ample opportunity for this kind of practice.

A teacher of Rhetoric ought to be a literary amateur. Without a love for literature himself he cannot make his pupils love it. Without literary taste himself, he cannot cultivate the literary tastes of his pupils. Ordinary teaching skill may suffice to make known the facts and rules of Rhetoric; but nature does not open her beauties here, nor anywhere, unless bidden by a loving heart.

PHILOLOGY.

The word Philology is used here to denote the science which treats of the origin and growth of language, or, in other words, its Natural History. Up to this point, language has been spoken of as a ready-formed instrument with which pupils desire to become acquainted, and methods of teaching how to read and understand it as such have been discussed. But a few remarks will show that it may be studied from another stand-point.

Language is itself a growth — a product evoked from human wants and evolved from human reason. It is concrete thought. God gave man reason and the power of speech, and he produced language. This growth of words was governed both in its origin and progress by certain laws. There are principles by which the forms and rules of Grammar can be accounted for. A language is not learned when we know its declensions, conjugations, and laws of construction, for the causes of these may be investigated. Words even do not arbitrarily change their pronunciation, orthography, or meaning. New words are introduced into a language, old ones drop out of it, and causes are ever at work changing its form and constructions, and the mere Grammarian who studies language as it is, or the mere Historian who notes these word-revolutions, may remain in ignorance of the subtle forces that ceaselessly operate to adapt human speech to the condition and wants of men.

Philology, if now properly apprehended, has the character of an Historical Science, with its facts and its philosophy, and as such, methods of teaching it belong elsewhere. They will be found to combine methods of teaching applicable to all the other sciences.

III. Learning to Compose in our Mother-Tongue.

Composition may be defined as the art of combining ideas and expressing them in words; or it may be called the art of speaking and writing. It is founded upon the sciences of Grammar and Rhetoric.

Without insisting that it is strictly philosophical, the following division of our intellectual faculties may be made: those by which we gain knowledge; those by which we elaborate it into systems; and those by which what we know is reproduced. The first class may be called the Perceptive faculties; the second, the Reflective faculties; and the third, the Expressive faculties. A perfect mind would possess the power of obtaining the material of knowledge, the power of working up this material into mind-products, and the power of conveying these mind-products back to the world without, in co-equal strength. As good reasons, therefore, can be given for the cultivation of the Expressive powers—the powers of speech, as for the cultivation of any other class of powers which men possess. Our intellectual light must not be hid under a bushel any more than our moral light. Writing and speaking are the candle-sticks by which this light is distributed about the world.

Besides, so closely connected is our mental machinery that we even use words in thinking, and facility in using them consequently promotes thinking.

The art of Composition may be learned, either by imitating the speaking and writing of others, or by applying the rules of Grammar and Rhetoric. Such a knowledge of Composition as can be obtained by the first method may be called *Elementary Composition*; and that obtained by the second, *Higher Composition*.

1. ELEMENTARY COMPOSITION. — A child is taking his first lessons in Composition when he begins to talk. If he enjoy the opportunity of hearing good language, a child at five years of age, will possess a large fund of words, he can construct them into sentences, and hold intelligible conversation about objects with which he is familiar. If at that age he be taught the written symbols which represent words, he will soon learn to write words, sentences, and little compositions about things he has seen. This is the manner in which the teaching of Composition should be commenced. As the child enlarges his vocabulary of words, notices a greater variety of sentences, and acquaints himself with more numerous objects, his ability to speak and write will become greater, and his instruction in Composition should be adapted to his increased capacity. Up to the age of ten or twelve, instruction in Composition should consist mainly in presenting pupils suitable models of speaking and writing for imitation, and in giving them ample opportunity to imitate them. Much in the art of Composition can be learned in this way at any age, but nearly all must be learned in this way in child-

hood. In teaching Composition to children, teachers ought not to be too critical — ought not to expect great accuracy or much elegance in expression. Their principal aim should be to evoke linguistic power; and when the power exists, it is time to acquaint them with the niceties of Grammar and Rhetoric. You must have the stream, before you can make its waters play about your grounds or sparkle in your fountains. There is nothing about which we are more sensitive than our speaking and writing, and teachers may do great harm to their young pupils by expecting too much from them.

Some lessons, well calculated to aid pupils in expressing their ideas in words, were described in the Chapter relating to Elementary Instruction, and they need not now be repeated. It is enough to indicate a few classes of appropriate exercises, and the intelligent teacher can expand them to any desirable extent.

First Class of Exercises.—The teacher may engage his young pupils in conversation about things with respect to which he knows they feel an interest; such as, *horses*, *whips*, *fishing*, *harvest-time*, *sleigh-riding*, &c., &c. The discipline in language obtained from lessons on objects as previously described is very valuable.

Second Class of Exercises. — Pupils may be taught to give in their own language the substance of their reading lessons. Attention should be paid in all recitations to the language used. All erroneous expressions must be carefully corrected.

Third Class of Exercises.—Pupils may be required to write sentences about things; as, *house, table, ball,* &c., &c.; or a word or several words can be given to be incorporated into sentences; as, *book, beautiful, strange; school-girls* and *rain; boy, mother,* and *cake; man, axe,* and *wood,* &c., &c. Some good exercises may be found in Sheldon's "Elementary Instruction," commencing at page 220.

Fourth Class of Exercises.—The teacher may present certain forms of sentences and require his pupils to imitate them. Writing from dictation with attention to forms of sentences, punctuation, capital letters, &c., is valuable. Pupils acquire the graces of style unconsciously upon reading or copying well-written composition.

Fifth Class of Exercises.—Lists of faulty sentences may be kept by the teacher, and now and then presented to the pupils for correction. Quite young children can be taught to point out the errors in large numbers of such sentences. Something can also be done in this way to train pupils to habits of correct speaking.

Sixth Class of Exercises.—The teacher may read striking narratives, interesting sketches, or lively descriptions, and require his pupils to reproduce them in their own language. This is an excellent exercise.

Seventh Class of Exercises.—At the age of eight or nine years, the teacher may begin to assign subjects upon which his pupils are expected to write original composition. These subjects ought to be simple, calculated to interest the writers, and to furnish them an opportunity of telling something they know as well as of finding something to tell. The teacher should assign the subject, and may make suggestions as to the matter and form of the composition. Every child can say something about *snow*, *flowers*, *birds*, *hay-making*, *husking-corn*, *gathering nuts*, *going to school*, &c., &c.; if not about *progress*, *government*, *the grandeur of nature's works*, or *the immortality of the soul.*

The preceding exercises will convey an idea of the manner in which children may be taught to compose, and further detail is deemed unnecessary. It may be remarked, however, that children should have daily practice in writing. It might, perhaps, be done in connection with reading lessons. No labored essays could be expected, but they would acquire the power of thinking and of saying what they think. What if the work thus done be crude and wanting in order, it would at least be original, fresh, and childlike. Great harm is done to children by giving them time and opportunity to resort to books and to older persons for help in writing compositions. Let them learn to write, as they talk, naturally. It is time those unmeaning forms of words, half nonsense, half plagiarized, called compositions, should be banished from the school.

2. Higher Composition.—The principal aim of instruction in Elementary Composition is to bring pupils to notice forms of expression, and to imitate them in writing freely and naturally what they

think and feel. Ability to compose having been thus acquired, the rules of Grammar and Rhetoric must now be applied to induce the additional power of composing correctly and elegantly; or the pupil must enter upon a course of study in language which I have called Higher Composition. This course may be commenced at the age of ten or twelve.

It will be remembered that the methods of teaching Grammar, considered the best, required pupils to exemplify every principle learned, in the construction of original sentences. Pupils thus taught, while learning the science of Grammar, will learn the art of Composition so far as Grammatical principles aid in the formation of sentences.

It will also be remembered that in treating of Rhetoric, it was stated that pupils should not merely study the compositions of others, but that they must have much practice in writing exercises in which they should be required to observe every principle learned. Such exercises would furnish a fine opportunity of learning to compose, from the forming of a sentence or the use of a figure to the construction of an oration or the writing of a poem.

If these views are correct, Grammar and Composition, and Rhetoric and Composition, should be taught together; and every suitable Grammatical and Rhetorical lesson should be followed immediately by a lesson in Composition. The manner of doing this is so obvious that there is no need of further illustration. It might be remarked, however, that the systematic correction of sentences, or more general discourse, which violates the rules of

Grammar or Rhetoric belongs appropriately to Composition. Science systematizes the true, art detects the false. Many pages of such exercises are not too much to furnish pupils with the practice they need. To be a good writer one must be a good critic both of his own productions, and the productions of others.

Not only in connection with Grammar and Rhetoric should Composition be studied, but such instruction should be given in connection with all studies. Pupils either write or speak when they recite, and it is always the teacher's duty to see that they speak and write well. Each exercise may thus be made to furnish valuable practice in writing and speaking.

Some useful exercises may be mentioned which are not usually found in works on Grammar or Rhetoric, such as paraphrasing; expressing sentiments in various forms; abridging diffuse compositions and amplifying concise ones; writing criticisms; and making analyses of orations, lectures, essays, or preparing outlines for such productions. Translating from a foreign language into our own or the reverse, gives discipline in all that relates to the use of language, hardly to be obtained in any other way. Taste in composing is greatly improved by reading good books, and by copying well-written productions.

In addition to a systematic course of instruction in Composition, as above indicated, teachers will find it advantageous with advanced pupils, at least, to have at stated times miscellaneous exercises in preparing and reading original compositions. I propose to answer the following questions concerning these exercises: At what times should such exercises be required? Who should assign the subjects? What should be the nature of the subjects assigned? In what manner shall the compositions be corrected? How ought the recitation to be conducted?

The work now had in view will require research and labor on the part of the student. It is not an example or an illustration that is wanted, but a systematically arranged composition, carefully prepared both as regards matter and manner. If pupils are engaged at the same time in the study of other branches, and have proper instruction in the details of composing in connection with their Grammar and Rhetoric lessons, the special exercises now referred to cannot very well be performed more frequently than once a week, if so often.

To give definite direction to a pupil's thoughts, to adapt the task to his capacity and requirements, and to remove from him as far as possible all temptation to plagiarize, it will generally be found best for the teacher to assign the subjects for composition, even to classes of advanced pupils.

The nature of the subject selected for a composition should be adapted to the pupil's capacity, requirements, and taste. In selecting a series of subjects, they should be chosen with reference to their fitness to furnish practice in composing different kinds of discourse and using different varieties of style. They should be such also as would be calculated to call forth the knowledge pupils have, or prompt them to search diligently for that which they have not. But while care is taken to train, equal care must be taken not to cramp. An exuberant flow of words in youth is a better indication of success in writing than a more correct, but more formal, style. Let the imagination of the young have free scope; do not cut out and trim off too much. Value most of all a spontaneous out-pouring of intellect, or a spontaneous out-gushing of feeling.

Teachers must inspect the compositions written by their pupils; but it will be found better merely to point out the errors they may discover than to correct them. If pupils are required to correct their own errors, they will be more careful not to make them; and, besides, the principle violated will be more strongly impressed upon their minds. The teacher must have some marks to indicate errors. For words incorrectly used or misspelled, wrong punctuation, or errors of any kind involving only a single word or mark, a short, perpendicular line may be drawn through the word or mark with respect to which the error occurs, and attention be called to it in the margin by an ☞. In case the error extends to several words, a sentence, or several sentences, the whole may be underscored, and attention called to it as before. More general errors as to style and arrangement can be best corrected at the recitation.

How ought a recitation to be conducted? Each pupil should write the errors which were pointed out by the teacher, upon the blackboard, together with the corrections made by himself. Each pupil should also read his composition; and, then, his whole work may become the subject of criticism, first by the class, and afterwards by the teacher.

II. Instruction in the Dead Languages.

The only Dead Languages that are taught to any great extent in our schools are the Latin and Greek, and special reference will be had in this Article to methods of teaching these languages, although the methods indicated will be found applicable to all languages belonging to the same class. The prominent place the languages of Greece and Rome have occupied in every liberal course of study would be a sufficient reason, if no other could be given, why some discussion of the methods of teaching these languages should be introduced into a work like the present one.

In regard to the benefits derived from the study of the Dead Languages, three opinions are entertained: first, that all other studies are less important than that of Latin and Greek, and that consequently the learning of these languages should occupy the most prominent place and the greatest portion of time in every liberal course of study; second, that the time now spent in the study of the Dead Languages might be employed to much better purpose in obtaining a more complete knowledge of our own language and the various sciences; and, third, that the study of Latin and Greek ought to occupy an important place in a course of study, but that school-time should be fairly proportioned between the several great departments of instruction, and that Collegiate and University honors ought not to be based upon proficiency in Latin and Greek any more than upon proficiency in other branches of learning.

The first of these opinions gives undue prominence to the study of the Dead Languages; the second wholly discards their study; and the third occupies a middle ground between the two extremes, and, while holding that Latin and Greek are not indispensable in a liberal course of study, still maintains that they are valuable auxiliaries in the work of education.

In supporting the last named of these opinions, the reasons will appear why it is considered that both of the other opinions are erroneous. That there are branches of instruction other than those of Latin and Greek which are worthy of careful study, will be generally conceded — conceded even by those whose practice does not correspond with their theory. Mathematics, Natural Science, Mental Philosophy, General Literature, History, the Modern Languages, and other branches of learning should not be omitted from a comprehensive course of study, and, as will be seen in the proper place, all of them furnish classes of facts and kinds of culture quite different from those derived from the study of the Dead Languages. Our duties as men of business and citizens may not be learned as well from the study of Latin and Greek as from some other studies, and this end of utility in study cannot be ignored in teaching.

The cause of education, however, is most likely to suffer detriment in this country, at this time, not from those who favor classical studies too much, but from those who oppose them altogether. The danger is not now great anywhere that Latin and Greek will absorb too much of the pupil's time and attention; but there are persons everywhere who attach little value to the study of these languages. As might be expected from the utilitarian character of our people, America has her full share of these advocates for the abandonment of the study of Latin and Greek, and the substitution in their place of other branches which are supposed to bear a closer relation to the work of the office, the shop, and the farm. In such circumstances, it may be well to state the principal advantages which may be derived from the study of the classical languages.

1. *The study of Latin and Greek assists in the study of our own Language.* — The English language, through the medium of the Norman-French and otherwise, derives at least one-half of all its words from the Latin. Almost all our scientific terms are of Latin or Greek origin, and no one who is unacquainted with these languages, can read a work on Law, Medicine, Theology, Teaching, or upon any science or art, without feeling sadly the want of such knowledge. The close analysis of an English author, such as Milton, is hardly possible for one who is unacquainted with Latin. The finer beauties and more hidden laws which characterize such a work can be fully appreciated only by the classical scholar.

2. *The study of Latin and Greek assists in understanding the Character of the People who spoke them.*— The character of the Greeks and Romans is well

worthy our study. Few nations have done so much that will live in History. The language of a people is closely related to its thought. In its language, as in a mirror, is reflected back an image of what a nation has thought and felt. Not even in the remains of their Sculpture and Painting, not even in their stupendous ruins, their Parthenons and their Colosseums, do the people of Greece and Rome represent themselves so perfectly as in the Poems, the Orations, the Histories and the Dramas, that have been preserved from the general destruction that overwhelmed them. Their noble languages are the richest legacy they could have left us, for in their study we may learn to sympathize with the master-spirits of the past, catch some of their inspiration, and commune with the sentiment which they embalmed in words that remain fresh midst the lapse of centuries.

3. *The study of the Latin and Greek assists in obtaining a Knowledge of the History of the Romans and Greeks.*—There were both Greek and Roman Historians of great celebrity. No translation can do them justice. They must be read to be appreciated. Besides, what these classic nations of antiquity accomplished best appears in the works of their Poets, Orators, Dramatists, and Philosophers; and no one has ever acquired the ability to read these books that did not acknowledge himself amply repaid for all his time and trouble.

4. *The study of Latin and Greek furnishes very good Intellectual Discipline.*—A recitation in Latin or

Greek, when well conducted, gives exercise to the memory, the judgment, and the reason. No better culture for the intellectual faculties can be found than that which comes from making nice discriminations between the meaning of words; carefully comparing constructions; earnestly searching the underlying thought in one language and the fit words to express it in another; and closely studying the modifications and relations among words, phrases, and clauses. It is not maintained that there are not other valuable means of intellectual discipline. The polished Greek himself probably obtained his culture without the study of language other than his own. But it is claimed that the disciplinary advantages of the study of Latin and Greek have stood the test of centuries, and nothing has been found that can be safely used to supersede them. The amount of practical knowledge gained from the study of the Classics may not be equal to that which can be gained in the same time from other sources; but the grand end of study is to increase mental power, to give general efficiency; and no way has been found better suited to the accomplishment of this end than the thorough study of the noble languages of Greece and Rome.

5. *The study of Latin and Greek furnishes fine Æsthetic Culture.*—No one can enter into the spirit of the classic authors without experiencing a refinement of his taste, and a more exalted flow of imagination. Relieved of whatever might have been gross, through the pages of Homer and Plato, Virgil and Cicero, the classic lands of Greece and

Rome reveal themselves to the student as pictures of surpassing beauty. They become his beau-ideals. He rises up from the sphere of the sensual as he contemplates them, and revels amid the ideal beauties of a world of purer thought and nobler sentiment. The classic scholar is known by his nice discriminations, his exact taste, his true sense of the beautiful, his lofty aspirations, his responsive thrill of emotion in witnessing whatever is manly and right in human conduct.

Several different methods of teaching Latin and Greek have been practiced. Before attempting a classification or an exposition of them, it will be well to determine the definite ends for which these languages should be studied.

Latin and Greek are not now studied for the purpose of acquiring ability to speak and write them. There was a time in the history of the principal countries of Europe when books were generally written in Latin, and the deliberations of ecclesiastical councils and learned assemblies were carried on in the same language; but that day has passed never to return. There were during the same period, and perhaps later, institutions of learning that required their students to dress up their poor ideas in the stately flow of what was meant for Ciceronian eloquence. Cicero's forms of expression, his very words, were committed with great labor and then servilely imitated. But even if this effort to acquire the ability to speak and write Latin was proper then, it is so no longer. Indeed, it is generally admitted by critics that no other than a Roman ever mastered the Latin language so perfectly as to speak and write it like Cicero or Virgil; and what Lipsius, Scaliger, and Milton, after many years of study, and with more inducements than exist at present, failed to accomplish, it is scarcely worth while for others, less gifted, and enjoying fewer advantages for such study, to undertake. Exercises in Latin and Greek composition are required wherever these languages are taught, but mainly for the purpose of fixing in the pupil's mind Grammatical forms and constructions. It is well known that the poems and orations written in Latin and Greek, and sometimes delivered at our college commencements, are at best but poor imitations. Besides, if ability to speak and write Latin and Greek with classic elegance could be acquired, the time and labor would be misspent. The Dead Languages, therefore, are not studied for the purpose of acquiring ability to speak and write them.

The purpose for which the Latin and Greek are studied, is to be able to read them, to obtain the rich stores of knowledge which they lock up, and to secure the disciplinary advantages which may be derived from their study. To accomplish these ends, spoken and written exercises may be used as means, but not as ends themselves.

If these views are true, it follows that the Dead Languages must be taught in a manner quite different from that applicable to Living Foreign Languages, inasmuch as the main purpose in learning the latter, is to acquire ability to speak and write them.

With a distinct object in view which is intended

to be accomplished by the study of Latin and Greek, it will be more easy to classify and define the methods by which that object can be attained.

With respect to our Mother-tongue, we first learn to speak it, next we acquire the power to read it, and finally study to know the laws which govern its forms and constructions. Pupils learning a Dead Language, may commence at any one of these points; and, hence, there may be three general methods of teaching such a language. These methods may be called, respectively: 1st, *The method that commences by teaching pupils to speak the language;* 2d, *The method that commences by teaching pupils to read the language; and,* 3d, *The method that commences by teaching pupils the Grammar of the language.* There have been practiced many particular methods, sometimes named after the teachers who used them; but I think it will be found that all of them are embraced in the preceding classification.

1. *The Method that commences by teaching Pupils to speak Latin or Greek.*—A native language is learned by associating certain verbal utterances with things or ideas. The child in learning to talk first hears particular names applied to particular things, forms an association between the names and the things, and finally, acquires the power of imitating the names. The children of Rome and Greece found no more difficulty in learning to speak Latin and Greek than English children do in learning English. If children now anywhere could hear these languages spoken, they could readily learn them. The celebrated Montaigne had a private tutor who spoke no

language in his hearing but Latin, and he learned to speak and read that language with considerable facility by the time he was seven years of age. At the present day, it is impracticable to study the Dead Languages in this way; and, if otherwise, it has been shown elsewhere that it would require the sacrifice of a great amount of time and labor to do so.

2. *The Method that commences by teaching Pupils to read Latin or Greek.* — Some teachers have taught their pupils to read the Dead Languages by having them read, first words, next simple sentences, afterwards sentences more difficult, and finally general discourse. Of course the meaning of the words must be learned either from the teacher or the book. This is substantially the method by which children learn to read their vernacular language; and, while it is admitted that the method can be applied to any language, it is denied that it would furnish that intimate acquaintance with the nature of the language studied, and that higher intellectual and æsthetic culture which is the main end of classical study. If it be said that a knowledge of Latin or Greek Grammar can be obtained after learning to read those languages, it may be replied that in such a case the reading of authors must be very superficial, a second reading after the study of the Grammar would have to follow the first, and the whole work would require much unnecessary time and labor.

Some teachers, too, instead of commencing with words, place in the hands of their pupils an easy, classical author, accompanied with a literal, interlinear translation, and expect them by this means to learn the meaning of words, the construction of sentences, and finally the sense of what they read. It is claimed that Hamilton and others had great success in teaching Latin according to this method; but it is evident that the same objections apply to it as to the preceding method. It may be a speedy way of acquiring the ability to read a language superficially, but it cannot be the best method of obtaining a thorough knowledge of it.

Other teachers select sentences from which particular Grammatical forms or principles can be deduced, teach their pupils to read them, and make them draw the required inferences and learn them in the form usually found in Grammar books. This method is Analytical, and as applied to one's native language, the best; but in regard to the study of the Dead Languages, it is defective in supposing the pupil can have a form of words or a sentence in his mind which he so well understands as to be able to analyze it. A Latin or a Greek sentence is at first wholly unintelligible to a learner, and its meaning can only be determined by the Lexicographic and Grammatical explanation of the single words which compose it. The meaning of each word in a sentence must be learned separately, and then in its relations to the other words with which it is used, before a clear idea of the meaning of the whole can be obtained. In teaching a language spoken by the learners, the method must be analytical; but in teaching one which they cannot speak, the method must be at first synthetical. A teacher of Latin and Greek must therefore begin with words; and in connection with an explanation of their meaning, he will find it greatly promotive of his object, if he acquaint his pupils with various Etymological forms which distinguish them as individual words, and the various Syntactical laws which control their place and relations in sentences. When ability to read a Dead Language has been acquired, no exercise can be more beneficial than the analysis of sentences.

3. *The Method that commences by teaching the Latin or Greek Grammar.* — In teaching according to this method, the pupil first learns the meaning and forms of simple words and the principles of Grammar which have been found by preceding analyses of Latin or Greek composition, and finally applies this knowledge in discovering the sense and beauty of classic authors. This process is similar to the manner in which a native language is learned in commencing with single words; but it differs from it wholly in commencing with words which represent Etymological forms and Grammatical principles. It was previously remarked that a person might learn to read any language without a knowledge of its Grammar; but it must be evident to any one competent to judge that an acquaintance with the forms of words and the laws of construction incident to such languages as the Latin and Greek, must greatly facilitate the work of understanding them. It is my opinion therefore that the first book which should be placed in a pupil's hands who desires to study a Dead Language is the Grammar — not an analytical Grammar as if the pupil already understood the meaning of sentences and was pre-

pared to gather facts and to infer principles, from them, but a Synthetical Grammar in which he will first find definitions, paradigms, and rules, and afterwards learn their significance in discourse.

It was formerly customary to require pupils to commit the whole Grammar, before being led to make an application of any of its principles, or being taught to observe how they might be illustrated by reference to sentences. Nothing could be less interesting to a child than the task of learning the senseless jargon (to him) of *hic—hæc—hoc* and ὁ—ἡ—το; and no word here said must be construed to mean anything in favor of such a method. I think, indeed, that the pupil should commence his study of the Dead Languages with the Grammar, but not with a Grammar book that contains nothing but dry forms and abstract principles.

The method of Studying Latin and Greek now presented, requires the pupil to commit Declensions, Conjugations, and rules; but it contemplates the accompanying of all such lessons with practical exercises calculated to enforce and enliven them. In detail, the proposed lessons might consist, first, of the forms or rules to be committed to memory; second, of sentences in which these forms or rules are illustrated; third, other sentences in which the principle of the lesson is violated; fourth, the construction of original sentences that conform to the principles of the lesson. At the recitation, these exercises should be properly varied, and given sometimes orally, and sometimes in writing. Numerous miscellaneous exercises, intended for review, should be distributed among them. With a book arranged upon a plan like this, an ingenious teacher cannot fail to make the study of the Grammar of any of the Dead Languages interesting.

What has been just said has reference to methods of teaching the elements of the Dead Languages. There is, of course, a higher department of Grammar which investigates the changes these languages have undergone, accounts for their forms, and reveals the great Philological laws which govern their constructions. Into this inviting field, the student, who is able, may enter; and it will be found that, if the Grammar is the proper book with which to begin a course of instruction in the Dead Languages, it is also the proper book with which to end it.

Having completed an elementary course in the Grammar, the pupil is prepared, in connection with further study of the Grammar, to commence the reading of authors in the language studied. Of these the teacher must make a judicious selection. Those works should be chosen which are the purest in sentiment, the most varied in style, and the best calculated to give culture to the taste, and impart information concerning the times in which they were produced. A student may read the whole work of an author or a part of it; but his course of reading should leave him ignorant of no writer who is distinguished in classic literature.

Some general directions may be given for conducting a recitation in the reading of a classical author.

1. Pupils should be required to give both free and literal translations; the purpose of the latter

being to obtain a clear insight into the sense of what is read, and that of the former to find appropriate English expressions for it. The practice of translating selections from Latin or Greek authors into English, and afterwards translating the same back again into Latin or Greek without reference to the original text, is very valuable. By means of this kind of double translation, Ascham says, Queen Elizabeth became one of the best Latin and Greek scholars of the age in which she lived.

2. Pupils should be required to explain the Etymological, Syntactical, Prosodiacal, Rhetorical, and Logical principles contained in the text. From this source comes much of the most valuable culture that is furnished by the study of the Dead Languages. The pupil must prepare his lessons with Grammars and Dictionaries open before him, and the teacher must lead him to see the great laws that regulate general human speech as they appear in the particular language studied.

3. Pupils should be required to account for the Geographical, Scientific, Historical, Mythological, and other like allusions and references that may occur in the lessons recited. Most pupils studying the Dead Languages soon acquire a deep interest in matter of this kind, and books containing such information should be to them a *vade mecum*.

A few additional suggestions will be made.

Constant use should be made of the blackboard in teaching the Dead Languages. This form of recitation is especially valuable while pupils are engaged in the study of their Grammar.

As one of the great objects in studying the Dead Languages is the discipline of the intellect and taste, I have found class criticism, judiciously managed, an excellent means of promoting it.

The teacher himself must be a good classical scholar, if he would make good classical scholars.

Teachers of the Dead Languages, who *love* their work, will have little difficulty in inspiring their pupils with a similar love.

III. Instruction in Living Foreign Languages.

The interests of commerce, correspondence, travel, literature, and science render a knowledge of several of the languages of Europe generally desirable. Besides, it is evident that the study of any language may be made advantageous in a disciplinary point of view. The new thoughts, the varied modes of expression, the nice distinctions in the meaning of words and sentences, the enlarged vocabulary, the comprehensive linguistic laws, the rich literary stores accumulated in other lands, with which a student of Foreign Languages becomes acquainted cannot but be valuable to him.

For these reasons, it is well to consider in this place the methods of teaching Living Foreign Languages; but the subject will not require a lengthy discussion.

A few persons study French, German, and other European languages for their literary and disciplinary advantages. For such persons, methods of teaching might be substantially the same as those just described as most appropriate in the case of the Dead Languages. Inasmuch, however, as the Etymological forms of French and German are less complicated than are those of Latin and Greek, an effort to learn to read the former without a knowledge of their Grammar, would be attended with more success than a similar effort in regard to the latter.

The most prominent object for which Living Foreign Languages are studied is to acquire the ability to speak, to read, and to write them. With these ends in view, no better way of learning them is possible than that by which we learn to speak, read, and write our own language. This is the natural method. We learn to speak by hearing others speak—by associating certain verbal utterances with certain ideas and imitating them. Next we learn the characters which represent words, and acquire the power of making them ourselves. When we know how to speak, read, and write our native language, we may commence the study of its Grammar. If circumstances favor, I am well convinced that this is the best way of learning a Living Foreign Language. Let the pupil be placed where he can hear the language it is designed that he should learn, spoken—spoken in its purity, let him hear no other, and he will soon learn to speak it himself. This done, he can acquire the ability to read and write it as he did his native tongue, and, when prepared, he can engage in the study of its Grammar. In writing this, I have in my mind children who are from three to ten years of age; and it might be remarked that foreign languages are learned at this age with great rapidity. If pupils are older than the age thought of, it might not be improper to combine the exercises in speaking, reading, writing, and Grammar.

It is not often, however, that the circumstances above supposed—circumstances in which the pupil can hear spoken in its purity the language he wishes to learn, are found to surround a pupil. They are seldom enjoyed by any who cannot pursue their studies in a foreign land, and hence some modification of this method must be adopted that will render it better suited to the condition of such as study under less favorable circumstances.

The pronunciation of a foreign language cannot be correctly learned from any one who does not pronounce correctly, nor can it be learned from a book, however carefully notated. A person well acquainted with the elementary sounds of our own language, however, can use this knowledge to considerable advantage in learning another. French and German for example, have very few sounds which are not found in English. If such a pupil first learn those sounds which are peculiar to the language he desires to master, and then use a carefully notated book or Pronouncing Dictionary, he can attain such a pronunciation as may possibly suffice to make him understood. But to speak a language correctly, something more is necessary than to utter its elementary sounds; there is a tone—a manner of speaking, that can never be acquired except from a correct model.

Where foreign languages are often taught by English teachers, as they are in this country, and where pupils use their native language always, except when preparing or reciting their lessons, the systems of such authors as Ollendorff, Woodbury, and Fasquelle are doubtless the best that can be used. After having given some directions in regard to pronunciation, these writers begin their lessons with brief, conversational exercises about the most familiar things, and follow them with other exercises in which practice is given in reading and writing such words and sentences as may have been introduced into the preceding conversational exercise. Each lesson takes for granted a knowledge of the lessons which preceded it, and new words and new constructions are presented for practice in speaking, reading, and writing. Grammatical forms and principles are introduced into all the exercises whenever it is thought that benefit can be derived from them. A course of lessons, arranged according to this method, will comprehend a well-graded series of exercises in speaking, reading, and writing a language, conducted with reference to its Grammar.

This method differs from that by which a person learns his mother-tongue in several particulars — in the use of books when teaching pupils to speak the language, and in teaching pupils to read and write the language and learn its Grammar while learning to speak it. For children not old enough to understand Grammar, it is not well adapted; but in the hands of a teacher who can present a correct model of pronunciation, it is perhaps the only method well suited to the teaching of a foreign language in American schools.

Pupils may learn to read a foreign language by

the method of interlinear translation; but the knowledge of a language thus acquired must be very superficial It is a great error to suppose that a knowledge of any language can be acquired in a short time or in a few lessons. Possibly some easy authors might be read profitably by means of interlinear translations before commencing a series of such exercises as those of Ollendorff. A good teacher might impart in this way a knowledge of pronunciation, the meaning of many words, and some idea of construction, all of which would be very advantageous in learning the Grammar.

Pupils might begin the study of a language like French or German by commencing with its Grammar; but the teacher will find it very difficult to interest pupils in the study of the abstract Grammar of a foreign language, and, besides, it is scarcely possible to acquire the ability to speak a language in this manner.

After a course of elementary instruction in which pupils have learned to speak, read, and write a foreign language with some facility, and possess a good knowledge of its Grammar, they may commence with profit the reading of authors. Easy authors must be first chosen, and afterwards those more difficult. Translations should be required and questions be asked upon the subject-matter in much the same way as has already been described in speaking of methods of teaching the Dead Languages.

CHAPTER III.

INSTRUCTION IN THE FORMAL SCIENCES.

THE Formal Sciences treat of the necessary *forms* in which truth presents itself or by which truth is conceived. They may be divided into two great classes, *Mathematics* and *Logic.*

Mathematics is the science of pure quantity. Its principles have no dependence upon material things. All its calculations and demonstrations may be made without reference to them. But its formulæ express the conditions under which matter exists in space and time.

Logic is the science of pure thought. Its principles are not derived from the manner in which thinking *is* done, but they show how it *must be* done. Its formulæ express the relations between the several parts of the thinking process.

The sciences of Mathematics and Logic are called Formal Sciences, because they relate to truth only in its abstract or ideal condition. The principles of both would be true if matter had no existence.

The following quotation from Sir William Hamilton will show that the object-matter of the Formal Sciences is exhausted by Mathematics and Logic. He says, "Formal Knowledge is of two kinds; for it regards either the conditions of the Elaborative

Faculty—the Faculty of Thought Proper—or the conditions of the Presentations or Representations of external things; that is, the intuitions of Space and Time. The former of these sciences is Pure Logic—the science which considers the laws to which the Understanding is astricted in its elaborative operations, without inquiring what is the object—what is the matter, to which these operations are applied. The latter of these sciences is Mathematics, or the science of Quantity, which considers the relations of Space and Time, without inquiring whether there be any actual reality in space or time. Formal truth will, therefore, be of two kinds—Logical and Mathematical."

The Formal Sciences are evolved from certain ideas and are founded upon certain axioms of which it is not their province to treat. These belong to the domain of Philosophy—a Rational Science.

If now we have correctly apprehended the nature of Mathematics and Logic, methods of instruction adapted to impart a knowledge of them must have much in common; and, therefore, it may be well before discussing the particular principles of instruction which apply to each separately, to speak of the general principles which apply to both alike.

I. The Formal Sciences in General.

The object-matter of a Formal Science admits division into three classes, as follows: 1. *Definitions* and *Axioms*; 2. *Deductions* and *Demonstrations*; 3. *Applications*. Its applications are not properly a part of the science; but they are very important in the work of teaching to illustrate and enforce scientific principles.

1. Definitions and Axioms.—Definitions, in the sense here intended, express the necessary limitations of particular conceptions. This is their meaning whether they relate to the explication of a term or to the nature of a thing.

Axioms, in the sense here intended, express the necessary relations of particular conceptions. Axioms in Mathematics express relations in space and time, and Axioms in Logic express the relations of one part of the thinking process to another.

It is exceedingly important that teachers should be careful in teaching Definitions in the Formal Sciences, where no real object can be presented to illustrate their meaning. We must understand the meaning of terms before we can use them properly. An object of thought must stand out before the mind distinct in itself, and separate from everything else, before one sure step can be taken in the investigation of its relations. Imperfect Definitions vitiate processes of reasoning, and it is to be feared that much of our teaching is defective in not requiring pupils to define fully, distinctly, and adequately.

The following are the most important laws to which Definitions must conform. Their meaning is sufficiently plain without any explanation.

1st. A definition must be a *truthful* representation of the conception defined. It must contain nothing that does not belong to it.

2d. A definition must be an *adequate* representation of the whole conception. It must contain all that belongs to it.

3d. All that is contained in a Definition should be self-evident. A Definition should not need defining.

4th. A Definition should be an affirmative proposition. Showing what a thing is not does not always reveal what it is.

5th. A conception cannot be defined by using the same terms in which the conception is expressed. In such a case, the unknown terms which darkened the conception would also darken the definition of it.

6th. Definitions should be stated in the briefest, strongest, and most expressive form of words.

Let pupils study closely the Definitions of the text-book, let them test them, and make others for themselves. They may commit them to memory, but it is much more important that they should understand them. If properly conducted, exercises in learning Mathematical and Logical definitions will prove an exceedingly valuable discipline for the mind.

All reasoning would be impossible without certain fixed principles from which to start. No man could ever convince another with regard to a truth or an error, if there were not some common point of agreement between them. Hence the necessity of Axioms in the economy of thought. And, although a formal statement of them is not always made, they constitute the bases of all sciences, and are especially prominent in the sciences of Mathematics and Logic.

As previously stated, the Formal Sciences borrow their Axioms from the Rational Sciences. From Axioms in general it may be their province to select such as belong to them; but they have nothing to do in determining the nature of Axioms, the tests by which they are to be distinguished, their number or their classification.

Mathematical Axioms are so well known that it seems unnecessary to enumerate them. They underlie as well the sciences which treat of number as those which treat of form.

Among Logical Axioms the following may be named—

1st. All thinking is governed by law.

2d. Every universal is composed of particulars.

3d. Every particular is comprehended in a universal.

4th. Whatever may be predicated of a universal may be predicated of all the particulars of which it is composed.

5th. Whatever may be predicated of all the particulars composing a universal may be predicated of the universal.

6th. If two terms agree with the same third term they agree with each other.

7th. If of two terms, the one agrees and the other disagrees with the same third term, they disagree with each other.

This enumeration is not intended to exhaust the Axioms belonging to the science of Logic, but simply to show that there are such Axioms.

With respect to pupils old enough to comprehend

Axioms, the method of teaching them presents no difficulty. Their simple statement will secure assent, and nothing more is needed. The discussion of their use in building up a science belongs further on.

2. Deductions and Demonstrations.—Deduction may be defined as the process of drawing out a particular from a universal truth by simple inspection or by a single step of reasoning. Demonstration may be defined as the method of finding new truths by the process of comparing definitions, axioms, and established propositions with one another. The first has the form of a direct inference or a single syllogism, while the second consists of a train of reasoning or a series of syllogisms. As the method of both is substantially the same, both may be considered together under the name Demonstration. This may be the case also if Deduction be used to designate a general method of reasoning, and Demonstration, an application of it.

In Pure Mathematics, all that cannot be learned directly, by intuition, must be learned by Demonstration. Inductive reasoning has no place in Mathematics.

In Pure Logic the same is true, for although an Inductive Syllogism may be used, yet, in a pure form, the conclusion must be just as much a positive truth as it is in a Deductive Syllogism. In Applied Logic as in Applied Mathematics, the conclusions are not always either certain or exact.

The Demonstrations of Logic consist essentially in showing the relations between the conclusions of syllogisms and their premises. In general, but a single step is necessary to be taken away from the first principles upon which the science rests.

Demonstrations in Mathematics, although like those of Logic in the circumstance that they concern pure conceptions and not the conceptions of material objects, differ from them in several particulars. In Mathematics it is not the doctrine of the syllogism as an exposition of the laws of thought that is to be demonstrated, but the relations of numbers and forms by means of syllogisms. Mathematics is a formal application of Logic to the conceptions of time and space. The student of Mathematics therefore cannot select any premises but he must select the right premises. He cannot often find the truth he seeks at the end of a single syllogism, but must frequently trace it through a long series of syllogisms.

So far as methods of teaching them are concerned, however, the Demonstrations of Mathematics and of Logic may be considered together; and the point now is to find the governing principles of those methods.

One who would become skilful in demonstrating must attend to the following rules:—

1st. Understand the proposition to be demonstrated and its relations to the definitions and axioms upon which it depends and to the propositions which may have preceded or are to follow it.

2d. Observe a rigid logical order in the successive steps of the demonstration.

3d. Argue closely and clearly.

4th. Attain positive conclusions.

5th. Use appropriate language.

These rules are sufficiently obvious without explanation. If any one of them is disregarded no perfect demonstration can be secured. They apply, however, to the demonstration of independent propositions. The object-matter of a Formal Science is composed of several kinds of propositions which must be divided according to certain laws, among which the following are the most important—

1st. The divisions should exclude one another.

2d. The order of the divisions should be determined by their logical relations.

3d. In the arrangement of particular propositions the simple and the independent should precede the complex and the dependent.

A child first learns to reason in connection with objects. The steps he takes are very short and very easy. Properly instructed, his skill rapidly improves until he can appreciate the abstract relations of things or thoughts. For first efforts at formal demonstration, easy propositions should be given him, and then those more difficult. Eventually he may be able to follow the most abstruse reasoning incident to Mathematics or Logic.

If teachers reason skilfully, their pupils will be likely to be benefited by their example.

Practice in detecting the different kinds of fallacies in arguments will be a good exercise.

A wise teacher will lead his pupils to discover their own errors in reasoning rather than correct them himself. The method Socrates so successfully practiced against the Sophists of his day may be just as usefully applied now.

3. Applications.—Mind and matter are correlative. For every ideal truth there must be a real thing—for every form of thought there must be matter to fill the form, or the creation would not harmonize. The world within must envisage the world without, or God could not have created it. Hence all abstract formulæ must be adapted to some concrete phenomena; or every Formal Science must have its Applications.

Mathematical principles may be applied to all things that appear under the conditions of space and time.

Logical principles are of universal application, for all things may be thought about.

In making an application of Formal truths three things are necessary: 1st, To have attained a clear conception of the truths themselves; 2d, To have carefully observed and colligated facts; 3d, To be able to apply the right ideas to the right facts.

Formal truths so far as they are not axiomatic are attained by the process of demonstration as already shown.

The collection and colligation of facts belong to the department of Empirical science and are to be treated of in the proper place.

The Applications of the Formal Sciences consist in fitting the right ideas to the right facts. This may be more a work of art than of science, but nature presents no more important work for human effort to perform. He who deals only with Formal thought is apt to become impractical and visionary. He may build up systems which seem beautiful, but at a touch they vanish into the thin air of which they were composed. He who absorbs all his time in collecting facts, who with eyes cast down to earth never looks heavenward, but occupies himself in examining animals, and plants, and stones, and fossils, until the eye of faith grows dim and matter seems omnipotent, does even less for himself and mankind than the speculative dreamer. But he who accustoms himself to apply the right ideas to the right facts, to prove his reasonings, to verify his theories, will be in no danger of becoming an impractical idealist on the one hand or a coarse materialist on the other. He finds that every fact rests in an idea; that each jewel has its casket in the crown of nature; that forms of thought existed in the God-mind and He made matter to fill them.

As hints to teachers giving instruction in the Applications of the Formal Sciences, it may be stated that sometimes facts may be given and pupils required to find principles, and sometimes principles may be given and pupils required to find facts; that easy applications should always precede those more difficult; that numerous examples and abundant illustrations should be furnished, arranged both with reference to specific principles and miscellaneously; and that close explanations should be exacted in all cases.

II. Mathematics.

After what has now been said respecting the nature of the Formal Sciences in General and the methods of teaching them, it is not deemed necessary to treat specially of methods of teaching Mathematics. Besides, what should be said specifically with respect these methods will appear in speaking of methods of teaching *Arithmetic*, *Algebra*, and *Geometry*.

Something will be expected, however, in regard to the advantages to be derived from the study of Mathematics.

Mathematics has occupied a prominent place in courses of instruction for the young from the earliest times. Some have thought that its disciplinary advantages were greater than could be derived from any other branch of instruction, while others have maintained that its study was rather hurtful than otherwise. In the hope of contributing something toward the settlement of the question, it is proposed here briefly to consider the value of Mathematical studies: 1. *In themselves;* 2. *In their objective relations;* 1. *In their effects upon the mind.*

1. *The Value of Mathematical Studies in themselves.*—All truth is worthy of study for its own sake. To decide otherwise would be to question the wisdom of God who created it. All kinds of truth, however, may not be of equal value, and the inquiry might be made as to the relative value of Mathematical truth. Truth may be divided into three kinds: *ideal* truth, *formal* truth, and *real* truth. Ideal truth is the truth which we know by simple intuition, which furnishes the basis upon which all other truth rests, and the criteria by which it is judged. Formal truth expresses the necessary forms in which all truth presents itself or by which it is conceived. Real truth is the harmonious relation between things or between thought and things. In compar-

ing the value of these several kinds of truth, no reasons appear why formal truth is not of as much worth as either of the other kinds. It seems as noble in itself, is of as much use, and manifests as fully the glory of the Creator. But formal truth is of two kinds, Mathematical and Logical, and we seek to know only the value of Mathematical truth.

As has been already shown, Logic contains a larger body of truth than Mathematics and is of wider application, but I can find no standard by which it can be determined that a truth in the one science is more valuable than a truth in the other.

Mathematics is a noble science. Many of its principles are exceedingly beautiful, and some of them almost sublime. It has won the admiration of great men in all ages, and his education must be considered incomplete among whose acquisitions a knowledge of Mathematics is not found.

2. *The Value of Mathematical Studies in their Objective Relations.*—No other science is so generally connected with the affairs of business as Mathematics. Arithmetic is used in keeping accounts and in all the transactions of buying and selling. In connection with Geometry, it is used in all mechanical employments. Geometry, Algebra, Trigonometry, Conic Sections, &c., cannot be dispensed with in the construction of machinery, nor in any of the departments of Engineering. All this, however, is so generally understood that it seems hardly necessary to mention it.

Mathematics is the hand-maid of the sciences. Working by means of this potent instrument modern philosophers have been able to make rapid advances in many departments of physical science. To it, we are indebted for what is most valuable in Mechanics, Optics, Pneumatics, Thermotics, Astronomy, and other sciences like these. It has its uses in Geography, Chemistry, Geology, and even Political Economy. Matter everywhere presents itself to us under Mathematical conditions. Laws that find their expression in Mathematics rule all that moves in the heavens, all that flies in the air, all that swims in the waters, all that springs up from the earth or that falls upon its surface, and the firm earth itself. Yonder yellow leaf that is lifted from its stem by the autumn wind, and after innumerable gyrations in the air, falls upon the surface of the stream and is borne onward by the current, makes no movement but in obedience to such laws. Mathematics has principles great enough to sweep the Universe, and hold suns and planets in their grasp, and delicate enough to poise the smallest atom on a point much too fine for human conception.

3. *The Value of Mathematical Studies in their Effects upon the Mind.*—One of the most important objects of study is to secure mental discipline. What is the value of Mathematics in this respect? In discussing this point, Sir William Hamilton says: "If we consult reason, experience, and the common testimony of ancient and modern times, none of our intellectual studies tend to cultivate *a smaller number of the faculties, in a more partial or feeble manner than Mathematics.*" In proof of this opinion, he quotes

a large number of authorities, a few of whom I shall take the liberty of citing here:

"*Bernhardi*, a celebrated Prussian educator, says: 'It is asked—*Do Mathematics awaken the judgment, the reasoning faculty, and the understanding to an all-sided activity?* We are compelled to answer—*No*.'

"'This also shows me,' says *Goethe*, 'more and more distinctly, what I have long in secret been aware of, that the cultivation afforded by the Mathematics is, in the highest degree one-sided and contracted.'

"*Descartes* stated in a letter in 1630, 'That he had renounced the study of Mathematics for many years, and that he was anxious not to lose any more of his time in the barren operations of Geometry and Arithmetic, studies which never lead to anything important.'

"'Thus it is rare,' says *Pascal*, 'that Mathematicians are observant, or that observant minds are Mathematical.'

"*Dugald Stewart* says, 'When the Mathematician reasons upon subjects unconnected with his favorite studies, he is apt to assume, too confidently certain intermediate principles as the foundation of his arguments.' And again, 'I have never met with a mere Mathematician who was not credulous to a fault.'

"*Bayle* says, 'It cannot be disputed, that it is rare to find much devotion in persons who have once acquired a taste for the study of Mathematics.'

"*De Stael*, to the same effect, 'The Mathematics lead us to lay out of account all that is not proved.'"

Sir William's argument against the use of Mathematics as a discipline for the mind is summed up in the following sentence. "We are thus disqualified for *observation, either internal or external*, for *abstraction*, and *generalization*, for *common reasoning*, nay, disposed to the alternative of blind *credulity* or of irrational *skepticism*." This argument he supports at much length with great ability and greater learning. When closely examined, however, the whole argument will be found to bear not so much against the use of Mathematics as a disciplinary study in its proper place, as against the injudicious claims advanced in its behalf in that regard.

No one should claim for the study of Mathematics that it disciplines the ordinary powers of observation. It is not concerned with either material or mental phenomena. Its province is not to collect facts. Pure Mathematics is quite indifferent to the existence of matter. There is a kind of observing power, however, which the study of Mathematics does cultivate — that power which sees truth in definitions and axioms and without which all demonstrations would be blind and unproductive of fruit.

Abstraction and generalization as used in the Empirical sciences have no place in Mathematics, and therefore that study cannot develop and strengthen the mental powers by which those processes are performed. But in another sense all of Pure Mathematics is abstract, and surely Mathematical truths admit classification and generalization. In every branch of Mathematics there are forms of demonstration which are true in particular cases, and there are others which must be true in all cases. In teaching, pupils may be made to advance from particular examples to general principles.

If by common reasoning is meant that kind of reasoning in which the conclusions arrived at are *probable* but not *positive*, it must be admitted that the study of Mathematics is not well calculated to increase ability in its use. As Hamilton forcibly remarks, "Mathematical demonstration is solely occupied in *deducing conclusions;* probable reasoning, principally concerned in *looking out for premises.* All Mathematical reasoning flows from, and, admitting no tributary streams, can be traced back to its original source: principle and conclusion are convertible. The most eccentric deduction of the science is only the last ring in a long chain of reasoning, which descends, with adamantine necessity, link by link, in one simple series, from its original dependence. In contingent matter, on the contrary, the reasoning is comparatively short; and as the conclusion can seldom be securely established on a single antecedent, it is necessary, in order to realize the adequate amount of evidence, to accumulate probabilities by multiplying the media of inference; and thus to make the same conclusion, as it were, the apex of many convergent arguments. In general reasoning, therefore, the capacities mainly requisite, and mainly cultivated, are the prompt acuteness which discovers what materials are wanted for our premises, and the activity, knowledge, sagacity, and research, able competently to supply them. In demonstration, on the contrary, the one capacity cultivated is that patient habit of suspending all intrusive thought, and of continuing an attention to the unvaried evolution of that perspicuous evidence which it passively recognizes, but does not actively discover. Of observation, experiment, induction, analogy, the Mathematician knows nothing."

The above is a true exposition of the nature of Mathematical reasoning; but it does not follow that such reasoning is of no value. It cannot accomplish what its nature unfits it for, but it may accomplish other ends quite as important.

The habit of rigid demonstration, of close thinking, which Mathematics inculcates, must be in itself very valuable. If no other kind of reasoning be practiced, it will no doubt lead to a one-sided culture; but, pursued with other kinds, any danger of this sort is avoided, and much is gained by introducing somewhat of Mathematical exactness and clearness, both of thought and language, into what has been called the "common reasoning of life." Need it be added that the loose forms of reasoning to which the majority of men are accustomed stand much in want of pruning?

Mathematical reasoning is necessary in Mechanics, Engineering, Navigation, Geography, Astronomy, and other arts and sciences; and when we consider that the principles of Mathematics are used in all transactions of buying and selling, the reasoning peculiar to that branch of study will not be considered very *uncommon*.

Hamilton himself admits that the study of Mathematics tends to correct the vice of "mental distraction," and to inculcate the virtue of "continuous attention." The attainment of this end alone would justify the study of Mathematics in our schools, for no one addicted to the vice of "mental distraction" can either become a scholar or succeed well in life.

It is easy to see how a mere Mathematician—a man who knows nothing but forms and numbers, might become *credulous* as to premises, and *skeptical* as to conclusions; but this danger cannot exist when instruction in Mathematics is combined with instruction in other departments of learning. Besides, it would seem that any one understanding the nature of Mathematics would scarcely expect to find elsewhere self-evident premises or positive conclusions; and hence be on his guard against allowing habits of thought engendered in demonstrative reasoning to influence him in inductive reasoning. The inductive reasoner, indeed, needs quite as much to be on his guard against bad mental *habits* as the Mathematician.

The sum of all is this: Man and nature correlate. It takes the whole of nature used as means to cultivate duly the whole of man. Instruction confined to one science, or to one class of sciences must be partial, one-sided, and productive of bad mental habits. Mathematics may receive more than its share of attention in some of our institutions of learning, and bad results may sometimes flow from it; but that such studies are valuable in themselves, in their objective relations, and as a discipline of the mind, is susceptible of the strongest proof. The only point that has been seriously questioned is their value for the purpose of mental discipline; but until it can be shown that demonstrative reasoning is valueless in itself, that the discipline of the mental faculties it calls into requisition is a superfluous work, and that it has no useful application in the sciences or in the affairs of life—all impossible, Mathematics will retain a prominent place in our courses of instruction.

Arithmetic.

Arithmetic may be defined as the science of Number. The idea of number, probably, has its origin in a consciousness of successive mental states constituting periods, and is therefore involved in the more fundamental idea of time. But whether this is a correct account of its origin or otherwise, it is certain that external objects furnish the *occasion* of its formation, and that children possess it at a very early age.

Arithmetic has its Definitions and Axioms, its Deductions and Demonstrations, and its Applications.

Among Arithmetical definitions, there must be those of *number*, a *unit*, a *fraction*, *ratio*, &c.; and among Arithmetical axioms, there must be the following: "Two magnitudes are equal when they can be divided into parts which are equal each to each;" "The whole is greater than any of its parts;" "The whole is equal to the sum of all its parts;" "If with the same means the same operations be performed upon equal quantities, the results will be equal."

It is maintained by good authority that "Pure Arithmetic contains no demonstration," but while the operations of adding, subtracting, multiplying, and dividing may, perhaps, be resolved into processes of simple intuition, there seem to be other

Arithmetical operations which cannot be so resolved; for example, that the product of the two means of a proportion is equal to the product of the two extremes, or that if the numerator and denominator of a fraction be multiplied or divided by the same number its value will remain the same. Arithmetic may require fewer steps of reasoning than Geometry, but its methods of operation are substantially the same. All the reasonings of Arithmetic are properly deductive or demonstrative. Some writers upon Arithmetic use the term induction with reference to certain methods of operation; but in all cases the truth sought is capable of being demonstrated without the series of facts from which it is inferred by induction, and, besides, universal truths which it is the special province of deductive science to attain, can never be arrived at by an inductive method.

The greater part of our treatises on Arithmetic is taken up with the Applications of the science. Its practical importance renders this desirable.

From what has been stated above, it will be seen that the general remarks made upon Methods of Instruction in the Formal Sciences, apply to Arithmetic; but as already intimated, it is my purpose to enter upon a more detailed discussion of Methods of teaching this subject.

Before proceeding to describe these methods, it may be well to state the principal ends for which Arithmetic is studied, and the most necessary conditions of their attainment. These ends are: 1st, *To obtain a knowledge of the properties of numbers;* 2d,

To give practice in mathematical reasoning; 3d, *To attain precision in the use of language;* and 4th, *To secure skill in the application of numbers to the concerns of life.* There are several secondary ends which must not be overlooked. Among them, the following: 1st, *Rapidity and accuracy in the solution of problems;* 2d, *Skill in the use of abbreviating artifices;* 3d, *An acquaintance with methods of proof.* The following may be named as the most necessary conditions for the attainment of these ends: 1st, *The object-matter of the science should be distributed in a logical order;* 2d, *Pupils should commence with the simplest Arithmetical operation, and be thoroughly grounded in each step of their progress before taking another;* 3d, *Arithmetical definitions and rules should be understood by pupils before they are required to use them;* 4th, *Pupils should be taught to explain their work in clear, concise, and appropriate language;* 5th, *Numerous, well-graded, skilfully varied problems, embodying every principle learned, should furnish ample opportunity to pupils for making a practical application of their theoretical knowledge.*

Arithmetic is usually divided into two parts, *Oral* Arithmetic and *Written* Arithmetic. These names are derived from the manner in which the operation is performed. All Arithmetic is "Mental," "Intellectual," and "Practical" in its character. Written Arithmetic may embrace all Arithmetical topics. In preparing their work, pupils write it out on slates or blackboards; and in reciting, they are expected to explain what they have done. Oral Arithmetic embraces only such topics as admit of a convenient oral discussion, and such problems as do not contain large numbers or require complicated fractional reductions. Pupils are expected to prepare their lessons in Oral Arithmetic without writing down their work, and to repeat the problems and solve them orally, upon hearing the teacher read them. Instruction in both Oral and Written Arithmetic should be given at the same time, and some advantage may be gained by making the lessons correspond. The peculiar advantage of the Oral method is that it enables a teacher to accomplish more disciplinary work in the same time than the Written method, and gives more exercise to the powers of conception and memory. Being unaided by written symbols it tends more to cultivate continuity of thought.

We shall now endeavor to present a series of Arithmetical exercises which will conform to the principles already indicated.

1. *Exercises in Counting.*—A child will be found to possess the idea of number at a very early age. He undoubtedly obtains it through the medium of objects. It is the teacher's duty to expand this idea in the way nature indicates. If a child can count ten when he enters school, the teacher must begin his instruction at that point and teach him to count twenty, fifty, and a hundred in the same way he learned to count ten. Convenient objects may be found for this purpose in beans, grains of corn, pebbles, strokes on a blackboard, or balls on a frame The pupils should be taught to count backwards as well as forwards, and without objects as well as with them.

2. *Exercises in adding, subtracting, multiplying, and dividing orally.*—These exercises must first be taught with objects; but the pupil must be gradually accustomed to do without them. Small numbers must be used until the pupil is prepared for larger ones. The manner of conducting such exercises is so obvious that no description of it here, is deemed necessary. Besides, any teacher who may need aid can obtain it from works on Oral Arithmetic.

3. *Exercises in combining these Processes.*—These exercises are of the same nature as the preceding and can be conducted in the same way. The teacher will do well to introduce into the lessons the names of the pupils in the class, the objects about the school-room, trees, flowers, sheep, horses, cows, dogs, &c.

4. *Exercises in learning the written Symbols for Numbers.*—Pupils have now the idea of number. They can readily count, and it is a task of no difficulty to make them acquainted with the nine digits. It is only necessary for them to make an arbitrary association between the number and the character which is used to represent it. The pupils may count while the teacher forms the characters, or the teacher may name the numbers, and the pupils either point them out or name them. The meaning of the cypher must likewise be taught.

5. *Exercises in Numeration and Notation.*—For the purpose of teaching Notation and Numeration, I

would arrange columns of figures upon cards or blackboards thus:

1	10	100	1000	10,000	100,000
2	20	200	2000	20,000	200,000
3	30	300	3000	30,000	300,000
4	40	400	4000	40,000	400,000
5	50	500	5000	50,000	500,000
6	60	600	6000	60,000	600,000
7	70	700	7000	70,000	700,000
8	80	800	8000	80,000	800,000
9	90	900	9000	90,000	900,000

This done, I would use the first two columns in giving the first lesson. One may be called the *units* column, and the other the *tens* column. We now suppose that the class have learned to read and write the numbers in the column of units, and we use it only to assist us in the task of teaching them to read and write the numbers in the column of tens. The teacher should call attention to the fact that there are single figures to represent any number of objects up to *nine;* but that *ten* cannot be represented by a single character. He may then arrange objects in collections of ten, and have his pupils count one ten, two tens, three tens, four tens, &c. If now he tell them that one ten is designated by the figure one with a cypher placed to the right of it, as in the column of tens, they will be prepared to understand that two tens are designated by the figure two with a cypher placed to the right of it, and so on to nine tens. The pupils should be exercised in pointing out two tens or twenty, five tens or fifty, seven tens or seventy, &c.; and afterwards in writing them.

The second lesson should consist in teaching the class to read and write numbers between ten and twenty, twenty and thirty, &c., to ninety-nine. The teacher may write the number 10 upon the black-board and ask how many added to ten will make eleven, twelve, thirteen, &c. He may then ask how these numbers are written, and if no one can tell, he may erase the cypher and put 1 in its place, and say the 1 on the left hand signifies one ten, and the 1 on the right hand one unit, and one ten and one unit are eleven. If when 1 is put in place of the cypher, the number becomes eleven, pupils will readily understand that when 2 is put in its place the number will become twelve; 3, thirteen, and so on to nineteen. The numbers between twenty and thirty can be taught in the same way, and so on to ninety-nine. Pupils must not only read the numbers but write them. Questions like the following will also be very useful: What number is that which it composed of two tens and seven units? four tens and three units? eight tens and five units? &c.; how many tens and units in twenty-four? in thirty-seven? in seventy-six? &c.

Pupils have now learned to read and write all numbers up to ninety-nine. The next lesson should make them acquainted with the third column, or the column of hundreds. To do this, the teacher will take the ten collections of objects of ten each, place them all together and ask the number. It is one hundred. He points to the number, has the pupils notice how it is written, and then they readily read and write the other numbers up to nine hundred. Any number may now be placed in the units column by erasing the cypher and inserting the number, and so with the tens column, or both columns at the same time.

It is unnecessary to describe further, as the same method applies to the column of thousands, tens of thousands, hundreds of thousands, &c.

6. *Exercises in Addition, Subtraction, Multiplication, and Division.*—A pupil who can read and write numbers is prepared to understand the operations of Addition, Subtraction, Multiplication, and Division; and, therefore, he should not only be taught how to perform these operations, but why they are so performed.

For the pupil to understand the process of Addition, it will be necessary for him to know that those numbers only which represent things of the same denomination can be added together. This he can be taught readily with objects. He will see at once that five grains of corn and three beans neither make eight grains of corn nor eight beans, and, hence, that units must be added to units, tens to tens, &c. He must know how to convert lower denominations into higher ones, that is units into tens, tens into hundreds, &c. This, however, more properly belongs to Notation and Numeration. Finally, he must be made to see that to render such reductions more convenient he must commence in adding at the right-hand column of figures.

To perform the operation of Subtraction nothing more is necessary than for that of Addition, except the converting of higher denominations to lower ones, and that is as easily done as its reverse.

There is no principle in Multiplication that is not found in Addition; and Division is but a different kind of Subtraction.

The first examples in Addition should consist of such numbers that the sum of those under each denomination can not exceed nine. The first examples in Subtraction should consist of such numbers that each number of a certain denomination in the minuend should exceed the number of the same denomination in the subtrahend. The first examples in Multiplication should consist of such numbers that none of the products of numbers in the multiplicand by the multiplier can exceed nine. The first examples in Division should consist of such numbers that the divisor can be contained in each number of the dividend without a remainder. The first divisors used in what is called Long Division should be less than ten. In all cases the progress of the pupils should be gradual; but one point of difficulty should be presented at a time. Much practice should be allowed them in order to secure rapidity and accuracy in the performance of their work. Solutions should be neatly written upon blackboards and properly explained. Forms of explanation may be obtained from text-books; but teachers should be careful to have their pupils understand them and not merely commit them to memory. Teachers will find the construction of Addition, Subtraction, Multiplication, and Division tables, by their younger pupils, a very valuable auxiliary in familiarizing them with the processes involved. The terms applied to the numbers used in Subtraction are Minuend, Subtrahend, and Difference. Any two of these being given, a third can be found. The same is true in Multiplication with reference to the Multiplicand, Multiplier, and Product; and in Division with reference to the Dividend, Divisor, and Quotient. I mention these facts here, in order to say that such problems present work of much value to learners.

7. *Exercises in the Solution of practical Examples involving the four fundamental Rules.* — Pupils not only need to know *how* to perform simple Arithmetical operations, but *when* they are required to be performed. For this purpose numerous practical problems must be presented. All text-books contain some such problems; but none of them within my knowledge contain one-fourth as many as are needed. The teacher must supply this deficiency. They are so well calculated to give interest to the study and to make pupils think, that I am disposed to consider them almost indispensable.

8. *Exercises in imparting the Idea of a Fraction.* — The basis of all Arithmetical operations is the unit. The unit may be multiplied or divided, and these processes really constitute the whole of Pure Arithmetic. All Integers may be called *multiplied units,* and all Fractions, *divided units.* Particular whole numbers denote the extent of the multiplication, and particular fractions denote the nature of the division.

The idea of a fraction is formed upon seeing things broken up or divided. Pupils have the idea when they enter school, but the teacher must expand it by exhibiting and naming the parts of objects. For this purpose, an apple may be cut into parts, a stick may be broken into pieces, or a line, a square, or a circle, drawn on a blackboard, may be divided into sections. Such instruction should be continued until the pupils can readily name the fraction upon seeing the object, or find an object which is represented by the fraction; or, in other words, until they learn to count fractionally.

9. *Exercises in adding, subtracting, multiplying, and dividing fractions orally.*—At this stage of their progress, pupils may perform orally with much advantage some of the simpler problems in Addition, Subtraction, Multiplication, and Division of Fractions. Such questions as the following may be asked: *In Addition:* What is the sum of one-half and one-half? one-third and one-third? one-fourth and two-fourths? one-half and one-fourth? one-half and one-third? &c.; *in Subtraction:* What is the difference between one and one-half? three-fourths and one-fourth? one-third and one-sixth? one-half and one-third? &c.; *in Multiplication:* What is the product of two times one-half? three times one-third? four times one-sixth? one-half times two? one-half times one-half? &c.; *in Division:* how many halves in one? in two? in five? how many times is two contained in one-half? in one-third? in two-fourths? how many times is one-fourth contained in one-fourth? in one-half? in one-eighth? &c. All this can be beautifully illustrated with squares drawn upon the blackboard and divided into the requisite number of parts. As soon as possible, however, pupils

should be taught to solve such problems without depending upon objects.

10. *Exercises in teaching Fractional Expressions.*—When pupils have attained a clear idea of a fraction, it will not be difficult to teach them to express it. The simplest fractions are those in which the numerator is unity, and, therefore, pupils should first be taught to write $\frac{1}{2}$, $\frac{1}{3}$, $\frac{1}{5}$, $\frac{1}{7}$, $\frac{1}{12}$, &c.; and afterwards fractions in which the numerator is greater than unity; as $\frac{2}{3}$, $\frac{4}{5}$, $\frac{3}{7}$, $\frac{11}{12}$, &c. Pupils may be required to write fractions representing the given parts of squares or circles drawn upon the blackboard, or they may divide such figures so that certain given fractions will represent them.

11. *Exercises in the Addition, Subtraction, Multiplication, and Division of Fractions, and their Applications.*—Pupils are now prepared to enter upon the work of adding, subtracting, multiplying, and dividing fractional numbers, and of making an application of them in the solution of practical problems. The work may be done orally or by writing. The simpler operations of fractions can be understood by inspection; but when pupils are prepared for it, the rules for finding the Greatest Common Divisor, the Least Common Multiple, and all other rules relating to Fractions must be rigidly demonstrated.

12. *Exercises in Decimal Fractions.*—With a knowledge of the Decimal Notation and of Common Fractions, it will be no difficult task for a pupil to learn Decimal Fractions, for there is no new prin-

ciple involved. A Decimal Fraction is a fraction whose denominator is always 10 or some product of 10. Such fractions are written by placing a point, called the Decimal Point, before the numerator. This point indicates that the number of figures in the numerator to the right of it is equal to the number of cyphers in the denominator, and hence does away with the necessity of writing the denominator.

Instruction in Decimals must begin by making pupils thoroughly acquainted with the Decimal Notation. They must be taught both to read and to write Decimals with facility. The Decimal Notation may be taught in the same manner as the notation of integers; but this trouble need scarcely be taken, as pupils can almost as easily read or write *tenths, hundredths, thousandths*, as *tens, hundreds, thousands.*

All the rules in the Addition, Subtraction, Multiplication, or Division of Decimals may be shown to be true either by reducing the Decimals to Common Fractions, or from the nature of the Notation itself. Text-books exhibit both methods, and it is unnecessary to detail them here.

13. *Exercises in Compound Numbers.*—In the Compound or Denominate Numbers, the units increase according to varying scales. These scales are fixed by some authority, and follow no regular law. Pupils must, therefore, commit them to memory; but when the tables of Weights and Measures are well understood, the Addition, Subtraction, Multiplication, and Division of Compound

Numbers present little difficulty to the learner that he has not already encountered in performing the same operations with abstract numbers.

14. *Exercises in Proportion, and Involution and Evolution.*—These exercises belong to Pure Arithmetic, but they are simply modifications of the four fundamental rules. They present no special difficulty in teaching.

15. *Exercises in Arithmetical Applications.*—A knowledge of Arithmetic is needed in almost every kind of business in which men are engaged, and, therefore, teachers should make its practica. applications a prominent part of their instruction.

In solving practical problems, pupils should be required to understand the words in which the problem is expressed, to point out the relation of the thing required to the thing given, to present a neat solution, and to explain their work in concise and appropriate language.

A few additional suggestions will be made. Problems that involve but a single principle should be given first, and, afterwards, those which involve several principles. Text-book or teacher may furnish a form of solution, but the problems should be so arranged that it cannot be followed mechanically. Pupils may be required to compose problems involving certain given principles or answering certain given conditions. Many miscellaneous problems add much to the value of an Arithmetic. These may be classified according to their relations. Important facts may sometimes be incorporated into Arithmetical problems.

The preceding series of exercises do not profess to cover the whole ground of Arithmetic; but it is believed that most that is essential in teaching it, has been presented.

ALGEBRA.

Algebra is not a distinct and independent branch of Mathematics. It is rather a method of representing quantities and of performing Mathematical operations, by means of symbols. These symbols may represent a portion of time, an extent of space, an amount of matter, value, or force, and, also, the relations of quantities and the operations which may be performed on them. These symbols are used in all the higher investigations of Mathematics, and they have been productive of results as wonderful as they are important. They have enabled mathematicians to abridge the processes of calculation, to overcome difficulties previously considered insurmountable, and to express in beautiful language the truths they elicited. All this should recommend the study of Algebra to the student.

Owing to the symbolic character of the language used, the truths arrived at by the process of Algebra are more general than the truths arrived at by the processes of Arithmetic and Geometry. Algebra is sometimes called General Arithmetic; in a larger sense, it might as appropriately be called General Geometry. In Arithmetic, particular numbers are given and particular numbers are required. When we have demonstrated a property of a figure in

Geometry, we are only sure that it is true of the class to which that figure belongs. But in Algebra, all kinds of quantity may be denoted by symbols, and the truths arrived at by their means are true of all quantities whatever when they are subjected to the same operations. From this it appears evident that common Arithmetic must be understood before its operations can be performed Algebraically, and Synthetical should precede Analytical Geometry in a course of study. Algebra should be commenced, however, before Arithmetic and Geometry have been completed.

In its ordinary signification, Algebra treats of the relations and properties of numbers by means of symbols, and it is in this sense that we design to speak of methods of teaching it. Thus considered, methods of teaching it must be quite similar to those of teaching Arithmetic, and a brief discussion of the subject is all that will be necessary. Any one who succeeds in teaching Arithmetic will succeed in teaching Algebra.

In the sense in which Algebra is now considered, its Fundamental Idea, and its primary Definitions and Axioms must be substantially the same as those of Arithmetic. Its Demonstrations differ only in being more general; and its Applications, in being more extensive. These, therefore, need no discussion here.

The Definitions peculiar to Algebra must be learned by the pupil, not perhaps, all at once, when he commences the study, but as he needs them.

No Algebraic operation can be performed without the use of symbols, and a knowledge of such as are necessary in the solution of simple problems must be imparted to learners in their first lessons. The others may be learned when they have made some progress in the study. All the symbols admit a neat classification, and a knowledge of them can be most readily acquired in that form.

In teaching beginners, it is best for the teacher to illustrate the meaning of the symbols by using them with respect to numbers. Thus: $4+2=6$; $8-3=5$; $4\times 3=12$; $9\div 3=3$; $7\times 4\div 2-4+2=12$; $\sqrt{16}=4$; $4^2=16$. He may desire to add 576 to 764; but instead of performing the operation Arithmetically, he may say "we will let a represent the first number and b the second, and the operation can be expressed by $a+b$." Nearly all the symbols used in Algebra can be illustrated in this way, and no one but a practical teacher can appreciate the value of such illustrations to the pupil just commencing the study.

The Algebraic symbols which are used to represent quantity are general in their significance, and in this respect, differ from numbers. Pupils can make little progress in the study of Algebra until they understand this difference. For this purpose the teacher cannot do better than to make a series of additions, subtractions, multiplications, and divisions with numbers, and then show that $a+b+$, &c., $a-b$, $a\times b$ or $a\,b$, and $a\div b$ or $\frac{a}{b}$ are general expressions for all of them in the order named, and for all others possible. Besides, it is easy to give illustrations showing that a, b, c, &c., x, y, z, &c., can be used to represent numbers in whatever manner or to whatever things they may be applied.

The Algebraic idea can perhaps be best communicated by requiring pupils to solve suitable Arithmetical problems Algebraically. Some of the problems in our works on Oral Arithmetic can be selected for this purpose, or, as some authors of text-books on Algebra have arranged it, they may be so placed as to be an introduction to the general subject. Pupils seem to see the practical value of Algebra more clearly when commenced in this way, and, consequently to take more interest in the study.

After such an introduction to the subject as is outlined in the preceding paragraphs, pupils can be taught to add, subtract, multiply, and divide Algebraic quantities, whether integral or fractional; but although some elements enter into these operations that are not found in similar ones in Arithmetic, they involve no new principle of teaching. The pupil must be allowed much practice to enable him to make a ready and intelligent use of the symbols.

The simplest step in mathematical reasoning may be expressed in the form of an Equation; thus, one added to one equals two may be written $1+1=2$. In idea the Equation is constantly before the mind of the pupil when engaged in the study of Arithmetic; and, consequently, the teacher will not find the task a difficult one to acquaint him with the Algebraic form of expressing it. A Pair of Scales can be made to furnish a very good illustration of the simple form of an Equation. The common weights can be placed in one scale, and any body or bodies whose weight is unknown can be placed in the other; and, when balanced, the Equation is formed, and can be represented by letting x, y, z, &c., represent the known quantities, and *a*, *b*, *c*, &c., represent the unknown. Having attained the idea of an Algebraic Equation, the pupil must next learn to reduce it to its simplest form. For this purpose, he must be taught to clear the Equation of fractions, and to transpose, collect, and reduce its terms. The method of performing these operations and the truth of the axioms upon which they depend can be illustrated by taking the simplest form of an Equation; as 4=4, and showing that equals may be added to or subtracted from equals, multiplied or divided by equals, and the results will be equal. In Equations containing two or more unknown quantities, the various methods of elimination must be explained and illustrated. The different methods of solving Quadratic Equations and the forms to which such Equations can be reduced must undergo thorough discussion. The theories of all kinds of Equations should be impressed upon the pupil's mind by practice in solving numerous, well-graded, and judiciously-selected examples and problems involving them. These problems may be divided into two parts: first, that which relates to the formation of the Equation; and, second, that which relates to the solution of it. The formation of the Equation consists in observing the facts given, in noting their relations, in finding the equality between the known and the unknown, and in expressing that equality in Algebraic language. Having attained the elements of a problem, the formation of an Equation expressing these elements is a synthetic, while the solution of the problem is an analytic, process The teacher may require one pupil to form an Equation for a problem, another to solve it, while still another is engaged in making a problem to answer the conditions of a given Equation.

Perceiving no necessity for pursuing the subject further, it may be well to remark in conclusion, that the ends for which Algebra is studied are similar to those for which Arithmetic is studied, that the general conditions which must be observed in their attainment are the same, and that the suggestions mentioned in reference to conducting recitations in Arithmetic or arranging its object-matter for study apply equally well to like questions in teaching Algebra.

GEOMETRY.

The Etymology of the word would lead us to suppose that Geometry has reference to *measuring the earth*, and no doubt it had this reference in early times; for the necessities of the race would compel them to adopt some means of measurement long before abstract truths like those now composing the science of Geometry could be appreciated, much less reduced to a system.

Geometry as now understood, may be defined as the science of form. Its Fundamental Idea is space. There are two kinds of form, pure and real. Pure form is a portion of space limited in idea but not in fact. Real form is a portion of space limited in fact. Geometry proper treats only of pure forms, but it may be applied to real forms.

Geometry furnishes the most perfect model of a deductive science. It may be considered a type of all the rest. No Mathematician doubts that its basis rests upon the Idea of space. Its Definitions and Axioms are better understood than those of any other of the same class of sciences. The Demonstrations which form the body of it, comprise a beautiful system of applied logic, each admitting an easy reduction to the syllogistic form. And its Applications are among the most important in the practical affairs of life.

The two most common divisions of Geometry are Elementary Geometry, and Higher or Transcendental Geometry. Elementary Geometry treats of the line and the circle. Higher Geometry embraces the consideration of all curves except the circle. A brief discussion of methods of teaching Elementary Geometry is all that is contemplated in this connection.

Elementary Geometry as we find it in books like those of Euclid and Legendre, is not a study for children. Its abstract conceptions and long processes of reasoning require for their full comprehension, minds of some maturity and some discipline. The idea of form, however, must be one of the earliest which springs up in the mind of a child; and it would seem to follow that he can receive instruction in Geometry at as early an age as in Arithmetic. It may be shown that this theoretical conclusion can be verified in practice.

Young children can learn to distinguish a great many Geometrical forms; as a *line*, a *square*, a *circle*, a *triangle*, a *rectangle*, a *cone*, a *pyramid*, a *cylinder*, a *prism*, &c., &c. For this purpose, they can be taught to draw them on their slates or on the blackboard, and they can be shown blocks which represent them as wholes, or are cut into sections of which they can be engaged in making them.

Young children can also be taught the meaning of many Geometrical terms. It is not meant that abstract definitions should be given; but certain Geometrical terms can be so illustrated as to render them comprehensible to children. The following are examples: a *plane*, an *angle* and *its different kinds*, *the different kinds of triangles*, a *perpendicular*, a *diagonal*, *parallel lines*, *the parts of a circle*, *chords*, *polygons*, *the kinds of prisms*, &c., &c.

Many Geometrical truths can be made known to children as matters of fact. They can perceive these truths without being able to demonstrate them, that is, they can perceive the particular truth, but cannot make it general. It is not a difficult thing, with blocks suitably made, or pieces of pasteboard suitably prepared, to *show* children that "If one straight line meet another straight line, the sum of the adjacent angles will be equal to two right-angles;" "When if two straight lines intersect each other, the opposite or vertical angles, which they form, are equal;" "In every triangle the sum of the three angles is equal to two right angles;" "Every triangle is half the parallelogram which has the same base and the same altitude;" "The square described on the hypothenuse of a right-angled triangle is equivalent to the sum of the squares described on the other two sides;" &c., &c. A well-graded course of instruction of this kind, if judiciously given, would furnish very valuable discipline to children of the age of ten or twelve years, and greatly diminish for them the labor of Geometrical demonstration when their minds become sufficiently mature to enter upon it. Besides, it seems to be the natural method. Solid objects first meet the eye, not points, and lines, and angles; and here, as elsewhere, the method of proceeding should be from the concrete to the abstract—from the particular to the general.

When pupils are prepared to understand Geometrical Demonstrations, they should be supplied with a suitable text-book. The first pages of such a book will present to them certain Axioms and Definitions relating to Geometry which must be carefully studied. If the author of the book has done his duty, its subject-matter will be arranged in a rigidly logical order, starting with the simplest and most independent propositions, and containing no missing, imperfect, or superfluous link in the chain.

Geometrical propositions admit of two kinds of demonstration; the first, with axioms, definitions, or previously proven propositions as premises, seeks to show that the proposition to be demonstrated is included in these premises, and is therefore true; while the second consists in forming hypotheses which contradict the proposition, and in reasoning upon these hypotheses until conclusions are reached which contradict truths before known, and thus prove the proposition by demonstrating that the hypotheses which contradict it are false. The former of these methods of demonstration is called *direct*, and the latter, *indirect*, or *reductio ad absurdum*. Both are equally philosophical; but where a choice is optional between them, the first as the more simple is generally preferred to the second. Some propositions admit both kinds of demonstration, and many can be demonstrated by different methods of the same kind. With such propositions, when a pupil has followed the text-book in one method of demonstration, he might be greatly benefited by an effort to find others. It would be an admirable feature in a text-book to present here and there undemonstrated propositions, because pupils ought not only to be trained to follow the reasoning of others; but to invent processes of reasoning for themselves. The connection between certain propositions is so obvious, that a pupil, after having demonstrated one, ought to be able to infer the next without being helped to it by the book or teacher. Original thinking is always much more valuable than that which is second-hand. If the teacher desire fully to impress upon the minds of his pupils the truths they demonstrate, he should teach them to make an application of them at once in the solution of well-selected problems. Mensuration might be very profitably taught in connection with Geometry. It might be well also to require the pupil sometimes to give Algebraic demonstrations of Geometrical propositions, and to solve Algebraic problems by Geometrical methods.

In conducting a recitation in Geometry, the proposition should be stated, and the diagram drawn, from memory; and the demonstration should be given clearly and precisely, in the pupil's own language. In placing letters or numbers to the diagram, it is best to use them in a different order from the text-book, or the practice of demonstrating without a diagram may be productive of benefit, especially in reviews. In addition to this, the pupil should be taught to give a complete analysis of each demonstration. He should be able to tell—

1st. The *kind* of quantity under consideration.

2d. The relation of the demonstrated proposition to those which have preceded it.

3d. The kind of demonstration used.

4th. The axioms, definitions, or previously demonstrated truths used as premises.

5th. The relation of the conclusion to the premises.

6th. The relation of Corollaries, Scholiums, and Lemmas, to the principal proposition.

III. Logic.

The aim of this book does not require that Logic should undergo a lengthy discussion. Much has to be omitted, and the vast majority of teachers will miss a discussion on Logic less than one on most other branches taught in our schools. Still something must be said, and it is proposed to say it under two heads: 1. *The utility of Logic as a study;* 2. *The methods of teaching Logic.*

1. *The Utility of Logic as a Study.*—Some extravagant claims have been made by Logicians in respect to the utility of their favorite study. It has been called the *Art of Arts*, the *Science of Sciences*, *Catharticon Intellectus*, *Caput et Apex Philosophiæ*, &c.; and these names indicate the estimation in which it was held by the authors who used them. But while these claims should be moderated, it will appear from what is to be said that the utility of Logic

is such as to demand for it a prominent place in every liberal course of study.

Logic is a useful study in itself. Thought, as thought, presents a noble object for investigation. It is man who thinks and thinking is his highest attribute. A thought is greater than a thing. Things pass away, thoughts are immortal. If science as science is worthy of study anywhere, it is surely worthy of it when it treats of the laws of thought. "And is it nothing," says a writer, "to watch the secret workshop in which nature fabricates cognitions and thoughts, and to penetrate into the sanctuary of self-consciousness, to the end that, having learnt to know ourselves, we may be qualified rightly to understand all else?"

Logic is a useful study on account of its objective relations. Men can do nothing well unless they think well. All science and all art are the fruit of right thinking. Wrong thinking is at the root of all error. In this sense, Logic would almost be entitled to be called *Ars Artium* or *Scientia Scientiarum.* It is only in theory, however, that Logic holds this place, for the best Logicians are far from finding all truth or escaping all error. All that can be claimed is that as reasoning takes place in every thing we do, the study of the laws of thought must aid us in reasoning correctly. Besides, nature in all its departments fills with matter certain logical forms, and cannot be well understood in itself or well arranged into systems of science without a knowledge of these forms. Logic is an indispensable instrument in scientific investigation.

Logic is a useful study because it disciplines the

Understanding. The Understanding is the faculty by which we reason. The end of Logic is to reason well. Hence it follows that the study of Logic disciplines the Understanding. It not only imparts skill but power, for reasoning about reasoning must be at least as capable of strengthening and developing the Understanding as reasoning about something else.

2. *Methods of teaching Logic.*—If the nature of Logic is as we have stated it to be, its subject-matter will be composed of *Definitions* and *Axioms*, *Deductions* and *Demonstrations*, and *Applications*.

Every one who has the least idea of Logic is aware the first step in teaching the science must consist in making pupils acquainted with the definitions of *concept*, *judgment*, *reasoning*; *term*, *proposition*, *syllogism*, *induction*, *deduction*, &c. Indeed, Logic consists in much greater part than Mathematics in definitions and explications of the products of the intuitions of the Reason. The axioms of Logic, too, admit as clear a statement as those of Mathematics and bear the same relation to the science. Hamilton speaks of Fundamental Laws of Thought, and states them as follows: 1. *The Law of Identity*; 2. *The Law of Contradiction*; 3. *The Law of Excluded Middle*; 4. *The Law of Reason and Consequent.* Other Logicians give substantially the same laws. But all of these laws admit of statement in the form of axioms, and many Logicians have so stated them.

The Body of Pure Logic is arranged by Hamilton, and substantially so by many others, into two great classes which may be expressed as follows: 1. *The Means of Thinking;* 2. *The Methods of Thinking.* The Means of Thinking include *Concepts, Judgments,* and *Reasonings.* Concepts are the products of conception. Judgments are the arrangement of concepts as subjects and predicates. Reasonings are processes by which one judgment is deduced from another, by means of a third which is intermediate. Reasonings, when fully stated, assume the form of syllogisms, of which concepts and judgments are the elements. The Methods of Thinking include the doctrine of *Definition,* the doctrine of *Division,* and the doctrine of *Proof.* Logical definition is the complete development of a concept. Logical division is the separation of a whole into its parts according to their relations. Proof consists in deducing one judgment from another known to be true.

This whole Body of Pure Logic is made up in the main of definitions and judgments which are known to be true only by intuition. A pupil who does not realize in his own mind the *thing* spoken of will not be profited in the least by the *words* of the Logician. A teacher of Logic must be constant in his efforts to induce his pupils to investigate the products of thought as they lie in their own minds. The study of Psychology should precede that of Formal Logic, both because the habit of introspection into one's own mind is a valuable auxiliary in the study of Logic, and because concrete mental phenomena are more easily understood than those which are abstract.

Logic has also deductions and demonstrations,

but their nature and the methods of teaching them have been sufficiently characterized in discussing the "Formal Sciences in General."

In regard to teaching Logic as a whole, it may be remarked further, that the method for beginners should be synthetic. Thought must be presented first in its elements, and afterwards in its connections. To analyze thought, requires a knowledge of thought, and this is what the pupil does not possess but seeks. Besides, a system of Logic is a growth. It commences with a germ in the Reason and develops all its parts into a compact system. This order of growth should be the order of study.

Logic has its applications in all the departments of science and art; and to attain skill in making these applications is the chief end of the study. Children begin to reason when very young. Throughout their whole course of study, it is the duty of parents and teachers to train them to reason well—to train them by correcting their mistakes, by teaching them to correct their own mistakes and the mistakes of others, by setting them a good example of logical reasoning. Thus taught they may become practical Logicians without learning Logic. All this training, however, is rather mechanical than scientific in its character. Valuable for children, with more mature minds it must give place to something higher. The science of Logic must be studied by all who wish to make an intelligent application of its principles.

The study of Logic in itself will not make a good reasoner. A person may know all the kinds, and figures, and modes of the Syllogism and still be unable to construct one that will answer the conditions of practical life. The teacher who would make his pupils good reasoners must not only show them how reasoning is done or why it has certain forms, but he must teach them to reason. The faculty of reasoning itself must be exercised in order to grow. The laws of thinking must be taught, and then practiced until all thinking is governed by them—until they "become identified with the spontaneous activity of the reason."

Logic as taught in the schools is too formal. More examples should be given; more practical applications should be required. Pupils should be exercised in giving definitions, in making divisions, in constructing syllogisms, in analyzing arguments and demonstrations, and in building up systems of science. Every lesson in science should be made a lesson in Applied Logic, and thus the young would be prepared for the great work of life.

CHAPTER IV.

INSTRUCTION IN THE EMPIRICAL SCIENCES.

FACTS are observed; these facts are arranged into classes; general laws are inferred from them, and thus the Empirical Sciences are built up. The Empirical sciences comprehend the systematic arrangement of the generalizations of experience. They embrace a large number of particular sciences: as Astronomy, Natural Philosophy, Chemistry, Meteorology, Geology, Botany, Zoology, Mineralogy, Geography, Physiology, Psychology, &c., &c. A classification of them may be made as follows: The Mechanical Sciences, as Astronomy, Mechanics, Optics, &c.; the Chemical Sciences, as Chemistry, Galvanism, &c.; the Classificatory Sciences, as Botany, Zoology, &c.; the Organic Sciences, as Physiology, Anatomy, &c.; and the Psychological Sciences, as those sciences of mind which are founded upon the facts revealed by consciousness.

It matters little here, however, what particular branches of study are included in the Empirical Sciences, or of what classification they are susceptible; since all of them consist of facts which must be observed, of classes which must be formed, and of inferences which must be drawn, or laws which must be applied; and, hence, all of them must be taught by the same methods.

It ought not to be necessary to say anything in regard to the importance of the study of the Empirical Sciences, nor would anything be said were it not for the fact that such studies are much neglected in our American schools. A large proportion of the student's time, both in Common School and College, is taken up with the study of Language and Mathematics, and he has little left to devote to acquiring a knowledge of the great science of nature.

Few sciences can be more useful to man than the Empirical Sciences. These sciences treat of the light by which he sees, the heat by which he is warmed, the air which he breathes, the earth from which he draws his sustenance, the animals and plants that minister to his wants, and his own body and mind. There is not one single occupation in which a person may not derive great advantage from a knowledge of some of these sciences. They relate to life in all its forms and circumstances.

Few sciences can furnish more valuable mental discipline than the Empirical sciences. They exercise the senses, the perceptive powers, the judgment, the imagination, and the reason. They present facts that a child may comprehend, and problems that men like Bacon, Newton, Franklin, and Humboldt have not been able to solve. Minds devoted exclusively to the study of the Abstract or Rational sciences, are apt to be dogmatic. They would like to control the universe with laws of their own making. They form their notions of what *ought to be*, and grow captious if these notions are not found to correspond with what *is*. They dwell in an ideal world which is sometimes quite different from the real. The results of this mode of thinking appeared in the dreamy speculations of the Scholastic Philosophy, the bad effects of which it required all the strength of the mighty mind of Bacon to neutralize. The human intellect can engage in no nobler task than the study of the Rational Sciences; but the discipline they furnish should be tempered by that which comes only from the study of the Empirical Sciences. With one hand we may clutch the ideal, if with the other we hold fast to the real. The study of the Empirical Sciences is calculated to make men patient in investigation, slow in the expression of their own opinions, and liberal toward the opinions of others.

The Empirical Sciences are peculiarly adapted to awaken love for the Creator. It is only the "fool" that "hath said in his heart there is no God." The wise find the footsteps of a God everywhere, and nowhere are they more clearly discerned than in the works He has made. These works teem with so many proofs of wisdom, evidences of goodness, and marks of beauty, that one who studies them must have his heart warmed in love and adoration to the Being who made them all. Truly, "An undevout naturalist must be mad." The Psalmist fitly exclaims, "Whoso is wise, and will observe these things, even they shall understand the loving kindness of the Lord."

In addition to the strong reasons in favor of the study of the Empirical Sciences, which have been just stated, two others of a less general application will be named.

A taste for the study of nature tends to lighten labor. Labor is not toil to the man that thinks while he works. All schemes that contemplate dignifying labor without educating the laborer will prove abortive. The farmer who, while he works, finds food for thought in animals, insects, plants, and soils; the mechanic who speculates upon the properties of matter and the nature of force as he deals with them; the miner who studies strata, and veins, and fossils, while he exhumes the treasures deep-buried in the earth's bosom, do much to convert the curse of labor into a blessing. Hugh Miller may have cut out and chiseled down as many stones as his companions in the quarries of Scotland; but he found a pleasure in the task which they could not, his head was kept as busy as his hands, he worked like a man, not like a slave.

The study of nature gives pleasant employment in leisure hours. Large numbers of persons in every community are engaged in indoor occupations. For these, linguistic, mathematical, or metaphysical studies would be inappropriate. They want exercise with study. This they can have by interesting themselves in studies like Botany, Mineralogy, Geology, or Entomology. What rich rewards in health, strength, and pure intellectual and moral enjoyment would accrue to merchants, mechanics, lawyers, teachers, and others who lead sedentary lives; if they would spend their leisure hours in the exploration of the neighborhoods in which they live in search of those objects that so much interest the student of nature. A taste for Natural History, too, may be gratified in travelling. Nature is so full of objects worthy our study, that they present themselves to the attentive passenger even in the swift-moving rail-car. If delays occur, and they will occur in travelling, while others grow weary and impatient, the naturalist gives himself employment, and keeps himself in good humour by reading a fresh page in the great book of nature. He needs no artificial help "to kill time," for the hours pass quickly when nature presents her truth and her beauty to his contemplation.

It is my purpose to speak, first, of methods of teaching the Empirical Sciences in General; and, second, of methods of teaching Geography. The reason I desire to discuss methods of teaching Geography more particularly, is because it is one of the branches almost universally taught in our Common Schools; and because by it can be illustrated the methods of teaching the other sciences of the same class. Geography, as usually taught contains matter which belongs to History, but this does not necessitate any change in methods of teaching it.

I. The Empirical Sciences in General.

The foundation of the Empirical Sciences is facts and phenomena that are open to observation. Children begin to acquire these facts and notice these phenomena as soon as they can use their senses; and by the time they are five years of age, their stock of knowledge of this kind may be made truly wonderful. Elsewhere, under the head of Instruction in the Elements of Knowledge, an effort was made to point out the method by which such information could be pleasantly imparted to children, here, therefore, on this point, no detailed discussion will be necessary. I will say, however, that I consider it the main business of teachers in Primary Schools to teach their pupils to observe, to make them acquainted with the facts and phenomena of nature. To do this, nature's own method must be adopted. A child in a ramble over a mountain, through a meadow, along a rivulet, about a grove, will notice objects and may observe phenomena that belong technically to all the Empirical Sciences. Nature scatters her treasures in rich profusion everywhere, and the child picks them up where he finds them. His attention cannot be confined, without a loss of interest, to one class of natural objects, much less to the minute differences which often distinguish genera and species, or the scientific terms which are applied to the peculiarities of individuals. Von Raumer in his *Geschichte der Pädagogik* has some excellent remarks on this subject. I quote from Barnard's American Journal of Education which expresses the ideas of the author very correctly. Von Raumer says, "A child commencing the study of Natural Science should first examine, in all directions, the neighborhood of his residence, and should make himself so thoroughly acquainted with it that he can call it up before his mind whenever he chooses. Such an acquaintance is the result of the unconscious and fresh pleasure which youth, joyful and free from scientific anxieties, will find for itself in such an examination, obtaining in this artless way a simple general impression of the vicinity, not forced upon him artificially by a teacher. He is not teased, while he is rejoicing in the blue heavens and the rapid motions of the clouds, in the oak woods and flowery meadows, where the butterflies play, by a professor with a cyanometer, to measure the blue of the sky with, nor by a recommendation not to stare into the woods, but rather to ascertain whether the oaks are *Quercus Robur* or *Quercus Pedunculata;* or, not to look at the flowers in the meadow all at once, as if they were a yellow carpet, but to take his Linnæus and determine the species of this ranunculus. No entomologist is setting him to chase butterflies and impale them. Neither is the youth, when inspired to devotion by the snowy Alps, glittering in moonlight, like so many spiritual, silvery forms of giants, annoyed by a geologist talking to him of granite, gneiss, and limestone, or of the junction and inclination of strata. The young enjoy the heavens and the earth as a susceptible painter or an ingenious poet does. In this first paradisaic pleasure is planted the seed of the perception of an intellectual world, whose secrets will not be fully ascertained and understood even after the longest and most active life of scientific effort. But most teachers, by the dispersion of these simple impressions of nature, forcibly destroy these earliest pleasures of children, the brightness of the imaginary world which they see. Even the great Pestalozzi falls into an error on this point, when he says 'It is not in the woods or meadows that the child should be put, to become acquainted with trees and plants. They do not there stand in the order best calculated to display the characters of the different families,' &c. That is, we ought to take the child into a botanic garden, arranged on the Linnæan system, so that he may study plants in the order of their species. To me this seems like saying that the child ought not to hear a symphony because that would be a mere chaos of sounds to him; he should rather have played to him, first, the first violin part, then the second, then the parts of the bass viols, the flutes, clarionets, trumpets, &c. It is true that in this way he would hear the separate parts, but not the bond of thought which makes them a symphony. Jahn was much more judicious in his gymnastic walks, when he said, not 'we are going botanizing, geologizing, or entomologizing,' but merely 'we are going to walk.' How much more naturally do our youth, when the bird-of-passage instinct seizes them at the university, wander through the father-land and rejoice in its grandeur, and lay it deeply to heart, without any idea of a premature, and painful, and usually repulsive studying of a particular subject. I hate this analyzing and lifeless elementarizing of the first youthful impressions of nature—this foolish, superficial, heartless, frivolous directing of the understanding prematurely out of its natural path—which is so sure to chill the youthful heart and render it old before its time. The utmost attainments of a mind thus trained must be—unless aided by remarkable natural qualities—to observe with the bodily eye; to use the reason, but not with pleasure; to derive mere lifeless ideas from creation; and to represent the objects thus conceived in equally lifeless descriptions, like the ghastly wax figures which afford a repulsive imitation of living men."

The sum of what has been said is that the first instruction of children in the Empirical Sciences should mainly consist in exhibiting to them interesting objects and phenomena; in allowing them to look, handle, and ask questions; and in giving opportunity for the free exercise of their youthful imagination. A teacher may guide them in their explorations of the neighborhood, direct their observations, make inquiries, give explanations, conduct experiments, call things by their right names; but he must be careful to do it in such a manner as not to check their play of fancy or chill their flow of feeling.

When pupils have acquired a taste for the study of nature, when they have learned to derive rich pleasure from a communion with her rocks, her hills, her valleys, her flowers, her trees, her insects, and her animals; when they stand with breathless interest while Air Pump, Magic Lantern, or Galvanic Battery reveals to them some astonishing phenomena, it is time for them to take a second step in the course of instruction of which we are speaking—to commence the analysis of the objects with which they have become acquainted and the study of their several parts. This task is heavy only to those who have no interest in it. Love here as everywhere lightens labor. What then is the best way of acquainting pupils with the particular facts of the Empirical Sciences? That is, how shall they proceed to analyze the general impressions which we now suppose them to possess?

It is well to remark first, that the facts to which the attention of pupils is called should be suited to their mental capacity. Nature is a vast store-house of facts; some of which lie open upon the surface, while others are so deeply hidden that it requires much searching to find them; some are so simple that a child can understand them, while others are still unaccounted for by the ablest philosophers. Among such an infinite variety of facts, the teacher will point his class to those which are calculated to interest and instruct them. As young children are not able to observe closely or study much, they cannot be confined to classes of facts belonging to any particular science; but must be permitted to acquire knowledge in the same *unsystematic order*, if such an expression is allowable, which nature evinces, when she throws together rocks, trees, flowers, birds, insects, running streams, and sporting fishes. When older, the attention can be more easily confined to facts belonging to the same science or subject.

The teacher should not rely upon verbal descriptions of facts or phenomena when a different course is open to him. The most skilful and enlivening word-painting makes a weak impression upon the mind in comparison with the real thing. The eye seems to be the most open inlet to the soul. Hence, children delight in examining curiosities in nature and art, in looking at pictures, and in witnessing experiments. The exhibition of a flower, a mineral, a shell, a fossil, a bone, the picture of a strange animal, or the falling of a feather and a guinea in the exhausted receiver of an Air Pump, will convey better ideas to a child at a glance than the most elaborate description of the same things.

Chemistry and Natural Philosophy require full experiments; Physiology can be illustrated by presenting the heart, stomach, bones, &c., of animals whose organic structure is similar to that of man; Botany, Mineralogy, Geology, and Zoology, are best learned where rich cabinets supply specimens, or in the field; and Psychology can only be appreciated by those who closely observe the actions of others, and that which passes within their own minds. Wherever possible, pupils should be required to repeat the experiments made by the teacher, to draw objects, and give written and oral descriptions of them. When specimens are wanting or facts cannot be tangibly presented, the unknown may sometimes be brought vividly before the mind by comparing it with the known which resembles it.

The pupil himself should be taught to search for facts. He should be appointed to conduct experiments, to make explorations, to give descriptions of natural objects. While the vast majority of men have eyes that see, they do not see, and ears that hear, they do not hear, much that takes place about them. They are blind and deaf to the beauty and truth of nature. It is the teacher's duty to awaken the dull senses of his pupils from their torpor, and send them out to gather fresh facts from the rich fields of nature ripe for the harvest. He should instruct them to make and handle simple articles of philosophical apparatus; to observe the phenomena of rain, hail, snow, dew, frost, ice, &c.; to notice the habits of insects, the growth of vegetation, the peculiarities of animals, &c.; to visit museums and menageries, &c.; to make excursions to quarries and mines, meadows and mountains, springs, rivulets, and rivers, &c. The pupils thus learn to depend upon themselves, and not to rely wholly for help upon text-book and teacher. If pupils can be taught to find pleasure in collecting facts, the work of teaching them is almost done; for to such, science is itself a pillar of cloud by day and a pillar of fire by night to guide them onward.

The third step in a course of study in the Empirical Sciences, is the classification of facts. Individual facts are so numerous that it is impossible to make much progress in the study of the Empirical Science without the use of classification. In the infancy of science, classifications were founded upon adventitious circumstances; but as further discoveries were made such classifications gave way to others founded upon inherent relationships. Guided by an intelligent teacher, pupils can be taught to classify objects properly, commencing of course with objects whose resemblances are obvious and passing on gradually to others in which they are more hidden. Many classes among plants, minerals, insects, and animals can be determined by the general appearance of the individuals composing them. I have succeeded best in imparting an idea of classification by descending from the general to the particular, from the class to the individual. My pupils have not experienced much difficulty, after having seen a few specimens of the Umbelliferæ or Violaceæ and heard their characteristics described, in finding the right place for other individual plants belonging to these Orders; and, so I think it would be with the Quartz family among Minerals, the Asteriadæ among Radiates, the Cephalopods among Mollusks, the Lepidoptera among Insects, the Ophidians among Reptiles, the Grallatores among Birds, the Rodentia among Mammals, and hundreds of other orders, classes, genera, and species equally well marked. The same method of teaching is applicable to the classes of facts and phenomena belonging to Astronomy, Chemistry, Natural Philosophy, Psychology, and other similar sciences. The only difference is that the principle of classification is not made so prominent in these sciences as in those previously referred to.

These remarks are made in full view of the fact that the lines separating the divisions which have been made in the sciences are sometimes very obscure. Men who have made certain sciences a life-long study are not always agreed about them. But the judicious teacher will confine his pupil in the beginning to the study of those classes which are most easily determined, and afterwards, when prepared, he can enter into the "debatable ground" of the subject.

In making original classifications, it may be well to remark that a sufficient number of facts should be collected before it is safe to form classes; that in forming classes, permanent and inherent relationships only should be regarded; that artificial systems should be wholly discarded; and that genera and species should be discriminated by never-failing marks.

A fourth step in a course of study in the Empirical Sciences is the inferring of laws or principles. The collection and classification of facts constitute only the introductory parts of the Empirical Sciences. Connecting principles must be found to bind these classes together into systems. Counting stamens, marking spots, measuring scales, or observing phenomena in general, is not science. Nothing takes place without law. We can only notice effects, their causes must be inferred. We have the consequents, but must find the antecedents. This process is called inductive reasoning; and the question now is, how shall pupils be taught to reason in that way.

A child reasons inductively when he learns that the hot stove burns his hand, that snow makes it cold, that a lump of sugar dissolves when placed in a cup of tea. In all these instances, the antecedent and consequent appear close together; a child has no difficulty in making the connection. With young children, the teacher must imitate this method; and, when nature conceals the consequent or places it at a distance from the antecedent, he must show their relation by carefully planned experiments and judiciously chosen illustrations. More advanced pupils, of course, need less help.

Text-books on certain of the Empirical Sciences sometimes present facts and afterwards state the principle involved, and sometimes announce the principle and then explain it by reference to the facts from which it was deduced. In building up a new science, the former method is the only safe one; but in teaching, either may be legitimately followed. The statement of a proposition, in treating of an Empirical Science before the facts which prove it have been presented, is merely a matter of conveni ence, and does not essentially change the method of reasoning which is from the particular to the general. Teachers will find it an interesting exercise to engage their pupils in deducing principles from given facts, and in accounting for certain facts by known principles.

It is proper to add that inductions should be made with much caution. Both teacher and pupil must be actuated by a sincere desire to obtain the truth —to interpret nature correctly. Hypotheses may be assumed, but they must be considered only as hypotheses until carefully tested by facts. The moment a teacher makes prominent some facts while he conceals others or distorts them through prejudice or preconceived opinions, the moment he adopts an hypothesis and begins to enforce it dogmatically, he becomes a false teacher and does his pupils a great wrong. Hasty generalizations have been the bane of science. The progress of the race has been greatly retarded by the resistance new truth has met from old opinions. A teacher had better communicate his facts and then tell his pupils to doubt in regard to their explanation, than to lead them into errors. Intelligent skepticism in matters of science is better than blind faith. He best studies nature who does it with a sincere desire to find the truth, and is willing to accept what he finds. Let no one be misled by "idols of the tribe," "idols of the den," "idols of the market," or "idols of the theatre." In searching for causes be sure that no active element lurks in the antecedent for which allowance is not made, and that which seems to be the consequent is not wholly or in part a mere contingency. The prominent elements in the character of a successful student of the Empirical Sciences are an enthusiastic love of nature and the most careful circumspection in its investigation.

The process which, after Mill, may be called the "Concrete Deductive Method," forms the fifth step in learning an Empirical Science. This method consists in bringing new facts or new phenomena under laws already ascertained inductively, or in determining the effect of such laws in new circumstances. Comparatively few new laws have of late been discovered in the Empirical Sciences, but the laws already discovered have received a much more extended application. The tendency of science now is to simplify laws, and to multiply facts. New effects are being constantly deduced from laws long since known. In this, indeed, consist mainly the triumphs of modern science. Such a standpoint has been reached by some of our best Naturalists that certain facts have been *anticipated* long before their actual discovery.

When pupils reach this stage of progress in their course of study, they will need little prompting to push forward. Knowing laws and the facts from which these laws were inferred, they will naturally feel an interest in testing their validity in new circumstances. Our text-books which treat of the Empirical Sciences should contain many facts and phenomena arranged miscellaneously, in order that pupils might have exercise in accounting for them; or nature herself might be used as the text-book. A pupil has but to go forth with his eyes open, and nature everywhere, above, around, beneath, will ask him to apply the scientific principles he may have learned. Hardly anywhere as yet do teachers estimate as highly as they should the value of scientific experiments. First made acquainted with laws by such experiments, pupils should be allowed to witness their effects in other circumstances — to repeat them, and to plan others for themselves.

There is a sixth step that must be taken before a course of study in the Empirical Sciences can be considered as completed. The observation of facts, the generalizations of experience, and the extension of known laws do not constitute the whole of science. Eternal, universal, and necessary principles control all facts and all inductions from facts. It is thus with mathematical, logical, and metaphysical principles. Aristotle says: "The general principles necessary to knowledge are *axioms*." An Empirical Science is like a ladder, it needs support at both ends — it cannot account either for the existence of facts, or for the genesis of the ideas which embrace them. Take an example: heat expands iron; heat expands gold, silver, copper, lead, &c. These are facts, and we infer from them that "Heat expands all metals." So far inductive science will take us; but mark the queries concerning the matter which remain unanswered: Are we sure that *all* metals *are* expanded by heat? In concluding affirmatively, what is the nature of the principle we take for granted? How do we become cognizant of such things as metals? How do we know one metal from another? Why do metals exist? Empirical Science is powerless in dealing with such questions as these, and yet similar problems lie about every inductive syllogism. The Inductive Philosophy in its own field has blessed mankind with rich fruit; but unaccompanied by the recognition of a higher philosophy, it would leave us without a personal Deity, without a united plan in creation, and would lead us finally into the dry Skepticism of Hume, the soulless Positivism of Comte, the philosophical Pantheism of Spinoza, the cold Logic of Mill, or the weak faith of Buckle.

The teacher who develops the Empirical Sciences in their higher departments, will be false to his trust if he does not exhibit to his pupils their limitations—if he does not show them what these sciences can accomplish, and where they must fail. The creation is the expression of an idea—is a thought embodied in matter. The great end of Empirical Science is, through facts and inferences, to reach this idea, and use it in the further interpretation of nature. The idea is not derived by any induction; but it is produced in the reason upon the occasion of some experience. Says Hickok, "Till we attain this eternal principle, which, as a living law, the Maker of the universe has diffused all through it from centre to circumference, we may stand outside and measure and weigh, and overwhelm the understanding with the summations of arithmetical reckonings, but we shall know nothing of that central working which makes and holds all in one concrete *cosmos* of perpetual beauty and harmony." No greater harm could be done to the human spirit than to teach it that all sure knowledge must be based on facts patent to the senses. It would be to dethrone God and cast the human intellect out upon a sea that has no shore, and from which no hope could lift the soul to Heaven.

Faithful to the study of nature, a few men of genius have mounted like Moses to the top of Mount Pisgah, up through facts and inferences, until, as a reward for their devotion, glimpses of the divine plan in creation were flashed into their minds, and praising God, they gave the heaven-born truth to men, by whom the revelation will be cherished until the end of their generations. I hardly dare to name—but among those that must be named, are Pythagoras, Plato, Kepler, Newton, and our own Agassiz. These, and such as these, hear the "Music of the Spheres;" discern the "Soul of the world;" "Think God's thoughts after him;" "Count themselves little children—standing on the shore playing with the pebbles, while the great ocean of truth lies spread out before them;" and recognize the "Facts of the world as the words of God."

This view of the steps necessary in a course of study in the Empirical Sciences is strongly confirmed by the history of their progress. A careful student may mark this progress by several distinct stages of growth.

First, the *Poetic Stage.*—The attention of uncultivated men is first attracted to objects by some quality which pleases their fancy or arouses their feelings. The African savage may deck his person with gaudy ostrich-feathers, the Arab may pitch his tent near some palm not only to enjoy protection from its shade but pleasure from its beauty, the

Indians of our own country may linger on some mountain summit to gaze at the river which winds along far below them, the lake which nestles among the hills, or the glories of the setting sun; and in each, it is easy to see the awakening of that interest in nature which in more highly civilized conditions of society will lead to study and knowledge. The Mythologies of the East are largely indebted for what in them is beautiful to this poetic interest in nature which characterizes peoples who have not made much progress in scientific knowledge. The most enlightened nations have had their ages of Fable, in which they personified the objects and powers of nature, and filled caves, and groves, and air, and waters, with creations of their lively fancies. It is not very difficult to see that the mental condition of men then was like that of children now.

Second, the *Mystic Stage.*—Wondering at the marvels which nature was constantly forcing upon their attention, men could not long withstand the temptation of trying to account for them. They could not but see that certain consequents followed certain antecedents, and the inquiry would become very natural as to whether this was always the case. Curious, indeed, would be that history which recounted the efforts made by the human intellect to find causes for the facts it observed. It may easily be supposed that the first inquirers would hurry to their conclusions, and that these conclusions would generally be mere guesses, contradictory and mystical. The ancient Hindoos, Persians, and Egyptians had their fanciful Cosmogonies; the speculative

Greeks found the principle of the universe in water, air, fire, and they placed the Titan, Atlas, under the earth to upbear it on his shoulders; and the Middle Age Mystics found a ready explanation for physical phenomena in supernatural causes. Both good and evil spirits play an important part in the affairs of men and the ongoings of nature, while nations are passing through the stage of progress now referred to. It is to be expected that children will now exhibit similar mental tendencies; but it is time that full grown men in enlightened countries should have passed beyond the stage of progress which we have called the Mystic.

Third, the *Observational Stage.*—Dissatisfied with the small return of fruit resulting from purely ideal speculations, students of nature began slowly and patiently to accumulate facts. Different observers explore the whole field of the Empirical Sciences—they experiment at home and travel abroad, and the treasures of thousands of volumes attest their industry. All feel that they have now struck the right path; and the faithful teacher must follow in it.

Fourth, the *Classificatory Stage.*—Facts accumulate; the memory is overburdened; the reaping of the rich harvests seems threatened to be stopped for want of barns in which to store the products. The necessity of classification is felt, and efforts are soon made to arrange the abundant material into classes. External resemblances or adventitious circumstances determine the first divisions into classes; but soon more hidden relationships are observed, and, in the light of these, better systems of classification are adopted and the great mass of material becomes moulded into manageable shape.

Fifth, the *Inductive Stage.*—Classification of facts and phenomena could not well be made without starting inquiries as to the causes which govern them, and, when once the search for these began, natural curiosity would prompt its vigorous prosecution. The fanciful guesses of the Mystic Stage of progress proceed from the same mental powers that give birth to the slow and careful generalizations of the Inductive Stage; but during the former, men leap to their conclusions without waiting to test them by an appeal to facts. The spirit of inquiry since the time of Bacon has been inductive. Guided by this method, earnest investigators have searched the earth, the air, and the heavens, the vegetable and animal kingdoms; and rich indeed has been their reward. Laws have been found, and superstitious influences have been discarded. Not only have busy hands revealed nature's curious hieroglyphics; but many a Champollion has decyphered them. The laws derived by induction may be very simple and applicable only to special cases, or they may be broad enough, like the law of gravitation, to comprehend the whole universe; but all safe inferences must be founded upon systematically arranged facts.

Sixth, the *Demonstrative Stage.* — Generalizations are often made in the Empirical Sciences long before all the facts which are embraced by them have been ascertained. Indeed, it is not possible to bring all the facts embraced by a single generalization within the limits of human experience, for that experience is finite and nature is infinite. But the laws of nature are uniform in their operations; and we feel quite sure when we ascertain a law applicable to several of the members of a class, it is true of the whole class, or when the tendency of a cause is to produce a certain effect in one set of circumstances its tendency will be to produce the same effect under other circumstances. It follows that inductions may be made, and then used in the search for additional facts or in the interpretation of different phenomena. We may even anticipate the existence of unknown facts. By a kind of demonstration we can prove that newly discovered gases must be subject to the law of chemical affinity, that the fossil plants or animals, just obtained from the strata of an unknown formation must exhibit the same plan of growth and structure as those to which we have been accustomed, or that the law of gravitation extends its influence to the remotest star just revealed by the powerful aid of modern Telescopes; and the same method is applicable to all departments of science.

From its very nature it is clear that the Inductive Stage of an Empirical Science must have preceded the Demonstrative Stage, and the history of all such sciences, is full of confirmatory evidence. Even now the most able Physicists are laboring in this stage, and the fruit gathered seems to show that the harvest is but ripening.

Seventh, the *Philosophic Stage.*—By our senses we observe facts, by means of the understanding we classify them and make inductions from them; but these faculties can never give us the universal principles which condition both the facts and the inductions. The atoms of matter may unite in certain definite proportions, the various organs of plants may be metamorphosed leaves, bodies may attract one another according to certain fixed laws; but there are reasons why all these things are so, and just so far as these reasons can be attained have we what may truly be called a Philosophy. He who observes the most facts and makes the broadest generalizations, will be best prepared to discern the eternal principles according to which the universe was made. Reaching a certain standpoint, these principles appear to the sincere investigator of nature, as the intuitions of the reason or as the perceptions of the quick eye of faith.

Eighth, the *Æsthetic Stage.*—Nature has beauties which lie upon the surface. They serve to attract attention. Nearly all persons, both young and old, derive enjoyment from them. Even the savage stops to gaze from some mountain summit upon the sleeping lake or the setting sun, and the little child claps its hands in delight when wandering about a garden of flowers or gazing at the richly-colored rainbow. But all this beauty bears little comparison to that which ravishes his soul who has gazed upon nature's teeming facts, who has constructed them into orderly systems, who has formed comprehensive generalizations, and who has at last caught glimpses of the eternal principles that are the archetypes after which things were made. It is a great mistake to suppose that those who are most ignorant of nature's works exhibit the most admiration for them. Study, indeed, sometimes curbs the light play of fancy and banishes forever her airy creations; but at the same time it reveals ten thousand real beauties of which the untutored poet never dreamed. All true art presupposes the highest conceptions of science; and he alone can drink in the full measure of nature's beauties who is able to comprehend the divine plan in the creation.

Ninth, the *Religious Stage.*—In the earliest states of civilization, men must have felt that there is a power above nature. The mind of the poor Indian "Sees God in clouds or hears him in the wind." Much of the ancient Mythology had its origin in the attempt to find God in some object of the visible creation or in some power that is manifested through it. Every event was regarded as a miracle. A darkened understanding prevented the Heathen world from discriminating between the Maker and the thing made. The most enlightened of these nations could do no more than erect an altar to the "Unknown God." Individual instances there were, of persons who seemed to apprehend a personal Deity, but they were such as had closely studied nature and themselves. All past history goes to show that those who have numbered the great variety of objects which nature contains, who have witnessed the working of her grand machinery, who have noticed the "foot-prints of the Creator" in nicely adjusting means to ends, who have marked the order that everywhere prevails and enjoyed the beauty that adorns the whole, and who have carefully inspected the revelations of their own minds, possess, other things being equal, the most adequate ideas of the Great Being who created the heavens and the earth and all that in them is, and pronounced it very good. "The heavens declare the glory of God; and the firmament sheweth his handiwork." God has revealed himself in the Bible; but he has also left his name labeled upon all his works and he who will may read it there, "For the invisible things of him from the creation of the world are clearly seen, being understood by the things that are made, even his eternal power and Godhead." The highest end of the study of nature is to find God in his works. The true philosopher finds Him, and his longing soul is satisfied.

II. Geography.

Geography treats generally of the aspects of nature and the works of man, and the causes which have produced or modified them. Its elementary facts as they relate to nature have the same basis as the Empirical sciences; and its elementary facts as they relate to man have the same basis as the Historical Sciences; but, in its higher departments, it may present the broadest generalizations of both. The difference between it and any special Natural or Political Science is that its object-matter comprehends a much greater variety of facts and principles. Geography is not so much a science in itself as it is a collection of matter belonging to a number of sciences.

The word Geography means a description of the earth; and a description of the earth is understood to include the changes man has wrought upon it. This meaning defines sufficiently well the Geographical matter that appears in many of our text-books on the subject; but Geography must now be considered not merely as a narrative of facts but as a system of principles controlling the facts.

Geography is easily divisible into two kinds; that which relates to Nature; and that which relates to Man. The first is called Physical Geography; and the second, Political Geography The terms Mathematical, Historical, Descriptive, Local, &c., as applied to Geography do not represent distinct divisions of the subject. If we follow the order of cause and effect, we must first speak of Physical Geography, and afterwards of Political Geography; but the teacher will find that he can best illustrate the subject and do more to create an interest in it on the part of his class, if he combine the two, and teach both together. Causes and their effects will thus be brought before the mind at one view and their relationship can be more readily shown. If this were otherwise, no necessity would arise for a corresponding division here, inasmuch as the same pedagogical principles apply to the one as to the other.

Many of our text-books on Geography adopt a very imperfect method of presenting the subject. They generally commence with some pages of definitions concerning the planetary relations of the earth, the general divisions of land and water, latitude and longitude, zones, government, races of men, stages of civilization, kinds of religion, changes of seasons, &c.; all of which it is impossible for a child to understand. Such lessons as these with others upon maps which are to the learner "a mere set of marks, without any equivalent conception in the mind of the thing represented," make the whole work a dull, dragging process; or, at the best, can only crowd the memory with forms of words, and images of dots, and lines, and ridges, which have little meaning. By and by, it is true, a healthy mental organization asserts its right to acquire knowledge in a rational way, and Geography may then be learned, not in accordance with this method, but in spite of it.

In teaching Geography, as in teaching all other studies, the teacher must first ascertain what knowledge his pupils already possess concerning the subject, and then make them familiar in a natural way with such new matter as may be most closely connected with it. The mind makes progress in knowledge only by the process of assimilating the unknown to the known. A child will have attained by the time he is eight years of age, a knowledge of many Geographical facts relating to the neighborhood about his home or his school. He will have seen water bubbling up from the earth in springs, and running away in rivulets; he will have walked up hills, and wandered about valleys; he will have noticed villages, and may have visited the market-town, the mill, shops, and manufactories—watched cars move on a railroad, or ships sail on a river; he will have become familiar with many plants, animals, reptiles, and insects; and with the general appearance of rain, hail, snow, ice, and frost; and possibly may have learned the names of some of the rocks and soils. This and other knowledge like this is what the pupil knows when he begins the study of Geography, and nothing can be more evident than that his instruction must start at this point.

If the proper place of beginning has now been found, it remains our task to arrange the object-matter of Geography, and exhibit the proper methods of making pupils acquainted with it. I know no better way of doing this than by presenting a classified series of lessons. These lessons are intended to follow a natural order of progression, and to include all the essential parts of the science of Geography. Each class of lessons may embrace matter sufficient for many individual lessons.

First Class of Lessons.—*On Objects relating to Geography, which Pupils can observe for themselves.*—The lessons to be given here are designed to extend the knowledge already in possession of the pupils by a method but little different from that by which it was acquired. Nature is the only text-book needed. Lessons may be given about the general aspects of a neighborhood—its hills, valleys, water-courses, forests; and, if, perchance, the school-house is located near a mountain, lake, river, or the ocean's shore, these objects will be an unfailing source of interest. The attention of pupils may be directed to the different kinds of land—farm-land, woodland, meadow-land, level, hilly, and rolling land; to the different objects composed of water—springs, brooks, creeks, ponds, dams; to the different kinds of soils—clay, sand, gravel, vegetable mould; to the different kinds of stone—quartz, sandstone, granite, slate, limestone, iron-ore; to the different kinds of trees—pine, oak, hickory, chestnut, poplar, ash; to the different kinds of productions of the neighborhood — corn, potatoes, rice, cotton, wheat, grass; to garden flowers and wild flowers; to domestic animals and wild animals; to reptiles and insects; to rain, snow, dew; to the changes of the seasons; to villages and towns; to the employments of the people; to shops, mills, manufactories, stores, school-houses, and churches.

It is the design of this enumeration of particulars to indicate to the teacher the sources from which he may obtain the materials for his first class of lessons in Geography. His own ingenuity must suggest which subject of those mentioned, or of other like subjects not mentioned, is most appropriate for any particular lesson. In giving this kind of instruction to young pupils, no strictly scientific discussion is expected or desirable. They should be taught those things in which they can be made to feel an interest; and this interest can be greatly increased by placing the object of the lesson before them in the school-house, or them before the object out of the school-house. Minerals, flowers, shells, fossils, &c., may be brought into the school-house; and the teacher and pupils may visit woods, meadows, mines, quarries, gardens, ruins, &c. These lessons, indeed, are Geographical Object

Lessons, and they should be given in the same mode and with the same spirit as other Object Lessons.

SECOND CLASS OF LESSONS.—*On similar Objects which can be found only in Localities distant from the School.*—Lessons on objects which they can see would prepare children to receive lessons on similar objects which they cannot see. In imparting such lessons, the teacher must rely upon comparisons made with things known, descriptions, and pictorial illustrations. The names of the countries in which the objects are found may be given; but the time has not come for formal instruction in regard to the relative positions of countries as exhibited upon maps.

Suppose the school-house in which these lessons are given is in Pennsylvania; then, the teacher may describe the natural features of countries unlike Pennsylvania—deserts, prairies, countries very cold or very warm, mountains covered with snow, hot springs, volcanos, &c.; such animals as the lion, ostrich, elephant, reindeer, camel, whale, &c.; such vegetable productions as the coffee-plant, the tea-plant, rice, bread-fruit, cotton-plant, banian-tree, palm, &c.; such people as the Esquimaux with their dogs and their houses of snow; the Chinese with their strange peculiarities of food, dress, and mode of life; the Arabs with their tents and horses; the Turks with their long beards and their clumsy clothing; the Hottentot in his hut, the Indian in his wigwam, the European lord in his stately castle. If given in simple language children will eagerly read accounts of travels and voyages, descriptions of countries and their inhabitants, and biographical sketches of distinguished men. Let a teacher tell his pupils of the Israelites crossing the Red Sea, Columbus on his way to America, Bonaparte at St. Helena; and if he does not interest them he will accomplish less than others have done.

Admit that in all these lessons much of the knowledge imparted cannot assume a definite shape in the mind of the child, admit that some of his impressions will be erroneous, and it is no valid objection against this mode of teaching; because *children learn nothing in any other way.* On the contrary, such teaching will impart many valuable ideas to children which they could obtain in no other manner so agreeable to them, and, what is of more consequence, it awakens a desire for knowledge and a taste for study which will render comparatively easy the task of learning formal Geography.

Pictures of the objects upon which the lessons are given are a valuable aid; and a Magic Lantern or a Stereoscope could be used to great advantage.

THIRD CLASS OF LESSONS.—*On the Topography of the neighborhood about the School.*—The two preceding classes of lessons, while they are intended to relate to Geographical subjects, are introductory in their character. It is proposed now to place the objects more definitely before the mind of the pupil by localizing the most important Geographical facts and introducing more system into the study of them. For this purpose the pupil must have communicated to him correct ideas of a map, and this cannot be very well done unless he is acquainted with the points of the compass. In this latitude, the direction of the sun at rising and setting marks with sufficient accuracy the points East and West; the direction of the sun at noon and of the north polar-star, or of a magnetic needle, indicates correctly the points South and North. A teacher can readily draw on the floor with a piece of chalk a line running east and west; another crossing it at right angles will run north and south. The respective ends of these lines can be marked with the letters E, W, N, S; and pupils will soon learn to name any point of the compass thus represented, or when drawn upon a blackboard. The class can stand up and point toward where the sun rises, toward where it sets, in what direction the sun is at noon, and in what direction the north polar-star is, if the teacher has previously taken the trouble to show them. Some questions should then be asked in reference to the direction from the school-house of certain prominent objects in the neighborhood. This done, the design and construction of maps must be explained.

Maps are intended to represent the earth's surface; but the various means made use of for this purpose, require considerable power of imagination to make them significant. The teacher must make his pupils realize the meaning of the marks, dots, and lines that are used in map-drawing. To begin, let the teacher draw, in the presence of his class, upon a slate or a blackboard laid *horizontally*, a plan of the school-house. He may make a line of a given length, and let it represent one end of the school-nouse, and then he may inquire of the pupils as to the length and direction of the other lines and the location of objects in the room. After this, the slate or blackboard may be raised to a *perpendicular* position, and the pupils required to imitate the plan drawn.

This lesson may be succeeded by a similar one upon the school-grounds. Different scales may be adopted in representing them, in order to guard pupils against the error sometimes fallen into by them of supposing that the size of a map must be proportioned to the size of the portion of surface it represents. Questions may be asked in reference to boundaries, and the relative position of the objects indicated upon the map.

Then may be drawn other maps representing the neighboring fields; the adjoining wood; the roads to the mill, store, smith-shop, factory; the town or the village; brooks, creeks, ponds.

Imaginary school-grounds may be drawn, ornamented with walks, shade trees, shrubbery, and beds of flowers; imaginary roads crossed by streams of water, bordered by fields and woodlands, and along which are located farm-houses, shops, stores, hotels, school-houses, and churches; imaginary streams spanned by bridges, and whereon are situated saw-mills, flouring-mills, factories, forges, and towns; imaginary farms divided into fields with wheat, cotton, corn, potatoes, &c., growing in them, with streams of water passing through them, and cattle grazing on the hills or in the meadows; imaginary plans of towns and cities with streets, gardens, public squares, and levees.

Such lessons as these, if accompanied with proper instruction, will prove very much more useful and interesting to children than committing to memory the little rivers of Turkey or the insignificant towns of Japan.

FOURTH CLASS OF LESSONS.—*On the Explanation of Common Geographical Terms.*—The preceding classes of lessons will prepare learners for entering upon the more formal study of Geography. But as clearness of thought very much depends upon clearness of language, some more definite ideas must be imparted concerning certain Geographical terms. A few examples will suffice to indicate the method of doing this.

Let the term be *River.* All pupils have seen rivulets, and they can easily understand that where several rivulets are conjoined a larger stream of water is produced. A number of these larger streams meet and form a creek, and a number of creeks joining their waters make a river. A river is, therefore, "a large stream of water." The representation of a river with its various branches can be drawn upon blackboard or exhibited upon Charts.

Let the term be *Isthmus.* A pupil can scarcely be found who has not seen at least a small piece of ground surrounded by water. He has noticed this in a creek, a mill-dam, or, if no where else, in a pond by the road-side. Two islands may be connected by a narrow strip of land, and this is called an isthmus. An isthmus can be represented as in the case of a river.

In like manner, passing from the known to the unknown, a pond can be *expanded* into a lake; a hill into a mountain; a piece of low land filled with water from a creek when flooded, into a gulf or bay; a township into a continent; a village into a city. Indeed, all that pupils really learn must be acquired in this way. A mere abstract definition cannot possibly be of any benefit to them. In order to ascertain whether pupils have formed a correct idea of such objects, they may be required to point out the pictures of them on Charts, and to draw either real or imaginary ones on the blackboard. Sets of Geographical models designed for imitation, and representing rivers, islands, straits, bays, lakes, mountains, &c., might be advantageously used. For this purpose, a distinguished English Educator recommends an article of apparatus which he calls a "Geographical box." It is made of wood, carved to represent a continent with its seas, bays, islands, lakes, &c. Mountains, table lands, banks of rivers, &c., are made with putty, and the whole painted in the natural colors of the objects represented. This model is made to fit in a box somewhat larger in size, and which when used is partly filled with water. Inside, the box is painted a bluish green, to imitate the color of the sea. The model must be so adjusted in weight that when placed in the water contained in the box, it will allow the water to pass about it in such a manner as to represent peninsulas, isthmuses, straits, bays, harbors, rivers, lakes, &c.

Pupils may be told that the earth about which they are going to study is round, and that it revolves upon its axis once in a day and passes around the sun once in a year. These facts must be illustrated by means of a globe or a Tellurian, may be made to seem probable from the ready explanation they furnish of certain phenomena with which even children are acquainted; but at the stage of progress indicated by the class of lessons now undergoing discussion, it would be folly to attempt to demonstrate them. Such facts may be received upon testimony, until children are able to understand the grounds upon which they are based.

It might be proper also at this stage of their progress to make children acquainted with the various lines which are employed to determine the relative positions of places upon the earth's surface. The most important of these are the equator, the parallels, and meridians. Some knowledge of the tropics, the polar circles, the poles, &c., may be imparted at the same time. Such instruction can be best given by means of a globe, although in the absence of one, some round object or the blackboard can be substituted. The teacher can point to the line which is drawn around the globe, show that this line divides it into two parts, and give these parts their proper names—*hemispheres*. Pupils will readily understand that it is easier to find a place in one of the hemispheres than it is to find one upon the whole globe. Other lines parallel to the equator may be pointed out or drawn, their names stated, and their purpose shown. Meridians can be exhibited and their use explained in the same way. Pupils should then draw maps of the hemispheres upon the blackboard representing the parallels and meridians, and numbering them; after which the teacher may engage them in determining the latitude and longitude of such places as he may think it proper to name. This done, a few minutes will suffice to make pupils understand what is meant by tropics, polar circles, and poles. Whatever concerning these things children cannot comprehend by such instruction must be left until their minds are more mature.

FIFTH CLASS OF LESSONS.—*On Detailed Geography.*—Having been instructed in the lessons previously described, pupils are prepared to commence the study of the details of Geography. For this purpose each country in turn must be brought under consideration; and the best order to be followed is to consider the school-house the central starting-point, and gradually advance further and further away from it, until the whole world is comprehended in the survey.

From the summit of a hill or the top of a house, the neighborhood of the school can be seen, its aspects and objects can be marked, and maps of it can be drawn. Pupils thus introduced to the subject could not fail to notice that the roads, rivulets, and hills gradually disappear from sight; and to realize that there was "more beyond." Then the teacher can gratify their curiosity by presenting before them a map of the town or township. If such a map cannot be purchased, the teacher can draw one for himself. In addition to the most important physical features, a map of this kind ought to have represented upon it, the public roads, the towns and villages, mills, manufactories, churches, post-offices, school-houses, and even some of the farm-houses. Exercises upon maps like this and in drawing similar ones can scarcely fail to interest pupils.

Next to the Geography of the town or township, the Geography of the county or district in which the school is located should be considered; then, that of the state, the country, and in succession the other countries of the world. Foreign countries need not be described so minutely as countries nearer home, nor those with which we have little intercourse as those with which we have much. Great teaching skill will be required to know what to include in these lessons and what to omit. In doing it, the teacher must be guided by the circumstances of his class, and no theorizing can supply that nice sense by which the true teacher adapts the mental food of his pupils to their mental appetites.

In leaving the neighborhood of the school where the pupil can use his own senses, reliance for communicating Geographical knowledge must be had upon maps and descriptions. The inquiry is important as to the form in which these are most effective.

With all the art of the most skilful Engraving, to crowd upon a flat surface of a few inches square, anything that will bear a close resemblance to the objects which are spread out upon a portion of the earth's surface hundreds or thousands of miles in extent is impossible. Maps with parts of their surfaces raised to represent the elevations of land, and profile maps may be better calculated to make correct impressions upon a learner's mind; but after all much must be left to the imagination to supply, and the teacher will do well to have his pupils frequently compare what they have not seen with what they have seen. Maps, however, must be carefully studied. Outline maps are very useful in teaching Geography. They train the pupil to remember by location and form. Having prepared lessons by means of common Atlases, pupils can have their knowledge tested upon Outline maps. The teacher can point out localities and the pupils name them, the teacher can name them and the pupils point them out, or some pupils can name them while others point them out. In reciting with Outline maps, chants are sometimes used; but while many names of towns, rivers, mountains, &c., can be quickly and pleasantly communicated in that manner, they are apt to be soon forgotten unless fixed in the mind by some interesting association.

Map-drawing may immediately follow the lessons on the maps, and it will be a test by which the teacher can always know how faithfully the work of preparation has been performed. Pupils will look much more closely at their Atlases, and perform with much more care their exercises upon the Outline maps, if they know that they will be immediately called upon to reproduce in the form of a map, what they have learned. The teacher should require his pupils to draw maps of every country the Geography of which they study. Beginners may copy their maps, but more advanced pupils should always draw from memory; or classes may be allowed to copy out of class, and be required to draw from memory in class. Maps thus drawn may present merely the outlines of countries, the outlines with a few of the principal localities, or they may give the full details that the best engraved maps contain. They may be rough, extemporized sketches on the blackboard, or they may be carefully prepared, and finely finished specimens of map-drawing. A teacher who gives instruction in map-drawing ought to be able to show how coasts, rivers, mountains, &c., should be drawn, and also to present rules for marking parallels, meridians, &c. Such instruction may be facilitated by the use of map-drawing cards, or blank, black globes suitable for drawing upon.

But all this map-drawing and this study of Atlases, and Outline maps, and globes, will be comparatively dull and profitless unless the teacher know how to enliven the lessons with interesting descriptions, narratives, incidents, and stories. Pleasant associations must be made to cluster about all the dry details of Geography. The earth must not be considered merely as a skeleton. It must be vivified with life. Its plants and animals must make revelations, and voices must come forth from mountains and valleys, from oceans and seas, from lakes and rivers, from great caves and mighty cataracts, making known their uses and revealing their beauty. It must be considered as the theatre upon whose stage the great drama of human life is being played. Scene has followed Scene for the past six thousand years, now a Tragedy, and now a Comedy, and still the play goes on. Mark yon uprolled curtain, teacher, and let your eager children view the wondrous spectacle. When thus taught, Geography is a very attractive study for the young. Here the teacher can pour out in rich profusion the stores of his knowledge gleaned from History, Biography, Voyages and Travels, and the explorations of scientific men, and he will be listened to with intense interest. Starting with the pupil's own village or township, the teacher can find an old church, a mound, a battle-field, the birth-place of some noted individual, a romantic pile of rocks, a beautiful glen, a bed of strange fossils, some mysterious legend, remarkable event, or curious incident, that will throw a charm about the formal dottings and tracings of the Atlas and the cold statistics of the text-book, that wins them a place in the pupil's mind and heart forever. The teacher of Geography has a wide field from which to gather his materials. He is at liberty to cull the choicest facts, the noblest truths, the richest beauties from all arts and all sciences, to furnish the intellectual banquets he provides for his pupils. No country is so poor that it cannot present something worthy of interest. Every state in this Union has much that if skilfully woven into the recitation would make its Geography one of the most attractive of studies. We have our Natural Bridges, our Mammoth Caves, our Niagara Cataracts; our noble rivers, our beautiful lakes, our picturesque mountains, our broad flower-decked prairies; we have Jamestown's ruins, Plymouth Rock, Independence Hall, Bunker Hill, Stony Point, Brandywine, Mount Vernon, Ashland, Marshfield, Shiloh, Gettysburg, and Missionary Ridge, and these, and such as these, have about them clustering rich beauties or hallowed memories. The teacher travels with his pupils in imagination. He should make their travelling seem real to them, by forming skilful combinations of the physical and political characteristics of countries and painting them in words or exhibiting them in pictures. Let a teacher take his class across the ocean, describing ocean life by the way; let him visit with them, Scotland, England, France, Switzerland, Germany, Italy, Greece, Egypt, Turkey, Palestine, India, China, and other countries of the East; and he will find that every step of the journey may be made full of the most absorbing interest. If the teacher speak only of those things which would attract the attention of the class if actually travelling, and others necessary to make them understood, he will have a delightful journey, and his pupils will return from it wiser and better. The teacher might be aided in this work by the use of a Stereoscope, a Magic Lantern, or a series of pictures which would exemplify the Geography of distant countries. With such aids the teacher might almost make his pupils think they were gazing upon the beautiful scenery, the rich cities, the gorgeous palaces, the ruined castles, the ivy-covered abbeys of the old world; or standing upon spots associated with the names of great men or noble deeds. He might almost make them conceive themselves as travelling in the snows of Lapland, riding in the gondolas at Venice, or marching upon the back of a rough camel across the desert with the slow-moving caravan—as rambling among the ruins of Rome, rebuilding in imagination from scattered fragments, great temples in Athens, climbing the Pyramids, or tracing the footsteps of the Man of Sorrows about the Holy City—as introduced among the wild Arabs in their tents, the grave Turks on their cushions or at their mosques, the superstitious Hindoos when performing their feats of jugglery, undergoing their penances, or carrying on their learned disputations, the self-conceited Chinese where they traffic in their shops or on their boats, where they dress their gardens or cultivate their tea, or where they crowd their temples or meditate in their schools of philosophy.

The design of all this is to exhibit the spirit with which Geography should be taught. The teacher must of course adapt his instruction to the age of the pupils and the circumstances of the class.

SIXTH CLASS OF LESSONS.—*On the Classification of Geographical Facts.* — To primary classes learning Geography there can only be imparted with much hope of success a knowledge of individual facts. Such facts must be chosen as will interest them, and their tenacious memories will not suffer them to be forgotten. As soon, however, as pupils enter upon the study of the minuter details of Geography, the teacher must aid their powers of recollection by a carefully arranged outline of classification. In the study of the detailed Geography of a particular country, it is not best to consider the facts to be learned in any order in which they may chance to present themselves, but they should be grouped together in classes. With such an outline of classification before him, the pupil could collect his matter and recite it, much more perfectly than it would be possible for him to do otherwise. He would also be likely to retain it longer in his memory. Many of our Geographical text-books are defective in their classifications. The following distribution of the object-matter of Geography will be found to answer the end now contemplated:

1. Boundaries.
2. Extent and divisions.
3. General character of the surface.
4. Internal waters.
5. Nature of the soil and climate.
6. Productions.
7. Cities and towns.
8. Facilities for internal communication.
9. The inhabitants.
10. Government, religion, science and art, education.
11. Miscellaneous facts.

At recitation, each pupil should be expected to reproduce the information he has collected respecting a particular country, and arranged under these respective classes. He need not be confined to the text-book in making preparation.

But the preceding classification is not broad enough to satisfy a teacher in the higher departments of Geography. The same principle should be so extended as to embrace the various Geographical facts relating to all countries. Mountains, rivers, islands, lakes, rocks, soils, climates, currents, winds, animals, plants, and men admit of classification. Indeed, it is impossible to study them thoroughly without it. If studied only as they appear in particular countries, the information gained will be comparatively of little value. Besides, the best way for advanced pupils to study the extent of countries, the population of cities, the length of rivers. kinds of religion, stages of civilization, and forms of government, is by comparison and classification

For beginners in Geography, the particular should always precede the general; but for advanced pupils the general may precede the particular, for they will possess sufficient knowledge to appreciate principles, and principles will guide them in further study.

It will be understood from what has been said that teachers of Geography ought not to be satisfied with a mere accumulation of disconnected facts, but they should lead their pupils to combine them into well-arranged classes and systems.

SEVENTH CLASS OF LESSONS.—*On the General Laws which govern Geographical Facts.*—Having found the facts of Geography and classed them, learners must be set upon the search for their causes. The form of the earth must be demonstrated, and its motions must be explained. The causes must be investigated that have tended to shape the continental masses, heaved up mountains, formed islands, scooped out valleys, graded plains, covered deserts with sand, and varied the nature of soils; that drive forward the ocean currents, swell the tides, determine the courses and cut out the beds of rivers, fill the lakes with water and keep them fresh or make them salt; that temper the weather, move the winds, distribute the rain, bring hail, snow, and dew, and build up and float away great bergs of ice; that adapt plants and animals to the countries in which they are found, and even modify the races of men; that control the employments of the people, inducing those of some nations to engage in manufacturing, some in farming, some in mining, and others in commerce, fix the boundaries of states, foment wars and keep peace, point out the locations for the founding of cities, the building of railroads, and the construction of bridges, and exert an influence upon government, the manners and customs of the people, science, art, education, and religion. This is a most inviting field; and the thoughtful teacher may find in it reasons so simple that a child may understand them, and principles so complicated that none but a mind like that of Humboldt could evolve them.

In teaching pupils to make inductions, they must be brought to compare the known with the unknown, by means of explanations, illustrations, and experiments. Finding out the reasons of things generally furnishes so much pleasure to learners, that the most the teacher will have to do is to provide a fit opportunity for the exercise of their reasoning powers, and they will gladly use them—and use them to some purpose. A text-book may state general principles and present a sufficient number of facts to prove them; but the pupil should be required to make an application of these principles in explaining new phenomena and solving new problems.

CHAPTER V.

INSTRUCTION IN THE RATIONAL SCIENCES.

THOSE who understand the sciences of which we have thus far treated can scarcely have failed to observe that they start out by taking something for granted, that they make no attempt to account for the ultimate premises upon which they base their conclusions.

The sciences relating to Language treat of the elements of speech and their relations; but every principle of these sciences may be traced back to laws of thought, and these again rest upon certain intuitions of the Reason.

The Formal Sciences confessedly erect their superstructure upon a foundation of definitions and axioms, the nature of which they do not pretend to investigate. Mathematicians merely state the definitions and axioms which relate to Mathematics; Logicians often enlarge somewhat upon those which relate to Logic, but merely as an introduction to the subject proper. Logic treats of the laws of thought, the treatment of the elements of thought belongs elsewhere.

The Empirical Sciences rest also upon a basis of definitions and axioms. Not a single observation can be made, class formed, or inference drawn without the aid of principles which no Inductive Philosophy can account for. By themselves they begin in assumption and end in assumption.

By means of the Understanding we can correct concepts, compare facts, form syllogisms, and apply ascertained principles, and this constitutes, apart from the collection of materials, the whole work the mind has to do in acquainting itself with a Language, a Formal or an Empirical Science. The products of the Reason are, of course, used, but they are assumed.

It is evident, therefore, that back of all the sciences referred to, there must be another class of sciences, whose province it is to treat of what is elsewhere taken for granted. We have ideas of space, time, cause, truth, beauty, right, &c.; but what is the nature of these ideas? and whence do they come? We deal with axioms; but what is an axiom? By what tests can axioms be distinguished? Upon what rests their claim to universal acceptance as truth? The sciences that embrace this object-matter must interpenetrate with their ideas and regulate with their forms all other sciences, must be the germs out of which they grow, the roots by which they are supported and nourished, the light in which they can be understood. The sciences whose object-matter may be thus characterized, have been called the Metaphysical Sciences, and, properly, since they are *over* or *above* Physics; but a better name, perhaps, is the *Rational Sciences*, since they are evolved directly from the Reason.

The Reason is that faculty of the mind which is, and by which it knows itself to be the source of necessary and universal principles. Out of such principles all the sciences grow, and by them life should be guided. By means of the Reason we rise above a servile independence upon material things, and, believing, lay hold on things unseen.

In searching the whole field open to his investigation, the most diligent student can predicate nothing in respect to what he finds that may not be arranged in one of the three following classes: TRUTH, BEAUTY, and GOODNESS.

The human mind has three great classes of Powers, viz.: the Intellect, the Feelings, and the Will. The activities of each class in their objective relations are subject to a distinct body of laws. The products of the right operation of the Intellect may be called *Truth*, the products of the right operation of the Feelings may be called *Beauty*, and the products of the right operation of the Will may be called *Goodness*.

The Reason reigns over the mind. All the mental powers operate subject to its control. Each looks to the Reason for an end to aim at, and a light to guide its effort. The Intellect knows nothing of truth; the Feelings of Beauty; the Will of goodness, unless the Reason furnishes criteria by which to judge them. These criteria are evolved from the Primitive Ideas of the TRUE, the BEAUTIFUL, and the GOOD; and based upon these ideas and outworking from them, we have the Rational Sciences, called respectively PHILOSOPHY, ÆSTHETICS, and ETHICS. The idea of God—an idea which unites all perfection in one Being, gives us THEOLOGY, but no discussion of this science will be indulged in here. Leibnitz, followed by others, has arranged the Rational Sciences into three classes, viz.; Rational Physics, or the science which treats of the World; Rational Psychology, or the science which treats of the Soul; and Rational Theology, or the science which treats of God. This classification is exhaustive, but not so well suited to the present purpose as that above named.

Among the ideas relating to the True are those of *space*, *time*, *substance*, *cause*, *infinity*, &c.; among those relating to the Beautiful are *order*, *proportion*, *harmony*, *grace*, *perfection*, &c.; and among those relating to the Good are *right*, *duty*, *liberty*, *virtue*, *holiness*, &c.

A few remarks are in place here as to the origin and nature of these ideas. It has already been shown that they cannot be derived from experience, but they are always formed upon the *occasion* of some experience. We notice something that is true, beautiful, or good, and immediately there uprises in the mind that ideal standard by which all that is true, beautiful, and good may be measured. Let experience be extended, be made as extensive as possible, still the ideal will outspan it. If in thought we can transcend all possible experience, can we in thought know the Absolute and the Infinite? To me it seems clear that our knowledge of the Absolute and Infinite must be confined to the fact that they exist; but of this fact we can be as certain as of any other. We cannot resist the conviction that there is nobler truth, richer beauty, greater good than any we can possibly conceive of; and rising in degrees it is impossible not to think that somewhere there must be the absolutely and infinitely

Perfect. Besides, as there is the Relative there must be the Absolute; as there is the Finite there must be the Infinite; as earthly truth, beauty, and goodness centre in the human Reason — in man, so the True, the Beautiful, and the Good, unconditioned in their perfection, centre in the Divine Reason — in God. The right conception of the human Reason leads necessarily to a conception of the Divine Reason, and to a Divine Personality in which it is enthroned.

We are just as sure of the existence of the Infinite as of the Finite; of the Absolute as of the Relative; of the True, the Beautiful, and the Good, as of truth, beauty, and goodness; of God as of man. What if into the pure regions where angels dwell the human mind is only permitted to *look* — that look reveals plainly enough the thing looked for, is a firm ground of faith, and furnishes a sufficient foretaste of the ineffable delight with which in the Better Land we shall behold its glories face to face.

Some great thinkers have denied that the human mind can attain to any knowledge of the Unconditioned, but at the same time have admitted that we *believe* in the existence of the Absolute and the Infinite, or of a Being absolute and infinite. That we may believe in the existence of a thing of which we have no *adequate* conception is clear for we do it constantly; but it seems to me that we never believe a thing without having some *ground* for the belief—an idea out of which it springs. With Dr. McCosh I hold "That when there is no positive conception, then faith ought to cease, and must cease." But God has not left mankind without a witness of Himself, without a light to guide those who will heed it, to Heaven. Through the spiritual eye, the Reason sanctified, the heart made pure, man can see enough of Heavenly things to make positive the evidence upon which he rests his faith in God and immortality.

Since the Rational Sciences are so far removed from what business men call practical, and since in this country there is so much prejudice against Metaphysical studies, it seems necessary to set forth the value which may be derived from the pursuit of such studies.

1. *The Value of the Rational Sciences in Themselves.*— To the unthinking, the value of the Rational sciences in themselves does not seem great. They can easily understand that Grammar is useful as it aids in speaking and writing, that Mathematics is useful in keeping accounts, that Chemistry may be useful in analyzing soils and selecting good fertilizers to enrich them; but the utility of truth so abstract as that of the Rational Sciences is not likely to be appreciated by those whose blind judgment estimates the worth of knowledge by the amount of money it will make. The age is intensely practical. Men are measured by the amount of work they can do. He who makes a great speech, wins a great battle, or heads a successful expedition receives the honors which he merits; but he who nobly devotes himself to the study of truth for its own sake is called a dreamer, a theorist, a transcenden-

talist, and is rather pitied than applauded. This condition of things may be excused on the ground that our country is new, and that in consequence great activity is manifested in all that relates to the external life; but the application of a test that would determine the true worth of knowledge might decide in opposition to the popular verdict. With a broader view even of the interests of our earthly life, it might appear that the most potent influence among men is exerted by the thinker — the thinker who studies at the root of things, and ever and anon announces principles that control church and state, and guide the affairs of men.

The value of a knowledge of the Rational Sciences appears in the nature of their object-matter. These sciences contain all that body of truth which is necessary, fixed, and fundamental — all else is contingent, fleeting, and dependent; and surely it is as important to understand the thought that furnishes the foundation and conditions the superstructure of knowledge as it is the work done by the laborers who simply adjust the materials. Besides, the Rational Sciences are the products of the Reason — the noblest of our mental faculties and the only one that distinguishes man as a being differing in kind from the lower animals.

The value of a knowledge of the Rational Sciences appears further in the fact that herein are found properly discriminated and expressed, all our Primary ideas without which all truth would be contingent, all beauty passing. all goodness relative — without which there would be no ground for a belief in a future life or in the existence of God.

It might be added, too, that their value appears in their relation to the Fine Arts. The Fine Arts are the efforts the Reason makes to realize its ideal forms. They impart their full meaning to him alone who can read the pure sentiment pictured on the canvas, enshrined in the marble, or uttered forth in poetry and music.

2. *The Value of the Rational Sciences in their Relations to other Sciences.*—The study of the Empirical Sciences exclusively is apt to exert an evil influence upon the mind. Accustomed to seek a cause for every effect, the student of these sciences is easily led to doubt the freedom of the will or the existence of a great First Cause. He cannot be made to understand how there can be an Unconditioned Being; and if he adopt any views at all concerning religion it will most likely be those of the Pantheist or the Fatalist.

No one by walking in the treadmill of the Formal Sciences can ever do more than demonstrate the particular truths that lie embodied in the general truths which he accepts without inquiry as to their source or nature. The stream of demonstration can never rise higher than its fountain.

The Rational Sciences constitute the bases of all other sciences. Unless grounded upon such bases, these sciences would be like floating vessels with no anchors. Unsubstantial as they may seem to the unthinking, all our knowledge rests upon the intuitions of the Reason. Take these from under the Empirical or Formal Sciences and beautiful parts might still remain, but there could be no scientific systems. Like the crumbling ruins of an ancient temple, they would lie scattered in disproportioned and disordered fragments. There must be conditioning principles for all perceptions, for all judgments, for all reasonings; and of such is the object-matter of the Rational Sciences composed. The intuitions of the Reason must work down to meet the intuitions of the Senses working up. Take away the Rational Sciences and you take away the heart of the other sciences—take away that which makes them sciences, that by which alone their facts and reasonings can receive an intelligent interpretation.

3. *The Value of the Rational Sciences as Means of Discipline.*—An end of study is discipline, what is the disciplinary value of the Rational Sciences?

These sciences concern the highest form of truth. They require the deepest insight, the clearest perception, the most exact definition, and the most careful reasoning of which the human mind is capable. They alone have furnished the great problems the solution of which has called out the full mental strength of such Philosophers as Plato, Kant, Cousin, and Hamilton.

These sciences employ all the powers of the mind. In its pure form, truth is apprehended only by the Reason, but in its applied form all the mental faculties may be engaged in dealing with it. But if the discipline to be derived from the study of the Rational Sciences, appertains to the Reason alone, no object in education can be higher than the development of that faculty. By it there is revealed to man a world of truth, beauty, and goodness; by it he is distinguished from the brutes that perish, by it he reigns sovereign of this world, and by it he claims heirship to a higher one

The mental discipline resulting from the study of Language comes in good part from the relations of Language to the Rational Sciences. This is more emphatically true of the Formal Sciences; and the hardest questions that may be asked in connection with the Empirical Sciences relate to ideas and not to facts.

4. *The Value of the Rational Sciences in preparing the Mind to accept Revealed Truth.*—Empirical Science finds facts, classifies and generalizes them, but here its work ends, as it can neither account for its facts nor make its generalizations universal. To it nature is but an endless chain of links. It can find neither a beginning nor an end. In the view of the Inductive Philosophy, if the human mind is anything different from matter, all its energizing is still subject to the inexorable law of cause and effect. According to it, there can be no free will, and, of course no right and wrong,—no God, and, of course, no inspiration, no revealed truth, no prophecy, no miracles. Empirical Science is well worthy of study in its own sphere, but it is incomplete by itself and needs Rational Science as a complement.

The Formal Sciences accept necessary and universal truths as facts, but make no inquiry as to what they are or whence they come. They carefully evolve from them particular principles relating to space, and time, and the laws of thought, but neither Mathematics nor Logic can solve the highest problems of life. They are means, not ends. They reveal truths, not truth. They treat of the *Formal* above nature but the soul asks for the *Real* above nature.

On the contrary, if we find a ground in the Reason for faith in the doctrines of human responsibility, the immortality of the soul, the existence of God, the way is open for an intelligent acknowledgment of the Bible as the inspired Word of God. Truth does come into the mind without reasoning, whence? May not God inspire it? Or, may He not so sanctify the Reason that He can use it to utter forth His counsel to a sinful world? May not prophets foretell future events, since from a certain standpoint all truths are universal as to time? And does not the power of free origination render miracles not only possible but necessary?

A God *in* nature if such a conception can be entertained, may be governed by the laws of nature; but a God both *in* and *above* nature, from whom nature came, must rule and regulate His works and can in no wise be subject to the laws that govern them. All skepticism has its root in an erroneous or incomplete philosophy. The highest office of the Reason is to *believe* without reasoning—to have faith in things unseen—to look up like Stephen through the opening Heavens and see revealed the mysteries of God.

Before we can treat intelligently of methods of teaching the Rational Sciences, we must characterize their object-matter more definitely. This object-matter consists, first, in *Primary Ideas*, or ideas of the True, the Beautiful, and the Good; second, in *Criteria*, or standards by which may be determined what is true, beautiful, and good; third, in *Axiomatic Truths*, or that body of principles from which deductions and demonstrations are made; fourth, in *Deductions* and *Demonstrations*, or the processes of evolving less general principles from those more general, and of bringing new truths under principles already established; fifth, in *Applications*, or the adapting of abstract principles to concrete facts. It is not pretended that the matter belonging to these several classes is entirely distinct, but the classification will be found convenient. Strictly considered, the Rational Sciences embrace only the matter indicated by the first three classes.

1. Primary Ideas.—I do not think there are any principles in the mind that are strictly innate. There are doubtless innate forces and laws governing these forces, but we never become conscious of them as principles except upon the occasion of some experience. An idea is the result of two factors—a subject thinking and an object thought. But while this is true as to the origin of intuitive principles, we are constantly making use of these principles in ways which show that they necessarily transcend all possible experience and therefore cannot be derived from experience. As soon as we understand what parallel lines are we know that such lines can never meet although we cannot follow them to the end. A single act of dishonesty is sufficient to suggest the principle that all dishonesty is wrong. In ordinary inductions many concurrent facts must exist before

we are safe in inferring a principle, and then we are not quite sure that the principle extends beyond the facts investigated. Here one fact suffices to bring up before the mind a universal and necessary principle. If a body of such principles exist, it follows that there must be a source in the mind out of which they come or out of which comes the power to recognize them. This source we call the Reason, and its legitimate products, its intuitions, we call Primary Ideas—Primary, because arising simultaneously with experience, it is only by their means that experience can be understood. God made the universe after archetypal ideas in His mind, and so our Primary Ideas give form to all we know and to all we do.

These Primary Ideas may be arranged as previously shown into three categories, the True, the Beautiful, and the Good. A final synthesis may unite them, but practically it is best to consider them separately, marking, as they do, the triune nature of man, and pointing, as perhaps they may, to a higher Trinity.

For information as to the number, nature, and relations of these Primary Ideas, students must search works on Metaphysics. Our purpose is to characterize them only so far as is necessary to make understood what we have to say concerning the methods of teaching the sciences of whose object-matter they form a part.

The idea of the true gives law to the Intellect. The Reason discovers directly only necessary truth, truth the opposite of which cannot be conceived, but such truth furnishes the conditions under which all contingent truth is made to appear. The truths of all the sciences rest ultimately in the higher truths reached by the insight of the Reason.

The idea of the Beautiful gives law to the Feelings. An object is noticed, say a rose, and in addition to those of its qualities which immediately effect the senses, it is found to possess something which leads us to pronounce it beautiful. What is that something? and whence the power that reveals it? To the first question no answer will be attempted here; but to the second no hesitation is felt in saying that the source of the idea of the Beautiful is in the Reason. We discover Beauty as we discover truth by means of an original power with which God has endowed us. The beauty of a particular object may seem to result from an analysis of objective properties, but further consideration will lead to the conclusion that the idea of the Beautiful, like the idea of the True, is not derived from but is necessary to experience; and that it furnishes the forms with which all beauty correlates. We are able, indeed, not only to criticise the beauties of nature, but to create ourselves forms of beauty and express them in a manner calculated to awaken emotions of the Beautiful in all beholders.

The idea of the Good gives law to the Will. A child knows but cannot be taught what is good. Without an idea of the Good native to the mind, the distinction of right and wrong would be as impossible to a man as to a brute. The idea of right and wrong cannot be a generalization of consequences, because it appears full formed on the first occasion. The Reason issues forth a voice to all who will listen to it demanding spiritual excellence — demanding love to man and love to God. There are appetites, passions, propensities ever tempting men to wrong-doing, ever leading them down to degradation and ruin; but the Spirit is at war with these influences of the flesh, it warns men of danger, and points out the way to life, light, and love.

2. THE CRITERIA.—How are we to measure what is true, beautiful, and good? "What is truth?" asked Pontius Pilate of Christ when brought before him, and the problem has been propounded thousands of times before and since. So, too, the questions, what is beauty? and what is goodness? have occupied a large place in the investigations of speculative Philosophers. It is not our intention to consider here the different theories which have been presented respecting the measure of truth, the standard of taste, or the rule of right. It appears to me, however, that these Criteria are neither found in the Objective nor the Subjective, but in the relation between the two. If I might venture to suggest a common Criterion for estimating truth, beauty, and goodness, I would do it in these words: CONFORMITY OF OBJECT AND IDEA. Expressed with reference to each, it should be stated as follows: *The measure of truth is conformity of the Objective with the Idea of the True; the Standard of beauty is conformity of the Objective with the Idea of the Beautiful*; and *the rule of right is conformity of the Objective with the Idea of the Good.* With God there must be complete conformity of object and idea, but with man this conformity can never be complete, because he

cannot comprehend the Absolute and the Infinite. We know, indeed, that there must be a Being having unconditioned perfections, but we cannot by searching find Him out. The Reason is the light of the soul—the spark of Divinity within us; but it is still human Reason with finite powers.

3. Axiomatic Truths. — An Axiomatic Truth is a self-evident, necessary, and universal principle, known to be true by intuition. Such truths under the names of Axioms, Canons, Maxims, Rules, furnish the foundation upon which all the sciences rest. The whole body of Axiomatic Truths belongs to the Rational Sciences. It is the province of these sciences to discover them, to test them, and to arrange them into classes. Those which are evolved from the idea of the True and can be tested by the measure of truth belong to Philosophy; those which are evolved from the idea of the Beautiful and can be tested by the standard of beauty belong to Æsthetics; and those which are evolved from the idea of the Good and can be tested by the rule of right belong to Ethics. Lists of such principles as are considered to belong to each of these sciences respectively might be given, but they are not essential to the purpose of a work like this.

4. Deductions and Demonstrations.—The Deductions and Demonstrations of Philosophy are those of Mathematics, Logic, Physics, which are, in the sense now contemplated, branches of it.

The Deductions and Demonstrations which relate

to the laws of taste, or the cannons of criticism constitute an important part of Æsthetics.

The Deductions and Demonstrations which relate to the rules which govern human conduct belong to Ethics.

All Deductions and Demonstrations are essentially the same, and, having explained their nature on a preceding page, it is unnecessary to repeat it here.

5. Applications.—Philosophy has its applications in the applications of all the sciences. The wise recognize in every single truth the evidence of a greater truth which involves it, and trace the most general of all truths directly to their source in the Reason. The Reason, if rightly used, carries the thoughtful inquirer up to God, who placed it midway, as it were, between earth and Heaven, where, not too distant to preside over the affairs of men, it could still see the glories of the Promised Land afar off.

Æsthetics has its applications in all that is beautiful in nature and art. No enumeration can be made of the beauties of nature. They are found everywhere, above, beneath, and around us. Then we have Architecture, Painting, Sculpture, Poetry, Music—what tongue can picture the beauties which they express? But neither nature nor art can furnish a type of beauty so perfect as that which may be seen in a *beautiful life.*

Ethics has its applications in what relates to human rights and duties. These have reference to all the relations of life, in the family, school, state, and church. Ethics teaches men how to live,

Religion prepares them for a state of immortality beyond the grave.

Thus would I construct into a system the object-matter of the Rational Sciences. In so doing, I desire to detract nothing from the importance or the dignity of other sciences. I am profoundly convinced, however, that all the sciences point upward toward a centre, and that that centre is the Reason; and I am as profoundly convinced that the Reason points upward to a Source, and that that Source is God.

It needs not now that much space be taken up in discussing the methods of teaching the sciences which have just been characterized. A teacher who understands them, and enters upon the work of instruction with a love for it, can hardly be mistaken as to the methods to be adopted.

All the education a child can receive in the direction of the Rational Sciences, is to increase his experience. He should be allowed every opportunity of seeing what is true, beautiful, and good; and his own heart should be kept pure that his sight may be free from distortion. A child can perceive truth, beauty, and goodness, and enjoy their contemplation long before he can analyze the powers or the process by which he does it, just as he can see long before he can understand the philosophy of vision. No department of education can be nobler than that which opens up to the young these sources of the purest enjoyment earth can furnish, and from which their minds and hearts can be filled with images of perfection that will ever tend to elevate and ennoble them; but this kind of education is rather a training than a teaching process; and, in its details, a discussion of it belongs more appropriately to "Methods of Culture" than to "Methods of Instruction."

Primary Ideas must be practically operative in the mind before their existence or potency can be recognized. A child cannot begin to think without their agency being involved in the process. A child knows that his mother's face to-day is the same face that bent over him yesterday; that another face differing from his mother's is not hers; that if the stove is hot it cannot be cold; and that if his hand is burned against the stove, something burned it; and, in these simple acts, may be recognized the great Fundamental Laws of Thought as stated by Logicians—laws according to which all thinking is done. But these laws have their ground in the Reason—in the idea of the True. So, too, a child is pleased with what is beautiful, and can determine what is good at a very early age; thus showing that the ideas of the Beautiful and the Good, as well as of the True, have a potential existence in his mind.

But while these ideas are operative in the mind of a child, and thus become an important element to be considered by the educator, no formal instruction can be given in respect to them before the mind is well matured. When old enough to notice what passes in his own mind, and to philosophize concerning it, the student may be taught to distinguish Primary Ideas, to investigate their nature and relations, and to arrange them into classes. These ideas are things to be observed and discriminated by the powers of internal perception. The mode of investigating them does not differ, as I suppose, from that followed in the investigation of the objects of sense; but the mind has great difficulty in studying its own products, and especially those which are as deeply hidden and as much beyond the power of analysis as those now under consideration. No forms of words, no analogical illustrations will convey to the pupil's mind clear instruction concerning such principles. He must use his own insight to detect them, his own powers of observation to individualize and characterize them. All he can learn of them must be realized in his own experience, or his knowledge will consist only of skeleton forms with nothing to fill them. It requires long, careful, tiresome labor to reach down into the mind's deepest self and study the secret foundations of knowledge; but all who possess the ability and the patience to accomplish the work will be well repaid.

The most a teacher can do for a pupil in these abstruse regions of thought is to lead him from the concrete to the abstract, from the limited to the unlimited, from the conditioned to the unconditioned. For example, take the idea of space. The pupil knows what constitutes a particular space, he can gradually add body to body until his idea of space is vastly expanded, and then, perhaps, he may rise to the comprehension of that space which contains the universal whole of things. The idea of perfection may be communicated by leading the pupil from one object to another, each more perfect than the preceding. These examples will serve for all cases as all are alike.

It ought to be remarked that our Primary Ideas, as a whole, have not been carefully studied by Philosophers. A master-mind is needed to present them in an order suitable for study.

Little agreement exists among writers as to the *Criteria* by which we determine what is true, beautiful, or good. Practically, however, there is less diversity of opinion, and men will coincide in pronouncing a thing true, beautiful, or good, who will differ as to the principles which guide their judgments. Here, as elsewhere, we can see more clearly with our eyes of sense than with our eyes of Reason. In teaching, therefore, it seems best, as has been already intimated, to acquaint pupils with things that are true, beautiful, and good—to widen their experience, as much as possible, in respect to nature, art, and life, before directing their attention to the abstract, ideal standards of perfection which the Reason furnishes. It is, indeed, only after such experience that any one can duly appreciate the noblest power God has given to men—the power of discriminating truth from error, beauty from deformity, right from wrong.

It has been stated that the common Criterion for determining truth, beauty, and goodness is Conformity of Object and Idea. This Idea is a direct product of the Reason; and in its abstract form is perfect and alike in all individuals. The Reason admits no culture; it sees, like the eye, at once and correctly; it is never inconsistent with itself. But the faculties that take cognizance of the Object are liable to err. It is scarcely possible for an Object to be so presented or represented to the mind as to stand out clear in its essential properties and relations. Hence men differ in regard to what is true, beautiful, and good, because their knowledge is imperfect. Practically, there never can be a complete conformity of object and idea; and, practically, each man has his own standard of perfection. His is the most perfect standard who possesses the highest culture. A child or a savage must have a low standard. It is the business of education, as applied here, to make observation more exact, the memory more tenacious, the imagination more faithful, the judgment more true, to set things in their proper light, to free thinking from all imperfections, to prepare the way for the Reason; and then will appear truth, beauty, and goodness in all the perfection which a human mind can appreciate.

Evolved out of Primitive Ideas and tested by the Criteria of the Reason, are *Axiomatic Truths*. These principles are operative in the mind from the first dawning of intelligence. No experience is possible without them, and yet it is only by means of experience that we become conscious of their existence, or can give them articulate expression. They have been called "generalized intuitions," and, perhaps, this name designates their genesis with sufficient clearness, as it certainly points out the mode of teaching them. With ordinary experience, Axiomatic Truths are recognized at once as self-evident and necessary; but they cannot be so recognized without a certain degree of experience. It ought to be added, however, that Axiomatic Truths are generalizations of an entirely different kind from those of the Empirical Sciences — the latter simply embrace what has been experienced, while the former transcend all possible experience.

Dr. M'Cosh, in discussing the nature of the truths now under consideration, uses the following language not less valuable to the Philosopher than suggestive to the Teacher. "The principle" (an Axiomatic Truth) "thus discovered and enunciated is properly a metaphysical one; it is a truth above sense, a truth of mind, a truth of reason. It is different in its origin and authority from the general rules reached by experience, such as the law of gravitation, or the law of chemical affinity, or the law of the distribution of animals over the earth's surface. These latter are the mere generalizations of experience necessarily limited; they hold good merely in the measure of our experience, and as experience can never reach all possible cases, so the rule can never be absolute; we can never say there may not be exceptions. Laws of the former kind are of a higher or deeper nature, they are the generalizations of convictions carrying necessity with them, and a consequent universality in their very nature. They are entitled to be regarded as in an especial sense philosophic principles, being the ground to which we come when we follow any system of truth sufficiently far down, and competent to act as a basis on which to erect a superstructure of science. They are truths of our original constitution, having the sanction of Him who hath given us our constitution, and graven them there with His own finger."

"It is ever to be borne in mind, however, that the

detection and exact expression of these intuitive principles is always a delicate and is often a most difficult operation. Did they fall immediately under the eye of consciousness, the work would be a comparatively easy one; we should only have to look within in order to see them. But all that consciousness can notice are their individual exercises mixed up with one another and with all other actings of the mind. It requires a microscopic eye and much analytic skill, to detect the various fibres in the complex structure, and to follow each through its various windings and entanglements to its source."

Reaching the stage of *Deductions* and *Demonstrations*, the Rational Sciences become virtually as to methods, Formal Sciences, the methods of teaching which have already been treated of.

Neither need much be said in this connection concerning the methods of teaching the *Applications* of the Rational Sciences, because wherever principles are applied to facts the process is the same.

The work of teaching must commence with Applications. All a child does he is impelled to do by some principle operative upon him. When he first learns to recognize truth, beauty, or goodness, he does it by applying principles active in his mind but of which he is unconscious. In the field of Philosophy, let the teacher present to him truth as it exists in the sciences, at first simple, afterwards, more complex. In the field of Æsthetics, let the teacher show him objects beautiful, grand, sublime, and teach him to love them. In the field of Ethics, let the teacher make constant appeals to his conscience, quickening it by exercise in determining right and wrong.

Thus growing in his knowledge of what is true, beautiful, and good, there will come a time when turning his mind in upon itself, the student can behold those great, universal, and necessary principles which condition all truth, all beauty, and all goodness; and, armed with these, he can then go forth, not as a child using intellectual instincts simply, but as a man applying the Divine gift of Reason, to interpret the world of matter, of mind, of life.

CHAPTER VI.

INSTRUCTION IN THE HISTORICAL SCIENCES.

HISTORY describes the past condition and actions of men, and investigates the causes which have operated to produce them. History may be thus either a Narrative of Facts or a System of Philosophy, and methods of teaching it must be chosen adapted to the different kinds of object-matter to which they are applied. We will therefore speak, first, of Methods of Teaching the *Facts of History;* and, afterwards, of Methods of Teaching the *Philosophy of History.*

I. Methods of Teaching the Facts of History.

The Facts of History comprise the sum of the events that man has brought about in all the teeming centuries since first he inhabited the earth. The number is beyond the power of the imagination to conceive, and Historians do not attempt to enumerate them. They describe some of the grandest and most interesting features of a nation's life, and leave the rest to be inferred or forgotten.

The great Masters of History relate how and by whom nations were settled; how they were protected in infancy, and what strength and prosperity they attained in manhood; and if fallen they have, how they fell. They tell the story of their civil and political affairs, their commerce, manufactures, agriculture, arts, sciences, and domestic life — their provisions for education, systems of religion, codes of laws, and forms of government. They describe the results of their wars at home and abroad, the revolutions through which they have passed, their manly resistance to tyranny on the one hand or their tame submission to slavery on the other, and those great throes which every healthy nation makes to cast off the evil influences that, cancer-like, threaten to eat away its life or those spasmodic death-struggles which mark a decaying nation's downfall.

Such are the Facts of History, and we will consider: 1. The nature of these Facts. 2. The peculiar difficulties which are encountered in their study. 3. A proper course of study in respect to them. 4. General suggestions in regard to teaching them.

1. The Nature of the Facts of History. — Sufficient has been said elsewhere in regard to the method of imparting to a child a knowledge of ordinary facts; but Historical facts generally differ from other facts in several important particulars.

Historical facts as taught in our schools must nearly always be furnished by testimony. A large number of the facts which constitute the natural sciences can either be observed directly or verified by experiment. The pupil is not compelled to rely upon what others say; he can examine for himself. In history, however, the case is different; his senses are of little use; he must rely upon authority.

Historical facts are connected by synchronal or

chronological relations, and not by relations of kind or quality. The reverse of this is the case with the natural sciences, and it must constitute a difference between these sciences and History.

Historical facts are the acts of Free Agents. All else is controlled by inexorable laws — moves only as it is moved by forces acting from without; but man is a law unto himself, and acts of his own will. These differences cannot be safely overlooked in teaching History.

2. The Peculiar Difficulties which are Encountered in the Study of the Facts of History. — Owing to the nature of the events recorded in History and the circumstances controlling their narration, peculiar difficulties are encountered by the student in obtaining a correct knowledge of them. These events occurred in the Past—many of them in the distant Past, and this alone is calculated to cast doubt upon their authenticity; but, in addition to this, when we consider the proneness of mankind to misrepresent their own actions, the prejudices of Historians, and their too often scanty and unreliable information, and the influences which may have subsequently tended to pervert what was originally fairly represented, we may well wonder whether there is any truth at all in History.

Writers upon the Natural Sciences lessen the labor of learners by making careful classifications— classes, orders, genera, species. Without this, the boldest student would hardly undertake the task of mastering the vast multitude of facts which these sciences now comprehend. The Facts of

History do not admit similar scientific classification. Cotemporaneous events can be grouped together, or an order of succession can be followed in narrating Historical facts; but that power of association, so valuable to men of science, which enables us to recall one thing from its resemblance to something else, cannot be used to much advantage in the study of History.

Science in almost all her departments reveals a series of effects and causes — conditions and conditioning. In nature, like causes produce like effects regardless of time or place. Hence the truths discovered by the ancient philosophers are valid today. The events of History are not uncaused. There may be chains of causation linking all of them together. But he who regards the Facts of History in the same light with which he regards the facts of other sciences, will but poorly comprehend them. Man has a spiritual, as well as a material, nature; and this enables him to move *against*, as well as *with*, nature. The building of a house, the making of a law, the fighting of a battle, are facts, very different in meaning, from the consolidation of a rock, the uniting of an acid and an alkali, or the rushing of a storm. The former class of facts are the results of a free choice, while the latter class are the effects of imperative laws.

These instances sufficiently exemplify the principal peculiar difficulties with which a student will meet in the study of History. The want of their appreciation has led both teachers and learners into the most serious errors.

3. A COURSE OF STUDY IN THE FACTS OF HISTORY. —If all other studies were neglected, a life-time is much too short to acquaint oneself fully with all the Facts of History which have been thought worthy of being recorded. Our schools can permit their pupils to devote but a small portion of their time to the study of History. Hence, the importance of the inquiry as to what parts of History should be studied; and what order should be observed in studying them.

The sources of Historical information open to the student, may be classified as follows: first, *Detailed Histories.* By these I mean Histories which contain a full account of some particular nation, state, or period of time. Some of these Histories are very voluminous. Second, *Universal Histories.* Universal Histories are such as profess to give an account of all the most important Historical facts in one connected narrative. They differ greatly in extent, the number of volumes in some instances being but a few, and in others extending to more than a hundred. Third, *Compends of History.* These contain brief outlines of some of the less interesting or less important parts of History, with fuller details respecting other parts. The most extensive Compends of History correspond in fullness and nature of details with the briefest Universal Histories. Fourth, *Fragments of History.* This class is intended to embrace the Biographies of individuals, Descriptions of particular places or events, Accounts of travels, voyages, &c. They constitute the materials of which History is made up, and may therefore be considered Fragments of History.

I will now indicate a course of study in History which will be found practical, and, I think, adapted to the condition of our schools.

The first Historical matter I would place in the hands of children to be read or studied would be what I have denominated Fragments of History. Children commence learning all things by fragments; and, if written in a suitable style, they will read the kind of writings now designated with remarkable avidity. Of this, the extensive sale of such works as Goodrich's and Abbott's Histories, and the Rollo Books, is a sufficient proof. This matter, in the form of voyages, travels, biographical sketches, historical narratives, may be arranged in lessons for reading in schools, it may be studied and recited, or it may be read at home. I cannot too earnestly insist that it is the duty of parents and teachers to encourage children in a course of reading of the kind now referred to. They can accumulate in this way a vast store of facts, before they reach the age of twelve, and before this age they are generally unable to enter upon a more systematic course of study.

I would next require children to study in detail the principal facts in the History of their native land. No one can well do without this knowledge, and to the citizen it seems indispensable. The law ought to require the History of the United States to be taught in all puplic schools. I am well aware that the History of one country cannot be fully understood without some knowledge of the Histories of other countries with which it has been connected; but teaching must begin somewhere, and less difficulty will be found in commencing with the History of one's own country than with that of distant countries, or with general History. The reason is that pupils are better acquainted with the events that have transpired in their own country than with those that have transpired in others, and are naturally more anxious to increase their knowledge in respect to the former than in respect to the latter.

A knowledge of the History of their own country is about all that can be expected of pupils in our common schools; but pupils in High Schools, Academies, and Colleges should study a good Compend of Universal History. This may be used as a text-book; but the teacher should enliven his instruction by imparting many additional facts, and more Detailed Histories should be at hand so that the pupils might frequently refer to them. In this way, quite an extensive knowledge of History can be acquired.

It does not frequently happen that the time allotted to History will permit a more comprehensive course than that now indicated; but, if so, I would recommend the study of the Detailed Histories of those Countries in which we feel the deepest interest, which have exerted the greatest influence upon us, or with which we are most closely connected. Among these countries I need scarcely name Judea, Greece, and Rome; England, France, and Germany. No one who aspires to be a scholar can neglect the reading of the Histories of these Countries, if he be under the necessity of pursuing the study by himself. The Bible is the most important of all Histories, since it is the History of God's dealings with men. Its truth is for all nations, for all tongues, and for all people.

4. GENERAL SUGGESTIONS IN REGARD TO TEACHING THE FACTS OF HISTORY.—There are two principal methods of arrangement followed in writing works on History, the Ethnographic and the Synchronistic. The Ethnographic method narrates the History of a particular race or nation, without reference to the History of other races or other nations any further than is necessary to illustrate or explain the main design. Detailed Histories, in the sense I have defined them, are Ethnographic in their method. Following the Synchronistic method, an Historian would group together and present in one view the events of a particular era wherever they might have occurred. Universal Histories and Compends of History are usually arranged according to the Synchronistic method. The teacher will at once perceive that the best method to be followed in teaching depends upon the object he desires to attain. When written, Histories may be studied in a Progressive or a Regressive order. It is evident that, if events are arranged in a chronological order, we can either ascend the scale thus formed or descend it—we can either proceed from antecedents to consequents or from consequents to antecedents. Teachers usually follow the progressive order, and for beginners, at least, it is the most natural and the most interesting. For advanced pupils and in reviews, I have found the Regressive method productive of good results.

A knowledge of Geography and Anthropology are very essential to the intelligent study of History. Geography treats of the physical features of the earth, and the present condition of society; and this forms the basis upon which rest the Facts, and, in part, the Philosophy of History. The *known* in History is the Present, and the Past can best be understood by a comparison with it; for the causes that modify our social relations; give form to Governments; advance the interests of science, art, education, and religion; promote reformations, and bring about revolutions—are the same now as in bygone centuries. Anthropology treats of man—his body, his mind, his relations to the world about him; and this science is even more intimately connected with the study of History than Geography. Man lived History; it is a record of himself; and can be understood only by understanding himself. Says Emerson, "Of the universal mind each individual mind is one more incarnation. All its properties consist in him. Each new fact in his private experience flashes a light on what great bodies of men have done, and the crises of his life refer to national crises. Every revolution was first a thought in one man's mind, and when the same thought occurs to another man, it is the key to that era. Every reform was once a private opinion, and when it shall be a private opinion again, it will solve the problem of the age. The fact narrated must correspond to something in me to be credible, or intelligible."

The Historical facts communicated, and the manner of communicating them should be such as to attract the attention and enlist the sympathy of the class of pupils for whom the instruction is intended. A Hume's or a Hallam's, a Gibbon's or a Guizot's Histories are works unsuitable for children, both in matter and in style. It is a common error in our schools to place Histories of the United States in the hands of children who cannot appreciate the facts contained in them, or understand the language in which they are written. The best that can be expected under such circumstances is the mere memorized recitation of the words of the text-book. Facts of History can be found adapted to pupils of any age, and expressed in forms which render them agreeable to every taste; and the teacher who fails to do his duty in selecting them can offer but a poor excuse.

Our works on History should present a lively picture of the Past. Even the best Histories contain much useless matter. It concerns us little to know the lineage of kings and queens, the intrigues of courts, or the plans of campaigns; but it would interest us much to be told how people in past times built their houses, worked their fields, or educated their children—what style of dress they wore, what kind of food they eat, what books they read. We want Encyclopedias and Gazetteers for reference, and they may be full of dates, statistical tables, and lists of names; but school Histories should present a true and life-like daguerreotype of things as they were—not a mere dead body with bones, muscles, and nerves minutely described, but without any soul in it. There is no good reason why History should not be as interesting to the young as Fiction. From School Histories, let bald, dry facts be omitted; let the customs, manners, and doings of bygone people —life's quiet ongoings as well as its comedies and tragedies, be described in vivid word-pictures, and

History will become a favorite study in all our schools.

History should be taught from a series of progressive stand-points. In the History of every nation, there are certain prominent events from which, as centres, other minor events have seemed to emanate, and to which they bear reference. These Historical nuclei with their connected circumstances should be minutely described, and, if well established in the learner's mind, he will recollect and understand other less important events from their relation to them. It is only of these great events that we need to know the dates or the minute particulars. It seems a useless waste of time and labor to commit to memory a great number of dates to be speedily forgotten. These centres of influence in History do not exist simply in the History of particular nations, but they mark certain periods in the History of the world. The whole of human life is exhibited in a great drama, containing a series of connected and dependent Acts—each separated from the others by intervals of comparative rest.

The style of Historical narrative should be clear, concise, and forcible. Long, elaborate, ornate sentences are out of place, at least, in Histories designed for school text-books. It would be unnecessary to make this suggestion, if the error it is intended to point out were less general.

A knowledge of History can be turned to good account in all the varied affairs of life; its study furnishes valuable intellectual discipline, and for the purposes of moral instruction its claims are of a higher order than those of any other branch of learning. No better opportunity of awakening virtuous feelings can occur to the teacher than is presented in the study of History, and it is nowise out of place here to urge that judicious advantage be taken of it. Moral examples have more influence upon the young than moral precepts. History presents many examples of good and great men and women who honored by their noble deeds the age and country in which they lived. The heart is more easily moved to virtue by incidental than by direct teaching; and the faithful teacher will not fail to improve the occasions which so frequently occur in reciting lessons in History by planting moral seeds in the open hearts about him, well knowing that they will germinate and eventually produce rich fruit. No study is so useful in the formation of character as History. In the study of all other sciences pupils come into the possession of interesting facts and valuable principles, but in the study of History they see life. Great deeds are done by beings like themselves, and they cannot resist the desire to do like deeds. This cultivates the will, forms character, makes men.

A teacher may be greatly aided in teaching History by using suitable maps, charts, engravings, and books for reference. The customs, manners, works of art, &c., which characterize the nations of the Past might be represented in a series of views by means of a Magic Lantern or a Stereoscope. An article of dress, an implement of warfare, the fragment of a statue, a coin used centuries ago, if presented to illustrate a point in History, would create much interest in the study.

II. Methods of Teaching the Philosophy of History.

The preceding discussion has had reference to the Facts of History and the methods of teaching them. Until quite recently, the Facts of History constituted the whole of History. In other departments of study, investigations were pushed beyond facts up to principles; but the Historian seemed to think his task well done when he had set in proper array the actions of men and accompanied them with such reflections as seemed to him calculated either to interest or instruct his readers. It is not hard to conceive why the science of History should be later in its origin and slower in its growth than other sciences. Its facts are less easily ascertained and more difficult to verify; the causes of these facts are many times so hidden as to be considered, even by wise men, inscrutable; its generalizations require broader views and a deeper insight; and its ultimate formative principles are the most profound which the human mind ever essayed to grapple. Besides, in a hierarchy of the sciences, History occupies the highest place. It extends its all-embracing principles around all science, all art, all human conduct, and combines them into one organic whole; finds unity in the diversity of the creation; and exhibits all things as the development of the primal ideas after which God made them. A true teacher will not stop when he has described the facts of some historic era, and moralized upon them. He will feel that something more is due to students whom he desires to make thinkers than to have them merely con life's fitful story, or gaze at the strange drama man has acted upon the world's broad stage.

The law of History has not been fully ascertained, data may now be wanting to ascertain it; but although all Historical phenomena cannot be followed back to their primary causes or forward to their ultimate effects, although no human intellect can tell where the series of events began or when it will end, to stop short of doing what may be done, is to dwarf the intellect and take away much that adds interest to the study of History.

If the condition of society is not the result of chance, it must be due to the operation of laws. When these laws are ascertained and formed into a system, they constitute the Philosophy of History. Upon the nature of this Philosophy must depend the methods of teaching it, and this consideration will determine the order of the present discussion.

No argument will be entered upon here to disprove the doctrine of chance. The doctrine is such that no one can entertain it whose mind is able to comprehend even the most common connexions and uniformities which are presented in the world about him. Nor is the doctrine more applicable to the actions of men than to the works of nature. In the latter case the regularities may not be so apparent, but they are sufficiently so to discard from the minds of all who rightly reflect upon them, the idea of chance; and, if otherwise, each individual knows that he has, and generally he can give, a reason, good or bad, for the acts he has committed.

If human actions are not the result of blind chance working from no motive and directed towards no end, they must be the effects of certain causes — the consequents of certain antecedents, and laws must rule the moral as well as the physical world. Philosophy presents no more important and no more difficult problem than that which relates to the origin of these laws. Solve this; and there is solved the great problem of History — the great problem of humanity.

The laws from whose operation human conduct proceeds, may originate from three sources: 1st, *From conditions imposed by matter upon mind;* 2d, *From conditions imposed by mind upon matter and upon itself;* 3d, *From conditions imposed by God upon both matter and mind.* Hence there can be three distinct theories of History, or three methods of building up a Philosophy of History; and, as a matter of fact, some authors have given great prominence to the laws that originate from the first source named, some to those which originate from the second, and others to those which originate from the third, and may thus be divided into three classes. The theories resulting from this disposition of the subject, may be termed, respectively, the *Materialistic*, the *Spiritualistic*, and the *Theistic*, Theories. Some inquiries will be made concerning each in turn.

1. The Materialistic Theory. — The advocates of the Materialistic Theory hold that all human

conduct is to be accounted for by the influences imposed upon the race by material agencies; that Free Will is a fiction; that God's Providence is a myth; that the human mind may act according to its own nature, but that its acts in all cases proceed from causes like those which govern matter. History judged by this theory is simply an Empirical Science, built up in accordance with the Inductive method. No self-originated principles are admitted. All causes uncaused are denied. Events march on, first as antecedents, then as consequents, uncontrolled either by man or God. Facts are collected, classifications formed, generalizations made, and scientific anticipations indulged in, with as little hesitation as in any other of nature's fields open for exploration, and with as much confidence seemingly in the applicability of the method made use of. Man is regarded as but a link in the endless chain of being; and, like any other link, fast in his place —each thought, each feeling, each volition, each act, necessitated by laws beyond his control. Human actions are accounted for in the same way as the falling of an apple, the growth of a plant, or the building of a beaver's dam. If God did create all things in the beginning, His hand is nowhere now apparent in the working world. If man was at first so made that he could choose between good and evil, we have now no evidence that he exercises of himself such a choice.

The best representative of the class of Historians who have adopted this theory, is Henry Thomas Buckle; and, that the reader may see for himself what they are, I will present some of his leading principles. 1st. The actions of men are caused by their antecedents. 2d. These antecedents exist either in the human mind or in nature. 3d. Those which are found in the human mind do not result from free-will, or from Providential interposition. 4th. The consciousness by which it is said we know that the will is free, is extremely fallible. 5th. It is gratuitous to assert that there is anything Providential in History. 6th. That History is the modification of man by nature, and nature by man.

With respect to the last proposition, it is hard to see how man can modify nature if he himself is bound by laws over which he has no control, unless it be in the same sense as a growth of trees, a school of fish, or a herd of buffalo modifies nature, or one part of nature modifies some other part. Allow man will in liberty and admit a Superintending Providence, and the problem of History might be expressed thus: History is the modification of man by nature, nature by man, and both by God. The incomplete notion of the problem of History entertained by Buckle is pointed out in this amended proposition; what are considered his fundamental errors will be pointed out as this discussion proceeds, but the great fact, that nature modifies man, which he so ably presents, and so richly exemplifies, must now be recognized.

Bossuet says: "And, as in all concerns there is that which prepares for them, that which determines their occurrence, and that which causes them to succeed, the true science of History is to observe the latent tendencies which have prepared great changes, and the important conjunctures which have brought them into fact." When closely examined, it will be found that nature has given rise to many of these "latent tendencies which have prepared great changes," and produced many of these "important conjunctures which have brought them into fact." The influences of nature upon man must therefore engage the earnest attention of one who desires to investigate the subtle laws that go to make up the Philosophy of History. Among the agencies most potent in their effects upon man, as mentioned by Buckle, are climate, food, soil, and the general aspects of nature. Others, as air, light, electricity, might be added; but, perhaps, the term climate, used in a very general sense, may embrace them. These agencies must have caused, to a great extent, the differences that now characterize the inhabitants of the earth: differences in size, form, features, color; differences in temperament and taste, in customs and habits, in manners and morals, in science and art, in religion. They must have done much to prompt emigrations and direct them, to determine the boundaries of nations, to control the employments of the people, to point out the locations of cities, to fix governmental institutions, to bring about revolutions, to incite conquests, to foment wars, to secure peace, and to give character to all that belongs to human civilization. No one at all acquainted with the present or past condition of the race, can be at a loss to find abundant instances illustrative of these effects.

Buckle infers from the regularity which is found to prevail even with respect to the actions of men which would seem least likely to be regular in their occurrence, that these actions "are governed by the state of society in which they occur." Statistics prove that nearly the same number of murders take place every year, and that they are committed in nearly the same way; that there are about as many suicides one year as another, and that about as many use the same instrument for the purpose of self-destruction; that the number of marriages annually contracted "is determined, not by the temper and wishes of the individuals, but by large general facts, over which individuals exercise no control;" that even the letters dropped into a Post-Office without superscriptions one year, about equals those similarly neglected other years. Facts like these do show in a surprising manner the influence upon man of causes existing without him — causes that can be ascertained only by investigating the facts. Nature modifies man, and no correct solution of the problem of History is possible wherein its influences are not allowed for; but the gravest errors have arisen from ascribing to these influences effects that other causes have produced. For example, to conclude that because certain actions of men occur with a good degree of uniformity in the same age and nation, that men never act from their own accord as free agents, is to draw a conclusion that the facts will by no means warrant. If some of our actions are regular, many more are irregular. Each individual does things every day of his life unlike others do them. New thoughts, new inventions, new discoveries in science and new works of art appear, and moral and religious duties are discharged — all as the products of a self-originating spirit. Men are all the time making choices, each unlike the choices of other men; but, in view of this, because the sum of the particular choices during one year may about equal the sum of the particular choices for another year — though the same persons may not do the choosing — are we to conclude that no man makes his choice freely? If men are free to act, does it follow that many will not act in the same way? If all are necessitated alike in their actions by causes existing without them, why do not all perform like actions? It decides nothing against the doctrine of free agency to show that in the great aggregate of human actions, men's choices — their likes and dislikes, their similarities and diversities — are uniform while their actions as individuals greatly differ; for this is just what would happen in the case of like beings who act partly from causes within themselves and partly from causes without themselves, but is wholly inexplicable upon the ground that all human actions are constrained by fixed laws. Social statistics may indicate the operation of general laws working independently of the human will; but all this, when well understood, is entirely compatible with individual freedom.

It is a legitimate mode of inquiry for the Historian to study the existing state of society in any or in all countries, to compare it with past states of society, and then to generalize into laws the uniformities, or correlations, which may be found to prevail. By such investigations it has been ascertained that as society advances men are distinguished more by mental and less by bodily qualities; that military occupations precede industrial; that men first are disposed to explain phenomena by supernatural agencies, next by metaphysical abstractions, and finally by observing the laws that govern them; that forms of government, modes of worship, the state of education and the arts, correlate with the condition of the cotemporaneous civilization. These and other such laws have been stated and expounded by the illustrious French Philosopher, M. Comte, and his followers. It is evident, however, that all these laws are simply the generalizations of effects, and constitute at the best but a body of Empirical truths. How can we account for the uniformities and correlations that are thus generalized? This is the great problem of the Philosophy of History. Materialists think they can do so by estimating the influences of circumstances, matter and mind acting as natural causes; but while they succeed in expounding one of its elements they entirely fail as we have seen in solving the main problem.

2. The Spiritualistic Theory. — It has been amply shown that men may be moved to act by the circumstances which surround them. No one seems to doubt that conditioned motives to action such as instincts and appetites, originate in his own nature. But the advocates of the Spiritualistic Theory of the Philosophy of History maintain that man was created with the power of choosing good or evil, that there is a sense in which the will is free, and though it may never act without a reason, it always acts with an open alternative. If motives to action can originate spontaneously in man's spiritual na-

ture, a full recognition of the fact will introduce a potent element into the Philosophy of History which has no place in a Natural Philosophy.

It is not proper here to enter upon a lengthy argument in favor of the doctrine that the Will finds motives within the spiritual nature which prompt it to act in contravention of all animal influences from within or physical influences from without, that it may reject all meaner influences and act solely with reference to absolute ends such as beauty, truth, and right, which are intuitions of the Reason, and cannot be derived from experience. Happily, however, little argument is needed, for the universal human consciousness affirms that the Will is free in the sense we have defined it to be so; men are everywhere held to be responsible for their conduct, and experience, legislation, language, all bear witness to this freedom.

But our consciousness is extremely fallible, asserts Buckle. Men believe one thing at one time, and the opposite at another. We are conscious at times of the existence of spectres and phantoms. This objection to the validity of consciousness arises from a mistaken view of its office. Consciousness merely reveals what exists or takes place in the mind. If I entertain one opinion to-day, and another to-morrow, my consciousness remains the same, assuring me that I entertained a certain opinion and changed it. The change of opinion takes place in the intellect. The outer senses deceive us in regard to spectres and phantoms, not the consciousness, which only informs us as to what impressions are made upon these senses. Indeed, we know that we see or hear things only by being conscious of the seeing or hearing; for all we know of anything we are dependent upon the consciousness, and, if the consciousness cannot be relied upon, the foundation of all knowledge gives way, and we have nothing but chaos. The consciousness, then, which reveals what takes place in the mind, enables us to know that there is a power within us which originates ends that no experience can account for, nor any logic discover, and that these ends may be freely chosen as against all other ends, come from whence they may. It is only by choosing the pure and noble ends furnished by the Reason that man lifts himself above the world of sense and expediency, and realizes that higher life—that true liberty, for which he was destined.

The abstract idea of History is that of a development. Plants and animals come into being and mature by an unfolding process, and analogy would lead us to presume the same of man. We know enough of History to say that its facts are connected together organically, that they are a growth not an aggregation; and this indicates, if it does not prove, their systematic evolution. Nothing moves unless set in motion, so development cannot begin without the application of power. Whence this power? Primarily, from the Creator; but man was created in the image of his Maker, and hence he too is a source of power, and the Historic development of his actions is modified by, if not mainly based upon, his own native forces. Unlike the plant or the animal, man can find a reason for many of his actions within himself: he may choose evil, and a growth of evil actions will be the result; he may choose good, and his life will yield abundant harvests of rich fruit. As a matter of fact, he did choose evil, fell, and the consequent disasters have weighed heavily upon the world; but he may accept the sacrifice made for sinners, rise again, and in a life of purity, fulfill the design of his creation. The growth of our animal nature is a development, but the conditions are all imposed from without; the perfection of the spiritual nature is a development but one of a wholly different kind, and arises from the realization in life, of the ideal conceptions of beauty, truth and holiness, which can only be inspired from within. From the antagonism of these two natures—antagonistic only on account of the disturbing element of sin—comes the warfare between the flesh and the spirit, which is to be overcome at last by the reconciliation of man to God. There is nothing in this view which does not harmonize with the idea of development. Our acts may be evolved partly from the animal and partly from the spiritual nature, may be partly good and partly evil, without necessitating the disruption of their organic unity. The same stream in one part of its course may have its waters wild, turbid, and foul; while further on, they may become calm, and the sediment that rendered them impure sinking to the bottom, may leave them clear and pure. To one, therefore, who can take in the vast sweep of the Creator's plan, there can be no conflicting potentialities, and no valid argument can be brought against the theory that allows Free Agency to man from this source. It does not follow because man originates an end in his own Reason with reference to which he acts, that a Science of History is impossible. Quite otherwise, unless he acts in view of such an end, there can be no true science of anything. Besides, each individual life in the unity of its several stages, exemplifies the life of the race, and self-reflection will enable one to solve some of the most profound problems in History; and no man who reflects about himself has ever failed to acknowledge his responsibility for his acts—a fact totally irreconcilable with the doctrine of Necessity.

Unless a spontaneous cause be found in the human mind, it seems impossible to account for the influence upon society exerted by belief and thought. Says Mill: "Every considerable advance in material civilization has been preceded by an advance in knowledge; and when any great social change has come to pass, a great change in the opinions and modes of thinking of society had taken place. Polytheism, Judaism, Christianity, Protestantism, the negative philosophy of modern Europe, and its positive science—each of these has been a primary agent in making society what it was at each successive period, while society was but secondarily instrumental in making *them*, each of them (so far as causes can be assigned for its existence) being mainly an emanation, not from the practical life of the period, but from the state of belief and thought during sometime previous." Can it be supposed that "belief and thought" from which come such results are attributable to the ordinary operation of physical causes upon mind? Can man move only with the wheel of nature? Did God make the world and then withdraw forever His creating hand? All we know of social phenomena seem to me to furnish a negative response.

The Philosophy of History has been more carefully studied in Germany than in any other country, and as the subject is one of the most vital importance, I will present the opinions of a few of the greatest German thinkers in illustration of the views here taken.

Kant says: "Reason is the faculty which furnishes the principles of cognition *a priori.*" If principles are furnished at all by the reason, it is evident that these principles may become objects of desire—ends of action, and thus move the will so to act that the conduct may be in conformity thereto. And, after all, the freedom of the will must be determined by determining the sources of knowledge. It is well ascertained that for every act of Knowing there may be an act of Feeling, and consequently an act of Willing. We know through the senses, and of course our conduct is influenced by the world of sense; but if the mind has power to cognize principles evolved from itself—and we have previously shown that it has this power—then, may the conduct be influenced by these principles, and man either is or may become a Free Agent. Had Kant written a Philosophy of History, he would not have overlooked the effects attributable to the autonomic potency of the human spirit.

Fichte's system consists of a Theoretical and a Practical division. The fundamental axiom of his Practical division is, "That the *not-me* is affirmed as determined by the *me.*" This proposition, whether true or false, indicates to those who understand it, with sufficient clearness, the author's opinions in regard to the Historic element now under discussion. But his views are further expressed by Morell as follows: "The mind has a purely rational nature, by virtue of which it sets before itself its own aim, the object of its own free activity. To deny this would be to deny the very existence of mind itself: to ask why it is so, would be to ask why truth is truth." Fichte's "Idea of Universal History" is that of a free spirit struggling to surmount obstacles of its own creation, "seeking to bring into actual existence all that lies potentially in its consciousness." This constitutes his "world-plan" and designates his place among writers on the Philosophy of History.

Schelling maintains the existence of a faculty which intuitively discovers the *Absolute*. A mind possessing such a faculty must be in some sense free in its actions. But we are not left to inference in regard to Schelling's views of History. Morell states them as follows: "History is the absolute combination of the freedom of the individual with the necessary development of the race. Every act of which History is composed is a free act; and yet man, with all his freedom, cannot help contributing to the accomplishment of the destiny of the whole nation and whole race to which he belongs."

Hegel starts out with the astounding proposition that *Sein* = *Nichts*, or that Being equals Nothing; and derives the idea of existence from the combination or contradiction of Being and Nothing. From this point he proceeds to expound in a series of logical triads the origin and laws of matter, the life of man, and the process by which God himself is realized—this last process in his Philosophy including the first two processes, or in other words all the on-goings of nature and all the thoughts and actions of men are but the unfolding of God. Hegel admitted no Creator. From nothing he developed existence, and then started a movement which in turn unfolded from it, logic, nature, mind, and God as a Divine personality. After assuming a series of conditions and annulling them, the Divine Spirit seems to attain freedom, in the freedom attained by men; but with Hegel there can be no such thing as individual Free Agency. Buckle binds mankind with the laws of matter, Hegel fetters him with the laws of thought. Buckle might admit a great First Cause, simply as an abstraction, while Hegel thinks he finds God only as the final product of all causation. The Philosophy of the former tends toward Atheism, and that of the latter is unadulterated Pantheism.

Schlegel's "Philosophy of History" was written at about the same time that Hegel delivered his "Lectures on History," and yet there is a wide difference in the doctrines of the two philosophers. Schlegel looks upon the freedom of man and the Providence of God as the two principal Historic elements. He writes, "Without this freedom of choice, innate in man or imparted to him — this faculty of determining between the divine impulse and the suggestions of the spirit of evil—there would be no History, and without a faith in such a principle there could be no Philosophy of History." And again, "Without the idea of a God-head regulating the course of human destiny, of an all-ruling Providence, and the saving and redeeming power of God, the History of the world would be a labyrinth without an outlet — a confused pile of ages buried upon ages — a mighty tragedy without a right beginning, or a proper ending."

3. THE THEISTIC THEORY. — The Theistic Theory recognizes God as the Creator of all things, and holds that He imposed and continues to impose certain conditions upon both nature and man, and that these must be taken into the account in philosophizing about History.

It is impossible to think that the creation did not begin to be—even Hegel's dialectic movement must *start*—and if so, it must have had an Author. Modern science has shown that new kinds of plants and new races of animals have been at various epochs introduced into the world, and if so, there is no alternative but to regard such facts as the result of the direct interposition of the same Power that originally called the earth itself into existence.

God evinces his power in History. Nations rise and fall. Whole races disappear and new men spring as it were from the ground to take their places. Great multitudes of people are moved by a common impulse, for which no one can account, to emigrate, to reform, to become religious. Inventions and discoveries are made just when most wanted. Genius gives birth to science and art. Great men seem born for the times in which they live. Crises occur in human affairs, and when all men despair, help comes, whence no one can [illegible]. These events and such as these, though to some extent the result of the potency of nature or the potency of will, indicate that the God who made the world still rules it. Without the idea of God regulating the affairs of men, History would be a grand chaos of disconnected facts and discordant elements, as already quoted, a "Confused pile of ages buried upon ages."

As individuals, nearly all persons acknowledge the Providence of God. The common instincts of mankind all point in this direction. The lowest grade of savages entertain it in some form or other, cultivated Heathen nations admit it, and Christians everywhere hold that God ofttimes strengthens them in the performance of good, and ofttimes speaks comfort to the sorrowing spirit. If these instances were few, distant, or isolated, no general conclusion should be drawn from them; but in all ages, in all climes, and among all people, the common belief has been that the hand of God is frequently apparent in the affairs of men, and it is a monstrous libel upon human nature to deny it. To me the same consciousness that reveals the idea of God, reveals Him as the Maker, Preserver, and Ruler of the universe; and I hold both revelations alike valid.

I have not yet referred to the Bible, nor need I. Those who believe it to be true, have already realized its effect upon mankind; and those who disbelieve it, would not be persuaded by arguments based upon it. Some good Christians, however, think that, with Christ and his immediate Disciples, God ceased to manifest himself by Special Provi dences; to them it might be said that the operations of the Holy Spirit must continue to be a special interposition of God, and the conversion of every sinner is a miracle. No man ever yet lifted himself up from sin and death, to purity and life. God must aid him in this work, and all such help is a Special Providence.

Much in History is Providential. Evidence of it comes from the creation, from the economy of nature, from the great events of the past, from individual experience, and from the Bible. All may have entered into the grand plan when first the creation was conceived, and may occur in accordance with that plan; but the plan itself may have embraced eras which God predetermined for his own glory or our good to distinguish by extraordinary manifestations of His presence or His power, or may have contemplated events which were to be specially guided by His omnipotent hand.

God's dealings with men cover three distinctly marked periods: first, that of Purity, before the Fall; second, that of Promise, from the Fall to the coming of Christ; third, that of Fulfilment, after the Resurrection. From both the nature and facts of the case, all these dealings resolve themselves into one grand plan for the protection of man from evil before the Fall, and for his restoration to holiness after it. This plan was undoubtedly made in view of man's Free Agency, and of physical influences, and, when well understood, harmonizes with them. Physical influences, indeed, must operate in entire subserviency to intellectual and moral influences — to the laws imposed upon them in the beginning; and if a man may be able to attain virtue and yet be unwilling to make the effort, and God in pity present a stronger motive and thus aid him in making a right choice, and save him from destruction, does that conflict with Free Agency? It does not, for it leaves an open alternative; and yet this is the simple mode in which God strives to save a lost world.

It remains only to say that Bossuet was the first to apply the idea of an overruling Providence in the solution of the Problem of History. He did it ably and eloquently. Schlegel's "Philosophy of History" is the most profound work written from a similar standpoint. Nearly all the German writers on the subject recognize God in History; but most of them seem to think that the Philosophy of History has other objects than that which Schlegel claims to be the chief one, "To point out historically, in reference to the whole human race, and in outward conduct and experience of life, the progress of the restoration in man of the lost image of God, in the various periods of the world."

Admit the theory now stated, and does it take away all foundation for a science of History? Must the world be a chaos because God rules it? By no means. God works in the light of absolute truth. The whole plan of the creation and the moral government of the world is consistent. The supernatural, no less than the natural, is subject to laws, but we can only catch glimpses of them. It is the fool that has said in his heart "there is no God."

Sufficient has now been said to render the truth

apparent that History results from the operation of three great causes: nature, man's Free Will, and God's Providence. These are the Historic factors. He who would construct a complete Philosophy of History must answer the following questions: What is the amount of influence nature exerts upon man? What is the amount of influence his own spiritual freedom exerts upon man? What is the amount of influence God exerts upon man? If he can fix the relative proportions of these influences in the events of History and harmonize them, his work is done. As History may be considered from these several standpoints, it is not to be wondered at that there have been propounded different Theories of the Philosophy of History. Each writer has some truth at the bottom of his system, but the whole of truth ascertained can only be known by a combination of the truths of all systems. The facts probably are that in the infancy of the race, physical causes had more influence upon man than when he advanced to higher stages of civilization, and God also presented himself in a more tangible form — walking and talking with men. But when nations emerged from ignorance, and reason mounted her throne and assumed her destined sway, nature succombed to a superior power, and God no longer reveals himself to the coarser senses, but only to the pure eye of faith.

It is not my purpose to apply the Theory of the Philosophy of History now arrived at to the Facts of History. If it were necessary to do so in order to exhibit the nature of the Theory now developed, it would not be very difficult to show that the three great Historic factors have each played an important part in the production of events like the downfall of the Roman Empire, the Crusades, the Reformation, the French Revolution, or the American Rebellion. I will only add that all the Facts of History to be understood, must be interpreted by the light of its Philosophy.

Having indicated the nature of the Philosophy of History, a few sentences will suffice to indicate the methods of teaching it. So far as the laws of History can be inferred from observed facts, it is an Empirical Science and must be taught according to the principles of the Inductive Method. To the extent that it is dependent upon truths derived *a priori*, it is a Rational Science and can be taught only according to the principles of the Deductive Method. When the designs of God's Providential interpositions cannot be determined, they must be believed. Thus the study of History requires the most extensive observation of facts, the broadest generalizations, the deepest insight into truth, the most careful demonstrations, and the most exalted faith. Methods applicable to all other studies, are employed in a higher sense in this; and, in addition, we are constantly reminded that human science has its limits, and that for light concerning the realm of pure truth beyond its ken, we must in this life trust to revelations from above.

Let me conclude by indicating the great lessons of History. Three kinds of influence make up our life; that from nature, that from our own free spirits, and that from God. In their deep significance, they teach these lessons: CHARITY, INDEPENDENCE, and HUMILITY. We find the follies, the faults, the wants and the woes of mankind much owing to nature and the circumstances of society—this excites our sympathy, and is designed to teach us *Charity;* we find motives within us which prompt us to act for ourselves—this is designed to teach us *Independence;* God in many ways makes us sensible of His overruling power and our weakness—and this is designed to teach us *Humility.* As now used, Charity is love to man; Independence is a true sense of our own manhood; and Humility is faithful obedience to God—equivalent to loving our neighbors as ourselves, respecting ourselves, and honoring God.

Our charities are bestowed in proportion to the helplessness of the recipient. Our toleration for the erroneous opinions of others is in proportion to their responsibility for them. We do not hold the Heathen strictly accountable for the violation of Christian principles, nor do we much blame the people of Constantinople for being Mahometans. If we could be convinced that differences of opinion in regard to politics, philosophy, morals, religion, were wholly owing to differences of soil, food, climate, the general aspects of nature, or the general condition of society, strife and debate, party-hate, and party-warfare would mostly cease, and the nations would learn the lesson of CHARITY.

To teach this lesson in this way, however, would necessitate the total annihilation of the distinction of right and wrong, and blot out forever self-consciousness and self-respect. We are governed by circumstances just so far as to form a social brotherhood, and to teach wise men charity; and for the rest we are made to find within ourselves the reasons for our conduct, and to feel responsible for it. Man, relying upon himself, gathers facts from earth, and air, and heaven, and finds the laws that govern them; he seizes the principles, his own reason furnishes and constructs systems of Philosophy; he produces—almost creates forms of beauty in the arts; he establishes governments, and when they fail to subserve his ends, he alters or abolishes them; he casts off the shackles of despotism and slavery, and becomes a freeman; he triumphs over his passions and rules himself, and thus he learns the lesson of INDEPENDENCE.

But with this Independence, come bigotry, pride, obstinacy, pertinacity, dogmatism, tyranny. In their foolish reliance upon self, men become self-righteous like the Pharisees of old, and vainly expect to purchase Heaven with merit of their own. They eat of the tree of knowledge, and would be gods. Then God stretches forth His hand, and flaming swords guard the entrance to Paradise which man has forfeited by disobedience; a flood cleanses the earth from wickedness; fire and brimstone rain down upon the devoted cities of the plain; Pharaoh's heart is hardened; thunders burst out from Sinai; prophets whose lips had been touched with fire from Heaven warn the nations; pomp and power are weighed in the balance and found wanting; men are afflicted, and, like Job, "abhor themselves, and repent in dust and ashes;" riches take to themselves wings and fly away; and the rebellious are all brought down in heart, and cry upon the Lord in their troubles. In the fullness of time, the meek and lowly One appears and calls, "Come unto me, all ye that labor and are heavy laden, and I will give you rest." Multitudes accept the call, and enter like little children into the Heavenly Kingdom; and thus learn the lesson of HUMILITY.

All goes to show that Independence ennobles Charity, and Humility softens Independence; and together they constitute the essentials of Manhood. We may now pluck the fruitage of all History: PEACE ON EARTH, LIBERTY TO MAN, and GLORY TO GOD.

CHAPTER VII.

INSTRUCTION IN THE ARTS.

ALL schools should impart instruction in *Writing*, *Drawing*, and *Vocal Music*, and methods of teaching these *School-Arts* will be presented here in some detail; after which a few general observations will be made concerning *Instruction in the Arts in General*. This order is the reverse of that followed in the preceding Chapters, and places the particular before the general; but by so doing, while care is taken that nothing shall be lost in perspicuity, something will be gained in symmetry to the book as a whole.

I. Writing.

Writing is the art of making letters and combining them in words. The instrument used for this purpose at the present time is called a pen or pencil; in ancient times it was called a reed or style. The characters used in writing and printing are undoubtedly modifications of the same forms.

It is hardly necessary to say that Writing is a useful art. It seems indispensable in transacting the complicated affairs of modern society.

In learning to write, two objects must be kept in view: first, to make the writing legible; second, to make it beautiful. Without the attainment of the first object, Writing would be of no use, and without the attainment of the second it could never gratify the taste.

Writing is partly a mental, and partly a mechanical operation. As a mental operation, it consists in conceiving the forms of the letters, and, as a mechanical operation, it consists in executing those forms. It seems evident, therefore, that lessons in Writing are divisible into two classes: those which are designed to teach the conception of the forms of the letters, and those which are designed to give culture to the muscles used in Writing.

1. Lessons designed to teach the Conception of the Forms of the Letters.—In art, the ideal precedes the real; the conception of form precedes its execution. Painters place their mental pictures upon canvas, sculptors realize them in marble, and architects express them in wood and stone. With an imperfect ideal, its realization must be correspondingly imperfect. All this applies to Writing as to other arts, and a teacher of Writing should have lessons calculated to impress upon his pupils' minds the most correct and beautiful forms of the letters.

Some lessons on Form in general may be made valuable auxiliaries to this end.

Young children may be amused and instructed with blocks of different shapes and sizes, out of which buildings and articles of furniture may be made; blocks cut into sections which can be formed into various figures; and diagrams and blocks representing the figures and bodies used in Mathematics. No article of apparatus can be used more advantageously in giving lessons in Form than the

Chinese Puzzle. It consists of eight pieces peculiarly shaped. The pieces may be so arranged as to form a square, a triangle, a parallelogram, and hundreds of other figures. A book accompanies the pieces containing diagrams of the figures to be formed, but not indicating the positions of the pieces; and the problems consist in having certain figures given, to find the position of the pieces in forming them.

Lessons requiring the discrimination of the forms of natural objects, such as leaves, crystals, fruits, &c.; make more vivid the impressions of form.

Some teachers have placed boxes of sand before their pupils and required them to make various figures in the sand, and others have exercised them in tracing figures in the air with rods.

The experience of many good teachers seems to prove that pupils should receive instruction in the elements of Drawing before they begin to write, and that such lessons are better calculated than any others to aid the pupil in attaining the power of conceiving forms correctly.

To impress upon the minds of pupils the particular forms used in Writing, the following exercises will be found valuable:

The letters which have in script the simplest form, such as *a*, *n*, *u*, should first be presented to the pupils. These the teacher should make upon the blackboard. He should make them as neatly as possible, and impress their correct form upon the minds of the class by exhibiting the common departures from it. Each lesson should include but a few letters, as this renders the discussion of their pecu liarities and the manner of making them more likely to be remembered.

After such an exercise as the preceding, the work of analyzing the letters may commence. Pupils can be readily led to see that the right line or "stroke" /, enters as an element into a number of characters, and so of the oval *O*, the hook *l*, the loop *ℓ*, &c.; and they will therefore take more interest in imitating them. A detailed analysis of the letters will not be attempted here; but it may be found upon reference to works on Penmanship that all the letters, both the small letters and the capitals, can be reduced to a very few simple elements. All that it is necessary to say now is that these elements must be exhibited to learners, they must be required to imitate them, and to embody them in letters and words. The making of letters and words should not be postponed until the whole analysis of the letters has been completed and the elements carefully practiced; but as soon as the elements composing a letter, or the letters composing a word, have been mastered, the pupil should be allowed to write them. Let it be remembered that one step must be taken at a time, that the pupils should commence with the simplest forms and become thoroughly acquainted with these before advancing to those more difficult, and that a correct knowledge of forms must precede a correct execution of them.

Not only is it important to impress upon the learner the correct forms of letters, but he must also be taught to give them the proper inclination, and arrange correctly the distances between them. In addition to the directions of the teacher and the model for imitation which the learner must have constantly before him, it might be well to use at first a copy-book so ruled as to indicate the length of the letters, their inclination, and spacing.

Some teachers have found much advantage in requiring pupils to "trace the letters." This tracing of the letters consists in following a model with the pen held above it or slightly upon it. Drawing the letters on slates or blackboards is an excellent exercise.

2. Lessons designed to give Culture to the Muscles used in Writing. — Certain muscles have to be trained in learning to sew, paint, play the piano; and such is also the case in learning to write. No one can make a more beautiful picture of a letter than that which he has in his mind; and he requires well trained muscles who can expect to make any close approximation to it. A good writer always has complete command of the muscles he calls into requisition. A teacher of writing must therefore so direct his instruction as to secure this end.

Some discipline of the muscles used in writing is obtained by a child who merely marks with his pencil upon a slate, or with a piece of chalk upon a blackboard; and, on the whole, I consider such exercises an advantage to the pupil in learning to write, although he may not hold the pencil or crayon as a pen should be held. A few days of patient training when he begins to write with a pen, will accustom the pupil to hold it correctly.

No better discipline of the muscles used in writing

can be had than that which is furnished by performing elementary Drawing-exercises. Close observers have remarked that pupils generally write best who have been taught to draw. Horace Mann in reporting upon his visit to the schools in different parts of Europe mentions this fact.

Works on Penmanship often contain special exercises designed for training the muscles of the arm and fingers. Such exercises are very valuable. No description of them is necessary here; but it might be remarked that they should be well graded, and that teaching should commence with the simplest.

Tracing the letters as noticed upon a preceding page is useful not only in aiding the pupil to conceive the correct forms of letters, but also in training the muscles in executing these forms.

Some additional suggestions are deemed appropriate:

Apart from the general exercises calculated to aid the pupils in conceiving the forms of letters or in getting command of the muscles used in making them, a recitation in Writing will consist mainly in calling the attention of the class to the forms of letters composing the lesson, describing these forms, analyzing them, showing how they ought to be made, and then requiring the models given to be carefully imitated.

Much the best copies for imitation are those which are arranged on loose slips. Copy-books with engraved head-lines may not suit the circumstances of the class. They may advance from easy lessons to those which are difficult, too fast or too slowly. Besides, in using them, pupils are apt, after writing two or three lines, to forget to look at the head-line; whereas, slips can be readily moved down the copy as the pupil proceeds with his work. It is an advantage many times, also, for the pupils to rewrite their lessons. If a teacher has ample time, writes a suitable hand, and has a prospect of remaining a long time in one school, it may be well for him to "set the copies" or write the models himself; but as these contingencies seldom exist, it is better for teachers generally to adopt some good system of Penmanship and follow it. Under the most favorable circumstances, pupils might take more interest in copying a teacher's hand-writing than in imitating models; but pupils lose so much much by being required to imitate the ungraceful characters made by poor pensmen, and by being compelled to change their hand-writing with every change of teachers, that it is time this practice of "setting copies" should be abandoned. A system of Penmanship adopted and a set of models chosen, the teacher must conform his instruction to it. This is very essential to success. The first lessons for children should consist of elements, letters, or words written in a clear, neat, and plain hand. The general length of the letters should be for first lessons about a quarter of an inch; but after some practice, pupils may be allowed to write both large and small hand.

In forming his style, the pupil ought to have the model constantly before him; but the manner of making the letters must become so familiar that he can preserve the same style in writing dictated copies without a model. Teachers will do well to require the pupil to observe in all his writing the directions given in the writing-class. Without such attention, pupils can never become habituated to the use of a uniform and correct style of writing.

There is the same reason for classification in writing as in other studies; and in conducting a recitation, much loss of time is avoided by introducing it, with such illustrations upon the blackboard as the lesson may require, and, in the same manner, during its continuance, exhibiting the errors made by the pupils in their work. If the blackboards are good, the pupils themselves may use them to great advantage in learning to write. All the pupils in a class should practice the same lessons at the same time.

Nothing need be said here concerning the kind of desks or tables best adapted for the purposes of writing, or of the manner of sitting and holding the pen, or of moving the fingers or arm, as all this is sufficiently discussed in works on Penmanship.

It is very important that the errors pupils make in their writing should be corrected. The best way to do this, probably, is for the teacher to pass to each pupil while engaged at his work, call his attention to his errors, and make such suggestions to him as seem necessary. The teacher may correct general errors by showing in what they consist upon the blackboard. Two or three critics may be appointed every day from among the members of the class to examine the copies and report the errors, or the copies may be exchanged for this purpose.

II. Drawing.

Drawing is the art of representing objects by means of lines and shades. Like writing, Drawing is partly a mental and partly a mechanical operation. One who draws must first conceive objects, and afterwards represent them. Drawing, however, aims to represent all objects, while writing is confined to the representation of a particular class of objects; and, in the case of Drawing, the objects are mostly concrete, while in writing they are always abstract.

As drawing is not generally taught in our Common Schools, some of the advantages of skill in this branch of study may be pointed out.

Skill in Drawing aids very much in learning and reciting other studies. Maps should be drawn in Geography; diagrams, in Mathematics; and plants and animals should be represented in the Natural Sciences. Elementary Drawing-exercises form a very good introduction to writing. Indeed, there is scarcely any study in which skill in Drawing may not be turned to good account. Skill in Drawing is indispensable in some kinds of business. It is so to the engineer, architect, and machinist. It is almost equally so to the farmer, the miner, the teacher, and the physician. There is no position or kind of business in which an individual might not find an opportunity to make an advantageous use of skill in Drawing. To draw well one must observe closely, and this gives valuable discipline to the senses and the perceptive faculties. Drawing is the language of the eye, and it often enables us to communicate what could not well be stated in words. A person desiring to have a new building erected or pleasure-grounds laid out, can communicate to his workmen more knowledge in a few minutes by drawing his plans, than he could by long hours of verbal explanation. So a traveller in a strange country can ofttimes convey more true knowledge by a rough sketch of some remarkable object in nature or art, than he could do by a labored description. In its higher departments, Drawing is well calculated to awaken the mind to the perception of new beauties, as it requires a careful study of nature; and when it rises from the sphere of an imitative art to that of a creative art, no other study can furnish higher or better culture for the judgment, the imagination, and the taste.

While it is agreed on all hands that children may begin to learn to draw when quite young—before they commence learning to write, teachers of Drawing differ very much as to the best method of instructing them. But although almost every system of Drawing differs in some of its details from all other systems, all of them may be arranged into two classes; and there are, therefore, two methods of teaching Drawing. The first commences with a straight line, as the simplest element used in Drawing, and may be called the *Abstract Method;* the second commences with objects, or the pictures of objects, and may be called the *Concrete Method.*

1. The Abstract Method.—All objects that can be represented by drawing them are either bounded by straight or curved lines. The simplest of the two kinds of lines is the straight line; and,

hence, many teachers of Drawing commence their instruction with exercises on the straight line. Before the pupils commence their lessons, however, it might be well for the teacher to draw the outlines of several objects bounded by straight lines, upon the blackboard, and have them notice the kind of lines of which they are composed, and the manner in which one line is added to another to build them up. In short, pupils may be led to see by such an analysis, the purpose for which they are required to make lines, and why they should make them correctly. The best way of developing this method of teaching Drawing is by presenting brief descriptions of a series of exercises.

First Class of Exercises.—*Straight Lines.*—These lines may be made of different lengths; they may be made perpendicular, horizontal, or inclined at different angles; they may converge, diverge, or run parallel; or they may be bisected, trisected, or divided into any required number of parts.

Second Class of Exercises.—*Combinations of two Straight Lines.*—These combinations will be better understood by examples than by descriptions:

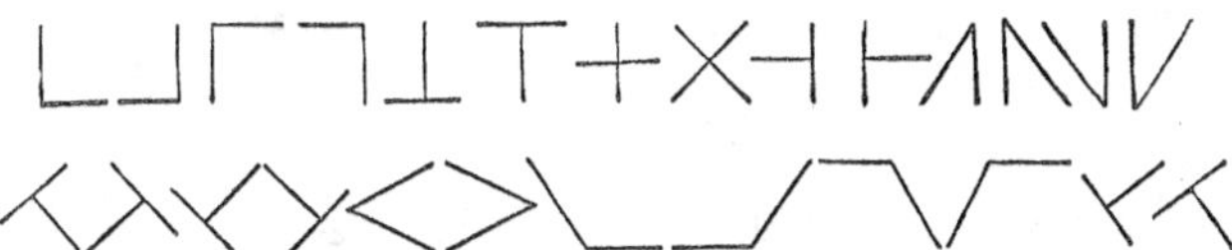

Such examples as these may be duplicated as follows:

THIRD CLASS OF EXERCISES.—*Combinations of three Straight Lines.*—The following figures are examples of this kind of combinations:

FOURTH CLASS OF EXERCISES. — *Combinations of more than three Straight Lines.*—Under this class there may be included all triangles divided by a single straight line, squares, rectangles, rhombs, trapeziums, all kinds of polygons, and an immense number of other figures that can be made to furnish a great variety of lessons.

FIFTH CLASS OF EXERCISES.—*The Imitation of real Objects bounded by Straight Lines.*—This class of exercises is intended to give pupils practice in imitating the pictures of real objects bounded by straight lines. Among the thousands of objects suitable for the purpose, the following may be named as examples: boxes, books, blocks, posts, milestones, stools, tables, stars, crosses, doors, windows, houses, castles, &c.

SIXTH CLASS OF EXERCISES. — *The Invention of Figures bounded by Straight Lines.*—Drawing is not only an imitative but a creative art, and pupils should have practice in inventing figures. The teacher may first exhibit a few original designs upon the blackboard. From this the pupils will understand what is wanted; and if there is not soon an interested class, and eventually some fine work done by it, it will be contrary to my experience. Such problems may be assigned as follows: given three, four, five, or any number of straight lines, to form a design of them; given a figure, a triangle, a square, or a parallelogram, to combine with straight lines; given one figure to combine with another; as triangle with triangle, triangle with square; squares, stars, hexagons, with one another.

SEVENTH CLASS OF EXERCISES.—*Curved Lines.*—A few simple curves may be presented as examples:

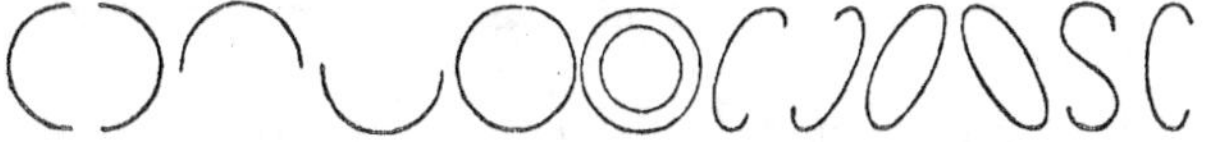

EIGHTH CLASS OF EXERCISES. — *Combinations of Curved and Straight Lines.*—Examples of such combinations may be found in sections of circles, sections of ellipses, cones, cylinders, many of the letters of the Alphabet, and thousands of objects.

NINTH CLASS OF EXERCISES.—*The Invention of Figures bounded by Curved or Curved and Straight Lines.*—This class of exercises opens a wide field for the display of ingenuity and taste.

After sufficient practice has been allowed in the preceding exercises, pupils may receive lessons in Shading and Perspective, but such remarks as I have to make concerning the methods of imparting such lessons will be postponed until something has been said of the second general method of teaching Drawing.

2 THE CONCRETE METHOD.—The concrete is the

most effective form in which knowledge can be communicated to children. We have found that lessons on objects should precede all other kinds of instruction; and it is very natural that children should take most interest in drawing the objects about which they are otherwise learning something. Any teacher can try the experiment for himself, and he will find that while children will be delighted to spend hours every day in trying to draw blocks, posts, houses, cats, or cows, they will soon grow tired of making lines, triangles, or circles. Nature thus indicates that the first lessons in Drawing should be in a concrete form. What if it be said that objects are not as simple as lines, or that it is impossible for a child to draw them correctly, the answer is ready, that in this way they learn everything else. Children do not first learn the *elements* but the *wholes* of things. Let them commence learning to draw as they commence learning other things, and it will be found that what is natural is the most effective. Children will even spend much time in "playing Drawing," if provided with proper materials. It is, doubtless, proper that pupils somewhat advanced should analyze figures, and commence with straight lines; but I am here speaking of instruction to beginners.

As with the Abstract method, the spirit of the Concrete method can be best appreciated from a series of exercises.

FIRST CLASS OF EXERCISES. — *The Pictures of Objects.*—It is more easy, and, I think, more interesting, for children to draw the pictures of objects than the objects themselves. The first lessons should consist of the outlines of the simplest objects, such as boxes, books, posts, gates, doors, houses, &c.; but, although more difficult, no harm can result from suffering children to attempt to draw cats, horses, fowls, dogs, human figures, &c.

SECOND CLASS OF EXERCISES.—*Drawing the Pictures of Objects from Memory.*—In the preceding class of exercises, it is presumed that the pupils have books or cards from which they copy the pictures. This done, it will be found of great advantage to reproduce them from memory. Drawing pictures from memory is more difficult than copying pictures; but its disciplinary advantages are proportionably greater.

THIRD CLASS OF EXERCISES.—*Drawing real Objects.*—Having copied the picture of an object, and reproduced it from memory, the pupil is well prepared to draw the object itself. For this purpose schools should be furnished with sets of model-objects, corresponding to the pictures upon the drawing-cards, or in the drawing-books. In the absence of these, however, the teacher need be at little loss to find things suitable for lessons with the world full of objects about him.

FOURTH CLASS OF EXERCISES.—*Inventive drawing.*—To succeed in the higher departments of Inventive Drawing, requires a highly cultured imagination, and a correct taste; but even children may be taught to draw objects and combinations of objects that are not copies of anything they have ever seen, and even to design the simplest kinds of monuments, gates, pleasure-grounds, landscapes, houses, &c. Indeed, this kind of work is done by children who have been well taught, with intense interest; and nothing can be better calculated to cultivate ingenuity, or give opportunity of growth to the budding imagination.

These four classes of exercises indicate all that is peculiar to this method. The method is particularly adapted to children, and aims only to communicate a popular knowledge of the art of Drawing. Pupils receiving instruction in Drawing up to the point indicated in the preceding exercises, according to this method, can enter upon the analysis of forms and their composition, as contemplated in the Abstract Method, with great profit. Thus here, as everywhere else, principles will be found to underlie appearances. The Concrete Method merely contemplates the imitation of appearances, while the Abstract Method contemplates, in addition, the study of principles. With pupils who are prepared for it, the two methods may be combined.

The time is now come when something must be said of Shading, Shadow, and Perspective.

Pupils will readily appreciate the effect of Shading if the teacher first draw the outline of a simple object, and then shade it. They may then engage in imitating the Shading of pictures, and, finally, practice the Shading of real objects. Much may be done in this way, according to the Concrete Method, to improve the pupil's taste and increase his skill, before he could learn the laws of Optics upon which the distribution of light depends. When the time comes for learning these laws, they must be learned and applied after the spirit of the Abstract Method, by commencing with the simplest and proceeding to the more difficult.

What has been said of Shading applies equally well to Shadow.

Distant objects do not appear to the eye under the same angle as near ones, and as Drawing must be true to nature, objects should be represented as they appear. Hence the necessity of Perspective in Drawing. Some idea of the nature of Perspective can be imparted to learners by calling their attention to the appearance of a long street, bridge, or hall, trees planted on each side of an avenue, or a railroad track. Illustrations of Perspective Drawing should be given by the teacher upon the blackboard. The pupils must be required to imitate a progressive series of models. It is all important to train the eye to judge accurately of Perspective, as it is impossible to take time to apply particularly all the laws of Perspective in drawing an object. Ruskin and other celebrated artists confirm this view. When the pupil is prepared for it, however, he should be made acquainted with these laws, and learn to demonstrate their truth.

It is only necessary to say further in regard to methods of teaching Drawing that, as in writing, they must have reference to the training of the muscles employed as well as to the conception of form. As in writing, too, the pupils should be taught in classes; the blackboard should be in constant use both by the teacher and pupils; good models should be at hand for imitation; convenient tables and seats, and suitable apparatus, should be provided; and great care should be taken in the correction of errors.

III. Vocal Music.

Vocal Music, when rightly considered, is linguistic in its nature, and closely related to Reading. The principal points of resemblance between them are that the words used in Vocal Music, as in Reading, are required to be correctly pronounced, and properly appreciated both in respect to thought and feeling; that while Speech is more the language of the intellect, and Song exclusively the language of the feelings, both are used for the purposes of communication by all races and conditions of men. The affinity of Speech and Song is so close, that they are sometimes combined in a kind of composition called Recitative. The most marked differences between Reading and Singing are that in Reading the common sounds of the voice are used, while in Singing these sounds are modified and receive the name of tones; that "no idea, thought, term, proposition, or meaning, is directly conveyed in Song;" and that Speech has no fixed clef for comparing one note with another, and can, therefore, neither give pleasure by presenting a melodious succession of notes, nor by observing their harmonious relationships.

The Study of Vocal Music is too much neglected, and it will not therefore be amiss to state some of the advantages which may be expected to result from its more general introduction into our schools.

Music gives pleasant employment during leisure hours. There are times of leisure in every family — evenings, Saturday afternoons, Sabbaths, and these seasons can be made to yield more true enjoyment if enlivened with or improved by appropriate Music. He who is fond of Music need never suffer from ennui, for he has a constant source of the purest pleasure within himself. Besides, temptations come to the young, especially to young men, during hours in which they are not employed. It is then that the dull family fireside is deserted for the enjoyments of the tavern, the theatre, the club-room, or the street-corner, vice presents her allurements, the unsuspecting are enticed into her toils, and thousands fall. Home should be made more attractive, and nothing is better calculated to give it charms than Music.

Music increases social pleasures. It has just been said that Music adds attraction to the circle of the family; it is now asserted that this is true with respect to larger circles of friends wherever they may meet. Rude choruses are heard in the rough cabins of wild savages, and grand concerts make echo the walls of great halls in civilized cities. Peasants sing in their cottages on festive occasions, and Music graces the banquets of kings in their palaces. The social party is comparatively dull unless enlivened by the influences of song. "The most joyous of joys is Music."

Music cheers men on in the performance of duty. The mother soothes her sick child with Music; with

Music the laborer lightens his toil; with Music our thoughts are turned heavenward in the house of God, and to the sounds of Music patriot soldiers march to battle. True, Music lends its attractions to the theatre; Music is employed to charm the ear, while the soul is led captive by the allurements of wine, cards, or other forms of wickedness; but this is a monstrous perversion of one of the most beautiful and excellent gifts of God.

Music purifies the taste. The taste is purified by contact with what is beautiful. It cannot be doubted that there is beauty in Music, and hence if the young be made to appreciate it, the rougher parts of their nature would be refined, their wilder passions would be calmed, and their tastes would revolt at what is low and degrading, and long for a universal harmony that would embrace both the world of matter and the world of spirit.

Music promotes good morals. It does this by furnishing employment for leisure hours, by increasing the pleasures of social life, by cheering men on in the performance of duty, and by purifying the taste. In addition to all this, the natural tendency of Music is to enrich and ennoble the whole emotional life. From a love of the beautiful, it is not difficult to attain to a love of the true and the good. There is something very much like Music in loving our neighbors as ourselves. The "Universal Harmony" of Pythagoras was more than the dream of an enthusiast; it was the vision of a philosopher. This position is taken in full view of the fact that vulgar and profane thoughts are sometimes expressed in song, and that vice often makes use of

Music to gild her deformities. But such perversions are not the misfortune of Music alone. The other Fine Arts, speech, the sacred rites of religion itself, have been forced into the service of sin.

Music induces a spirit of devotion. The Bible contains ample evidence that blessed spirits and angels chant their choruses around the throne of God; St. Paul commands the Colossians to teach and admonish one another in psalms, and hymns, and spiritual songs; and during the whole past history of the Church, since the children of Israel sang unto the Lord on the banks of the Red Sea, until the present, Music has been employed for the highest and holiest purposes.

All these uses are general; Music is specially valuable in school, both in relieving the tedium of study and in promoting good order. Its influence upon a school, when well directed, is valuable physically, Æsthetically, socially, morally, and religiously.

Poetry is the beautiful as expressed in rhythmical words. Music is the beautiful as expressed in measured tones. Such words uttered in such tones constitute Vocal Music, or Song.

Apart from the Pronunciation of words and the appreciation of the thought and feeling of discourse, both already treated of, methods of teaching Vocal Music as designed to be discussed here, embrace: first, the *Training of the Vocal Organs;* second, the *Culture of the Musical Taste;* and, third, *Musical Execution.*

1 THE TRAINING OF THE VOCAL ORGANS.—Music

like Reading is a vocal art, and the voice has the same general capabilities in both. Music as a vocal art concerns the Quality, Compass, Movement, and Quantity of the voice. By the Qualities of the voice are meant its tones; but since tones form the bases of Musical composition, their utterance bears the same relation to Vocal Music that the Pronunciation of words does to Reading. Hence the Quality of the voice comes first in order, and vocal training with respect to music may be considered under the following heads:

1st. *The qualities of the voice, or Tones.*
2d. *The height or lowness of tones, or Melody.*
3d. *The length or shortness of tones, or Rhythm.*
4th. *The loudness or softness of tones, or Dynamics.*

Harmony, including both the perception of simultaneous, concordant tones, and a knowledge of the laws which govern them, is purely a product of the intellect, and not of the voice.

Having very little practical knowledge of Vocal Music, it is right to say that what follows is mainly the result of theory, and of observations upon the teaching of others.

Elementary Music books are very full of well-arranged exercises intended to be used in training the voice to sing, and it is not deemed necessary to attempt to give here detailed descriptions of them. My end will be gained if I succeed in announcing some general principles that will be of advantage in guiding the teacher in the use of such books

1. *Teachers of Vocal Music should be careful to secure those Qualities of Voice which enable the Pupil to utter Tones correctly.*—Some persons are naturally endowed with voices which render it easy for them to learn to sing; but there are others who have voices so defective that they can scarcely utter, without training, the simplest tones. If a teacher find among his pupils those who have rough, shrill, harsh, nasal, or weak voices, or voices otherwise incapable of uttering pure tones, he must, by Physiological means, do what he can to correct them, before much progress is possible in learning to sing. Pupils with defective voices must be brought to perceive their defects, good models must be presented to them for imitation, and they must be made to engage in vocal exercises calculated to impart the needed culture. In many cases it may be sufficient to connect practice in uttering simple tones with practice in Pitch, Time, and Force.

2. *Teachers of Vocal Music should exhibit Musical Sounds to their Pupils before requiring them to commit their Names.*—Tones should be uttered by the teacher in all their varieties, high and low, long and short, loud and soft, and the pupils be engaged in distinguishing them as uttered, and in uttering them themselves, before they receive names. Things naturally precede words. A child learns to speak by imitating the sounds he hears; and so a child must hear tones before he can imitate them, or form any idea as to what their names signify. The same gradual progress from the easy to the difficult must be made here as in other studies. The teacher

must first give the simplest tones, require his pupils to imitate them, and learn their names; and then proceed in the same way to dispose of those more difficult.

3. *Teachers of Vocal Music should acquaint their Pupils with Musical Sounds before they require them to learn the Musical Notation.*—Children are often taught the symbols used in musical notation before they have any true conception of the thing signified by them. They are expected to sing by note before they can sing by air. This is as great a mistake as to attempt to teach a child to read before he can speak. The difficulty learners have in reading Music, probably arises to some extent from this fault. It cannot be doubted, however, that musical notation properly used is of great advantage to the learner as it represents to the eye and fixes in the mind the more easily-forgotten conceptions that are formed through the ear.

4. *Teachers of Vocal Music should begin their course of Instruction to Children by teaching them Little Songs and Hymns.*—Vocal Music is no exception to the principle that the concrete is the most effective form in which elementary instruction can be given. No great profit can arise from requiring children to begin a course of systematic instruction in Vocal Music before they are ten years of age. Indeed, if great care is not taken to confine them, even at that age, to such exercises as will not overstrain their vocal organs, much injury may be done them. But a child can begin to learn to sing as soon as he

can talk. From this time on, both parent and teacher must furnish him with opportunity to sing and give all needful help. Up to the age of ten years, therefore, the instruction of a child in Vocal Music should consist in teaching him to sing by air suitable songs and hymns. Our language contains some such musical compositions. The common rhymes of the nursery are better than nothing, though they are susceptible of great improvement. So well convinced am I of the intellectual and moral benefits which might be derived from this form of instruction, that I do not hesitate to say that this age could produce no greater benefactor to the race than he would be who could succeed in placing a collection of songs and hymns, adapted to the capacities and tastes of children, within the reach of every family and primary school in the land.

5. *For Pupils from the age of ten to fourteen, Teachers of Vocal Music should have two independent courses of Instruction: one intended to give practice in Singing, and the other to impart Systematic Vocal Culture.* —If a teacher could find suitable songs corresponding to abstract vocal exercises and in which these exercises could be applied, it would be well to combine the two courses from the beginning; but it is presumed that this is impracticable; and, since neither can be omitted without harm, instruction in both may proceed independently. By two independent courses of instruction, it is not meant that the singing and the vocal training should have no relation to each other; but the design is to allow the teacher to select a number of songs to be sung,

and a series of vocal exercises to be practiced, without necessarily adapting the former to the latter. Both kinds of instruction may be combined in the same recitation.

From the age of fourteen, pupils may be taught to apply the disciplinary vocal exercises in songs. At this age, both kinds of exercises can be made mutually illustrative. A song can be sung, and the pupils can be required to write the music; or they can be asked to find words suited to music already written.

6. *Teachers of Vocal Music should be careful to adapt their Musical Exercises to the Vocal Powers of their Pupils.* — It is a well-known Physiological law that the human muscles are weakened by either too much or too little exercise. This law must be observed in training the vocal organs. It is equally well known that muscular strength can be imparted only by the patient application of a well-graded, progressive series of exercises. Children's voices, too, are more limited in Pitch and Force than are those of older persons, and any vocal training conducted without regard to this fact will be hurtful.

7. *Teachers of Vocal Music should make their instruction very exact and thorough.*—Exactness and thoroughness should be a characteristic of all teaching; but there is a special reason for it in a study like Music. The misstatement of a fact or the misunderstanding of a principle can be readily corrected; but pupils whose taste is vitiated by listening to unmusical sounds or whose vocal organs are habituated to the

utterance of them, can scarcely be expected to overcome faults thus produced. The very essence of Music is order among sounds; and lessons in Music should be so well adapted to the capacity of pupils, so carefully graded, and so thoroughly taught that pupils may have constantly before them an ideal, approximating as nearly as possible to perfection.

Vocal exercises are made more effective if an instrument be played in connection with them as an accompaniment. The instrument guides the voice. Practice in composing musical exercises is very advantageous. Pupils can commence the composition of simple pieces very early in their course, and such instruction should be continued as a necessary part of musical instruction. Each pupil in a Vocal Music class should be taught to sing by himself as well as in concert with others. There is no better reason why pupils should be relieved from personal responsibility in reciting a lesson in Vocal Music than in reciting a lesson in any other study.

2. The Culture of Musical Taste.—By musical taste is meant the power by which we perceive and appreciate what is beautiful in tone. It is the mental part of Music, and includes both an intellectual and an emotional element. A person may possess a voice capable of uttering tones in all the varieties of Pitch, Time, and Force, and yet be a very unskilful musician. The voice is merely an instrument used to express in tones, the thought and sentiment which have their birth in the soul. Skill in Vocal Music requires not only the perception and

appreciation of the beautiful as expressed in tones, but also as expressed in words.

The teacher of Vocal Music must give culture to the musical taste. Every individual has likes and dislikes, meets with some objects which are agreeable and with others which are disagreeable, notices what he conceives to be beauties and deformities. The power of discriminating between what pleases and what displeases is taste — a power universally possessed by men. Taste differs among individuals and among nations. Rude, ignorant people have very different tastes from those who are refined and educated. The laws of taste are the generalizations of what has been found agreeable to such persons as by nature and by education are most competent to form correct judgments. The idea of the beautiful is a projection from within, and not an induction from without. Upon occasions given, we express our likes and dislikes; and these, when expressed by the best critics, constitute the laws of taste.

The teacher will find his pupils in possession of some degree of taste; our query is how to purify and elevate it?

Taste in all the Fine Arts is improved by furnishing fit occasions for its exercise. In abstract Vocal Music, these occasions may be found at every step of the pupil's progress. All true Music is beautiful, from the simple chord to that complicated contrasting and blending of tones which characterizes the compositions of the masters of the art. In concrete Vocal Music, these occasions may be found in the songs they sing. These should be rich in beautiful and noble sentiments. Children should sing of home, of country, of truth, of liberty, of love, of Heaven, of God. The songs of a people have much to do with their character. I can think of no better way of filling the heart of a child with high and noble aspirations than by teaching him to sing beautiful songs and hymns.

It must be remembered, however, that all Music, whether abstract or concrete, must be adapted to the capacities of the pupils for whom it is intended, or they can see no beauty in it. Music has its simple, surface beauties, and those which are complex and hidden — beauties which delight the unthinking fancy, and beauties which only the highly-cultured imagination, inspired by genius, can appreciate. Between the tune whistled by the peasant boy to cheer his toil while he works in the fields, or sung by his sister as she watches for his return to the cottage, and the divine inspirations of a Beethoven or a Mozart, the difference is almost infinite. Let the teacher first open the way for the little stream of love for the beautiful to come up from the infantile heart, and then lead it gently on until it become a rivulet, and, at last, swell into a river as it gushes forth from the bosom of manhood.

3. Musical Execution. — Given, a well-cultured voice and good musical taste, and pupils are prepared to compose, arrange, or perform musical compositions.

Musical execution, with respect to Vocal Music, consists in Composing Music, in adapting tunes and words to each other, and in singing.

Composing Music is a work of high art. All the

varied feelings that agitate the human bosom admit expression in tones. It is thus that Music is the universal language of the heart. Here can be applied all the laws that give beauty to Melody, Rhythm, Dynamics, and Harmony — the laws that govern the relation of sentiment, and its expression in tones.

To adapt tunes to words requires a nice appreciation both of Poetry and Music. In all serious Music, there must be a correspondence between the sentiment embodied in the words, and the sentiment expressed in the Music. In comic songs alone can unexpected contrasts be appropriately introduced; and, then, they must be subjected to the rules that elsewhere control the expression of the witty and the humorous. To observe these correspondences and create these contrasts, requires good taste and great skill.

Singing is the utterance of sentiment in tones. Prepared, in respect to voice and taste, ready with tunes composed, notated, and adapted to words, students of Music can enjoy themselves in song, for this is the fruition of their and their teacher's labors.

IV. The Arts in General.

The Arts in the sense now contemplated embrace the whole product of man's regulated activity. The Sciences are what he knows, the Arts are what he does. Some authors have limited the meaning of Art to that which is produced without physical or social restraint — which springs from spontaneous impulses; but here it is convenient to consider as works of Art all that men do, whether they do it from necessity and duty, or with the design of realizing in a concrete form the ideals of their Reason.

Art both precedes and follows Science in the order of time. Says Whewell, "In all cases the arts are prior to the related sciences. Art is the parent and not the progeny of science." And McCosh, "Art has in general preceded science. There were bleaching, and dyeing, and tanning, and artificers in copper and iron, before there was chemistry to explain the process used. Men made wine before there was any theory of fermentation; and glass and porcelain were manufactured before the nature of alkalies and earths had been determined." The same writer states numerous other facts to the same effect.

On the other hand, Mill maintains that "Art necessarily presupposes knowledge; art, in any but its infant state presupposes scientific knowledge." James Harris states more positively that "If there were no theorems of science to guide the operations of art, there would be no art; but if there were no operations of art, there might still be theorems of science. Therefore science is prior to art."

Both of these views are correct. Art in its infancy precedes Science properly so called. Driven by necessity primitive men made rude efforts to provide themselves with food, clothing, shelter, and other conveniences before they began to philosophize. True they acted in conformity with principles capable of being expressed in a scientific form, but of these they were wholly unconscious. As society advanced towards civilization, and the

Sciences began to be formed, their principles were used as a guide to Art, and finally many Arts grew out of the related Sciences, and could not exist without them. Art is therefore older than Science as a matter of fact and younger as a matter of logic. In all enlightened communities Art and Science advance together, giving each other mutual aid Mill in referring to their reciprocal influence remarks, "The relation in which rules of art stand to doctrines of science may be thus characterized: The art proposes to itself an end to be attained, defines the end, and hands it over to the science. The science receives it, considers it as a phenomenon or effect to be studied, and having investigated its causes and conditions, sends it back to Art with a theorem of the combinations of circumstances by which it could be produced. Art then examines these combinations and circumstances, and according as any of them are or are not in human power, pronounces the end attainable or not."

From what has been stated it is obvious that all the Sciences may have their related Arts. There are Arts connected with each of the great classes of knowledge as we have formed them — Arts connected with Language, the Formal Sciences, the Empirical Sciences, the Rational Sciences, and the Historical Sciences. Methods of teaching some of these have been referred to under the head of Applications of the different Sciences. Of others no notice need be taken here; and what remains to be said of all in general must be presented in a brief space.

The Arts may be divided into two great classes, which may be called respectively, the *Empirical Arts*, and the *Rational Arts*. An Empirical Art is the accomplishment of an end of utility. Such an end is always found without oneself, and is a labor. A Rational Art is the realization of an ideal of perfection. Such an end is always found within oneself, and is a delight. The first class of Arts is dependent upon the faculties of the Sense and the Understanding, while the second class is based upon the intuitions of the Reason. The Empirical Arts are sometimes called the Useful Arts, and the Rational Arts, the Fine or Liberal Arts; but the terms here applied to them are deemed preferable.

1. INSTRUCTION IN THE EMPIRICAL ARTS.

The Empirical Arts include all Arts that relate to the practical affairs of life as Agriculture, Manufactures, Commerce, Mining, &c. They are the Arts by which we obtain food, clothing, houses to live in, facilities for travelling, and all the ordinary comforts of society. They constitute what is called business.

In discussing the methods of teaching the Empirical Arts, it will be convenient as well as logical to speak: 1, of their *End*, or the purpose to be attained; 2, of their *Means*, or the agencies to be employed; 3, of their *Execution*, or the manner of doing the work.

1. THEIR END.—The end of all the Empirical Arts is some physical or moral good—a utility. The farmer proposes to produce food; the mechanic, to

construct houses, bridges, mills, machinery; the merchant to collect together and expose for sale various commodities which conduce to the comfort of life; the physician, to cure the sick; the judge, to secure the ends of justice—all of which are utilities, and come within the province of the Arts now under consideration.

The Empirical Arts, grow out of our necessities. Man must earn his bread by the sweat of his brow. He must labor or suffer from hunger, the elements, or the attacks of wild animals. He must conquer nature or be crushed out of existence. Among uncivilized tribes, wants are comparatively few and easily supplied, and consequently the Arts are simple; but in highly enlightened communities wants become very numerous and complex, and the result is a growth of multitudes of Arts. All of them, however, whatever may be the stage of civilization in which they are produced, are prompted by wants real or supposed. If the history of every Empirical Art, of which we know anything, could be written, it would be found to have arisen from a pressure of circumstances. Facts appertaining to the Arts may have been observed by accident, but these facts were always pressed by necessity into the service of the Arts.

Nor is it unworthy of a man to labor—to engage in any business that will promote his own welfare or that of his fellow men. Our farms, and shops, and mills, and stores, and offices, have their place in the social economy. They provide for the interests of self, and the interests of society. The great world-traffic must go on. But it ought to be said that in this country the so-called practical absorbs over much attention. Money-making is the besetting sin of the age. Mammon is served rather than God. The public cry is, "down with theories," "give us the practical, in business, in books, in teaching, in preaching." We worship banks, railroads, coal-mines, steamships, printing presses, and Parrott cannon. These may all tend to personal comfort and national greatness; but life has higher ends. The Bible asks: "Is not the life more than meat, and the body than raiment?" Education is compelled to lower its standard to meet the pressing demand for the practical. The branches of study most popular are those which seem best calculated to make successful business men. Agricultural Schools, Mechanics' Institutes and Polytechnic Colleges are founded and flourish. Every city boasts of its Mercantile College with hundreds of students whose highest ambition it seems to be to fit themselves for calculating cargoes of dry-goods or for balancing the two sides of a ledger. To the practical, in its proper place, no objection can be made, but that place is a subordinate one in a liberal scheme of education. God never intended this beautiful world to be converted into a great shop for hucksters, or that His temple should be profaned as of old by such as would make our "Father's house a house of merchandise." It is melancholy to reflect that there are educational theorists who estimate as of greatest worth that knowledge which is only capable of administering to the material interests of life, and undervalue that which is calculated to subserve the higher interests of man — which ennobles him here and fits him for the world to come. In the words of Carlyle, "An irreverent knowledge is no knowledge; may be a development of the logical or other handicraft faculty inward or outward, but is no culture of the soul of man."

The Empirical Arts have ends more or less noble, and the first step a student must take in acquiring such an Art is to obtain a definite idea of its end. Confusion here will vitiate the whole process, because appropriate means of accomplishing an end can only be selected and fitly applied when the end itself is clearly known. Most of the Empirical Arts are practiced blindly, it is for the true teacher of such Arts to substitute science for guess-work.

2. THEIR MEANS.—With its end plain before him the student of an Empirical Art will next need to seek the means of attaining it.

Man is a maker by instinct. As the bee and the beaver build, so does he. In his primitive condition, he feels certain wants and tries to supply them by an unconscious power of adapting means to ends.

Somewhat further advanced in civilization, he is ready to take advantage of what others have done by using his powers of imitation. He may imitate nature, or he may imitate the works of other men. His first imitations are those of natural objects, and these in turn are imitated. The largest number of persons who now practice the Empirical Arts are still imitators. Such persons are found among farmers, mechanics, merchants, and professional men.

They simply do what they see others do, but make little attempt to comprehend the principles which ought to guide all the operations of Art. They may accomplish the end aimed at, but they do it mechanically.

The Empirical Arts are all based on scientific principles, and these principles furnish the means by which their ends may be surely attained. The farmer proposes to increase the fertility of his soil, Chemistry points to the means; the engineer proposes to locate a railroad or navigate a ship, Mathematics aids him in the work; the physician proposes to amputate a diseased limb, Anatomy must guide the operation; and so throughout the long category. Farmers may fertilize their fields as they see others do it, engineers may construct railroads and navigate ships by rules which they do not understand, physicians may amputate diseased limbs by guess; but this would be false Art, quackery, and, when the interests of others are concerned, criminal quackery. What Blackstone says of one preparing for the practice of the legal profession, is true of one preparing for practice of any kind. "If practice be the whole he is taught, practice must also be the whole he will ever know; if he be uninstructed in the elements and first principles upon which the rule of practice is founded, the least variation from established precedents will totally distract and bewilder him."

Each particular Art has for a basis a body of rules or principles derived from science. They sometimes come from one science and sometimes from several sciences. Surveying is an Art with a simple basis of Mathematics. Teaching is an Art with a complex basis, composed of principles derived from all the sciences relating both to matter and mind. Without a knowledge of the principles underlying an Art, the Art itself cannot be understood. Some skill, it is granted, may be attained by an instinctive adaptation of means to ends, and by imitation, but such skill is mechanical, not artistic.

If what is above said is true, the teacher of Art must borrow from science the means of instruction in the Arts; and as methods of teaching the several sciences have been discussed, nothing further concerning them in this connection is needed.

3. Their Mode of Execution.—Facts show that there is a natural difference among men in their ability to do particular kinds of work. All men would not make equally good mechanics, equally enterprising merchants, equally skilful physicians. For each man there is an appropriate sphere—something he can do better than anything else, if not better than anybody else. Of these differences education must take account.

Ingenuity in making things can be cultivated in childhood. Blocks can be used in building little houses, towers, bridges, &c. Very beautiful models of objects can be made of terra cotta. A great variety of things can be cut from pasteboard and paper. Suitable tools with suitable material to work upon may be given to children.

Imitation is a faculty largely used in executing

all works of Art. Exclusive dependance ought not to be placed upon it, but, working side by side with the understanding, it is a valuable auxiliary in attaining success in Art. The child should have models in learning to draw, write, or sing, and so in all other Arts. The best model, however, is a skilful workman. Pupils who see work well done will be apt to do it well; but if the teacher be a bungler, his pupils will not be likely to excel him.

The maxim, "Practice makes perfect," was designed to apply to the execution of works of Art. There may be a well-defined end before the mind's eye, the scientific principles involved in the accomplishment of it may be understood, his powers of imitation may be active, and still, unless a pupil enjoy ample opportunity of practice, he will most likely be wanting in skill. Skill in Art is attained by a training rather than a teaching process. Pupils in our schools are probably not allowed to *do* enough. Sufficient practice is denied them. The argument seems strong in favor of combining work and study. Knowledge applied will be remembered. It is by *doing* that character is formed. Life makes the man, not study.

2. Instruction in the Rational Arts.

The Rational Arts are the free productions of our ideals of perfection. A generalization of these ideals of perfection gives us the *True*, the *Beautiful*, and the *Good;* and the Rational Arts admit, doubtless, a corresponding three-fold division. He who construct, a system of Philosophy or of Ethics for the purpose of realizing his ideas of truth or goodness, is not less an Artist than one who bodies forth his ideas of beauty on canvas, or in marble. Either may work for an end of utility, but in that case the production belongs to the Empirical, and not to the Rational Arts.

In what is to be said, here, however, we shall mainly keep before our mind's eye the Arts which are expressions of the beautiful, usually called Fine Arts — Gardening, Architecture, Sculpture, Painting, Music, and Poetry; not forgetting that everything may be made, in the language of another, "The basis of an exquisite Art, for Art being universal disdains no field of ministration however humble, but avouches its redeeming virtue most in descending to what is lowly, and exalting that which is despised. It sheds a divine splendor over the meanest things, and glorifies the infinite riches of its resources in the exact ratio of the intrinsic poverty of its materials."

What we have to say concerning methods of teaching the Rational Arts may be said under heads similar to those adopted in treating of the Empirical Arts: 1, *End;* 2, *Means;* 3, *Execution.*

1. Their End. — The end of the Rational Arts is the expression of ideals of perfection in concrete forms — is the production of *things* of beauty.

To those who use only the senses which acquaint them with material objects, to those who so mix up in the world's affairs that their hearts become dead to all that is beautiful, an end that cannot be measured by some practical standard is counted as of little worth. But as we rise above mere animal wants and are freed from their pressure, our higher nature begins to seek expression in forms that fitly embody its ideals of perfection. It is thus Angels act. It is thus God creates. The soul has interests as well as the body, and the educator ought not to overlook them.

No one can be an Artist who has not born within him an ideal of beauty. It is this ideal which he paints on canvas, chisels out of marble, expresses in tones, or writes in measured words. It is his model. It is his light. It is what he struggles to body forth. Every work of Art is a new birth. Nothing can emanate from emptiness. Up from the depths of the soul comes this image, and we fitly call its coming inspiration, and can say no more.

2. Their Means. — We seek now the means of expressing the ideals of perfection born in the soul.

There must be a suitable body. It may be form, color, tone, word, but there can be no Art without a body. Without it, the image might exist in the mind, but it could not be expressed. Nor is the relation between the ideal and the body used to express it a matter of indifference. An Artist may exhibit exquisite taste in the selection of his forms, his colors, his tones, his words.

There must be appropriate accessories. The central thought of a master of Art cannot be penetrated at a glance. It is a study, and can only be approached by steps. There must be an adjustment of surrounding details each co-operating to heighten the general effect, or to make more impressive the main design.

There must be a knowledge of scientific principles. An Artist cannot dispense with certain principles of the Rational Sciences, for from this source he must draw all his knowledge concerning the pure ideas under whose inspiration he works and the criteria by which he judges in matters of taste. All the rules of Art and canons of criticism are the deductions of Rational Science. Artists are aided, too, by a knowledge of the Empirical Sciences. The Architect needs to know the strength of materials and the laws of mechanics; the Sculptor should understand Anatomy; the Painter, the properties of pigments and the effects of light and shade; and the Musician the laws of Harmony.

There must be genius. Rules of Art do not make Artists. By long practice, men can become mechanics, imitators; but Art requires originality, invention, the poet's fire, genius.

3. THEIR MODE OF EXECUTION.—Young Artists usually seek the studio or the shop of some famous master of the Art they wish to acquire, that they may study his style and imitate his models. For the same purpose they visit collections of pictures, galleries of statues, concerts and rehearsals, and study poems and compositions. This is all very well, but it can never supply the want of genius or of acquaintance with the works of nature. Per-

haps, something has been lost to Art by the practice of imitating the style of the masters. All men can work in themselves better than out of themselves. No Artist can execute like another. All attempts to do it will prove failures. Each must be himself or nothing. A work of Art is a growth, the vital force of which exists in the Artist's mind, and extraneous influences may nourish but must not constrain it.

It is earnestly maintained by some that all Art is an imitation of nature—that it is by the study of nature alone that the true Artist can find instruction. Ruskin gives the following advice to young Artists: "They should go to nature in all singleness of heart, and walk with her laboriously and trustingly, having no other thought but how best to penetrate her meaning; rejecting nothing, selecting nothing, and scorning nothing." Doubtless all the elements of beauty are found expressed in the works of nature, and the first part of Ruskin's sentiment is worthy of acceptation, that young Artists "should go to nature in all singleness of heart, and walk with her laboriously and trustingly." But Art is not simply an imitation of nature. The grapes painted by Zeuxis that the birds came and pecked at, were a work of high Art, but there is a higher. The Artist has an ideal of beauty in his own mind, the presence of beautiful objects is necessary for its manifestation, but when manifested it becomes a criterion by which nature herself can be criticised. The capacity of conceiving the beautiful exists in every mind; it needs only that a spark from the outer world should light it up, and all things become illuminated in its blaze. Cousin quotes Plato as follows: "The artist, who, with eye fixed upon the immutable being, and using such a model, reproduces its idea and its excellence, cannot fail to produce a whole whose beauty is complete, whilst he who fixes his eye upon what is transitory, with this perishable model will make nothing beautiful." And Cicero, to the same effect: "Phidias, that great artist, when he made the form of Jupiter or Minerva, did not contemplate a model a resemblance of which he would express; but in the depth of his soul resided a perfect type of beauty, upon which he fixed his look, which guided his hand and his art." God gave man Reason; and the word of the Reason becomes the flesh of Art, the latter only finds its nourishment on earth, the former looks to Heaven for its inspiration.

Success in Art is not likely to be reached without much practice in efforts to express the ideal. A divine image may struggle for utterance in the soul, nature may be full of forms, colors, sounds, motions, symbols suited as a body to its expression, but to free the one by finding the other generally requires practice and patience. The Sculptor may see his ideal in the rough block of marble before him, but how many the trials, how great the toil, before the breath of beauty is breathed into the dead stone. The Painter may see his ideal on the dull canvas, but tired hand and aching head are his before that canvas will speak like a voice from Heaven to listening worshippers. Fairer ideals dance before the

Poet's imagination than he has ever been able to clothe in the drapery of words, and richer symphonies swell in the ear of the Musician than were ever sung save upon the harps of angels. From this cause, a true Artist is seldom satisfied with his productions. He feels capable of more than he has accomplished. More perfect ideals dazzle him with their beauty, and seem to challenge his powers of expression. Fired with poetic frenzy, he works and works on, with chisel, with pencil, with pen, but to find repeated, at the end of every struggle, the same longing to touch that higher beauty which still lies beyond his reach.

It may be in place to say here, that all true Art is pure and truthful. Out of the idea of the beautiful nothing unchaste or false could come, for otherwise the child would destroy the parent. All the Arts have been turned to base uses, as sin dragged down the angels from Heaven, but their mission is to promote virtue among men. From a love of the beautiful to a love of the good there is but a single step.

In the highest sense, Art is universal in its end. It aims to dignify all that is low, to beautify all that is deformed, to make all labor a delight, to lift up the world from sin and ignorance to holiness and light. Says Ruskin: "Remember that it is not so much in *buying* pictures, as in *being* pictures that you encourage a noble school. The best patronage of art is not that which seeks for the pleasures of sentiment in a vague ideality, nor for beauty of form in a marble image; but that which educates your children into living heroes, and binds down the flights and fondness of the heart into practical duty and faithful devotion."

The highest of all Arts is the Art of living well. Beyond the beauty of Sculpture, or Painting, or Music, or Poetry, is the beauty of a *well-spent life.* Here all can be Artists. Every man can be a hero. Obedience to the command, "Be ye perfect even as your Father in Heaven is perfect," would ally man to God, and make earth a Paradise.

VALUABLE EDUCATIONAL WORKS
FOR
SCHOOLS, ACADEMIES, AND COLLEGES.

Selected from Messrs. J. B. LIPPINCOTT & Co.'s Catalogue, which comprises nearly Two Thousand Works in all branches of Literature. Catalogues furnished on application. *Liberal terms will be made for Introduction.*

Haldeman's Outlines of Etymology. By S. S. Haldeman, A.M., author of "Analytical Orthography," "Elements of Latin Pronunciation," etc. 12mo. Fine cloth. 90 cents.

"This is a most scholarly presentation of the science of etymology, . . . to which is added an appendix of inestimable value to the student of language. . . . It is a marvel of conciseness."—*New England Journal of Education*, July 5, 1877.

"There is, probably, no man living who has studied and analyzed the English language so thoroughly and so successfully as this distinguished savant of Pennsylvania, and this little treatise is the latest fruit of his ripe scholarship and patient research. No newspaper notice can do justice to the work, for it cannot be described, and must be studied to be appreciated."—*Philadelphia Evening Bulletin.*

Walker's Science of Wealth. A Manual of Political Economy, embracing the Laws of Trade, Currency, and Finance. Condensed and Arranged expressly for Use as a Text-book. By AMASA WALKER, LL.D., *late Lecturer on Public Economy, Amherst College.* Student's edition. 12mo. Extra cloth. $1.50.

"I have, during the past year, made use of Dr. A. Walker's 'Science of Wealth' in the new and condensed form he has given it, in giving instruction to the senior class in Political Economy, and have found the book better adapted than any other with which I am acquainted for use in a college class-room. It is clear, compact, and ample in its illustrations."—PROF. JULES H. SEELYE, *Amherst College, Massachusetts.*

"It is, in my opinion, the best work on this subject."—W. T. HARRIS, *Superintendent of Schools, St. Louis, Missouri.*

Berkeley's Principles of Human Knowledge. A Treatise concerning the Principles of Human Knowledge. By GEORGE BERKELEY, D.D., *formerly Bishop of Cloyne.* With Prolegomena, and with Illustrations and Annotations, Select, Translated, and Original. By CHARLES P. KRAUTH, D.D., *Norton Professor of Systematic Theology and Church Polity in the Evangelical Lutheran Theological Seminary; Professor of Intellectual and Moral Philosophy, and Vice-Provost of the University of Pennsylvania.* 8vo. Extra cloth. $3.00.

Prof. A. C. Fraser, of the University of Edinburgh, says of "Berkeley's Principles:" "It would be difficult to name a book in ancient or modern philosophy which contains more fervid and ingenious reasoning than is here employed to meet supposed objections, or to unfold possible applications to religion and science."

Atwater's Elementary Logic. Designed Especially for the Use of Teachers and Learners. By L. H. ATWATER, *Professor of Mental and Moral Philosophy in the College of New Jersey.* 12mo. Cloth. $1.25.

"This manual shows the hand of a master, and will speedily take its proper place as a valuable contribution to the cause of liberal education."—*Congregational Quarterly.*

"I observe in Atwater's excellent Manual of Elementary Logic a disposition to unite the real improvements of the analytic with the established truths of the old logic."—DR. JAMES MCCOSH, *late Professor of Logic in Queen's College, Belfast, Ireland.*

Dr. Blair's Lectures on Rhetoric. Abridged, with Questions. 60 cents.

The want of a system of Rhetoric upon a concise plan has rendered this little volume acceptable to the teaching and reading public. Many who are terrified at the idea of travelling over a ponderous volume in search of information, will yet set out on a short journey in pursuit of science with alacrity and profit.

Samson's Art Criticism. Comprising a Treatise on the Principles of Man's Nature as Addressed by Art; together with a Historic Survey of the Methods of Art Execution in the Departments of Drawing, Sculpture, Architecture, Painting, Landscape Gardening, and the Decorative Arts. Designed as a Text-Book for Schools and Colleges, and as a Hand-Book for Amateurs and Artists. By G. W. SAMSON, *President of Columbia College.* 8vo. Cloth. $3.15. ABRIDGED EDITION. 12mo. Cloth. $1.60.

"Art criticism, boiled down into small doses for amateurs and students, is the function of Dr. G. W. Samson, President of Columbia College, Washington."—*Philadelphia Bulletin.*

"This work should be in the possession of every lover of the beautiful, and the abridgment deserves to be introduced into all our high schools, and made a part of common education."—*North American.*

Malcom's Butler's Analogy. The Analogy of Religion to the Constitution and Course of Nature. To which are added Two Brief Dissertations. I. On Personal Identity. II. On the Nature of Virtue. By JOSEPH BUTLER, D.C.L. With Introduction, Notes, Conspectus, and ample Index. Prepared by HOWARD MALCOM, D.D., LL.D., *President of the University at Lewisburg.* 12mo. Extra cloth. $1.15.

"We fully justify the editor's reasons for offering another edition of Butler, viz., that he had found none satisfactory as a text-book. . . . His Introduction is valuable, but his admirable Conspectus, of nearly fifty pages of fine type, gives a key to the work which will make the study of Butler a new kind of business. We have been surprised and delighted with this new aid afforded by President Malcom. In our opinion this edition will be the text-book used by all intelligent instructors who once give it an examination. Persons who have been repelled from studying Butler by the difficulties both of the argument and the style, will find these difficulties chiefly disappear by the facilities Dr. M. has afforded."—*Southern Baptist.*

Studies in the English of Bunyan. By Prof. J. B. GRIER. 12mo. Cloth. $1.25.

SANFORD'S SERIES OF ARITHMETICS.

SANFORD'S ANALYTICAL SERIES.

COMPRISED IN FOUR BOOKS.

The Science of Numbers reduced to its last analysis. Mental and Written Arithmetic successfully combined in each Book of the Series.

By SHELTON P. SANFORD, A.M.,
Professor of Mathematics in Mercer University, Georgia.

FIRST BOOK.

Sanford's First Lessons in Analytical Arithmetic. Comprising Mental and Written Exercises. Handsomely and appropriately Illustrated. 16mo. Half roan. 27 cents.

SECOND BOOK.

Sanford's Intermediate Analytical Arithmetic. Comprising Mental and Written Exercises. 16mo. 232 pp. Half roan. 45 cents.

THIRD BOOK.

Sanford's Common School Analytical Arithmetic. 12mo. 355 pp. Half roan. 80 cents.

FOURTH BOOK.

Sanford's Higher Analytical Arithmetic; or, THE METHOD of making ARITHMETICAL CALCULATIONS on PRINCIPLES of UNIVERSAL APPLICATION, without the AID of FORMAL RULES. 12mo. 419 pp. Half roan. Cloth sides. $1.25.

From Prof. HUGH S. THOMPSON, *Principal Columbia Male Academy, Columbia, S. C.*

"Sanford's Arithmetics are superior to any that I have seen in the fulness of the examples, the clearness and simplicity of the analyses, and the accuracy of the rules and definitions. This opinion is based upon a *full* and *thorough test* in the school-room. To those teachers who may examine these Arithmetics with reference to introduction, I would especially commend the treatment of Percentage and Profit and Loss. No text-books that I have ever used are so satisfactory to teachers and pupils."

From Capt. S. Y. CALDWELL, *Supt. of Nashville (Tenn.) Public Schools.*

"Your Intermediate and Advanced Analytical Arithmetics are among the best I have examined.

"It is contrary to my practice to write testimonials or recommendations, but the high merit of your book certainly justifies it in this instance."

From Prof. B. MALLON, *Superintendent of Atlanta (Ga.) Public Schools.*

"I think they [Sanford's Arithmetics] are the best books on the subject ever published; and I trust it will not be long before they will be introduced into every school in our State. In my judgment they are the very perfection of school-books on Arithmetic."

CUTTER'S SERIES

ON

Analytical Anatomy, Physiology, and Hygiene,

HUMAN AND COMPARATIVE,

FOR SCHOOLS AND FAMILIES.

By CALVIN CUTTER, A.M., M.D.

During the past ten years more than two hundred thousand (200,000) have been sold for schools. This is the only series of works upon the subject that is graded for all classes of pupils, from the primary school to the college, the only one that embraces Anatomy, Physiology, and Hygiene for schools, and the only one arranged so as to be used advantageously with illustrating Anatomical Charts.

NEW SERIES.

First Book on Analytic Anatomy, Physiology, and Hygiene, Human and Comparative. 196 pp. With 164 Illustrations. 12mo. 80 cents.

Second Book on Analytic Anatomy, Physiology, and Hygiene, Human and Comparative. With QUESTIONS, DIAGRAMS, AND ILLUSTRATIONS for Analytic Study and Unific Topical Review. 309 pp. With 186 Illustrations. 12mo. $1.35.

New Analytic Anatomy, Physiology, and Hygiene, Human and Comparative. With QUESTIONS, DIAGRAMS, AND ILLUSTRATIONS for Analytic Study and Synthetic Review. 388 pp. With 230 Illustrations. 12mo. $1.50.

OLD SERIES.

First Book on Anatomy, Physiology, and Hygiene. Illustrated. 12mo. 70 cents.

Anatomy, Physiology, and Hygiene. Illustrated. 12mo. $1.50.

Human and Comparative Anatomy, Physiology, and Hygiene. By Mrs. E. P. CUTTER. Illustrated. 12mo. 45 cents.

NEW OUTLINE ZOOLOGICAL CHARTS,

Or Human and Comparative Anatomical Plates. Mounted. (Including Rollers, etc.) Nine in number. Three feet long by two feet wide. $15.00. Half set. Five in number. $9.00.

CLASSICAL WORKS OF REFERENCE.

GARDNER'S LATIN LEXICON.

A Dictionary of the Latin Language, particularly adapted to the Classics usually studied preparatory to a Collegiate Course. By FRANCIS GARDNER, A.M. 8vo. Sheep. $3.00.

LEVERETT'S LATIN LEXICON.

A Copious Lexicon of the Latin Language. Compiled chiefly from the Magnum Totius Latinitatis Lexicon of Facciolati and Forcellini, and the German Works of Scheller and Luenemann, embracing the Classical Distinctions of Words, and the Etymological Index of Freund's Lexicon. By F. P. LEVERETT. Large 8vo. Sheep. $5.50.*

This work contains all the words in the Latin language, embracing those used by authors of the classical, ante-classical, and post-classical periods, with words of modern origin coined for scientific and other purposes.

LEMPRIERE'S CLASSICAL DICTIONARY.

Containing a full account of all the Proper Names mentioned in ancient authors, with Tables of Coins, Weights, and Measures in use among the Greeks and Romans; to which is prefixed a Chronological Table. 8vo. Sheep. $3.25.* ABRIDGED EDITION. 12mo. Extra cloth. $1.50.

The original text of Lempriere has in this edition been carefully revised and amended, and much valuable original matter added. The work is now a complete Bibliotheca Classica, containing in a condensed and readily accessible form all the information required by the student upon the geography, topography, history, literature, and mythology of antiquity and of the ancients, with bibliographical references for such as wish to get fuller information on the subjects treated of.

GROVES'S GREEK DICTIONARY.

A Greek and English Dictionary, comprising all the Words in the writings of the most popular Greek authors, with the difficult inflections in them, and in the Septuagint and New Testament. Designed for the Use of Schools and the Under-Graduate Course of a Collegiate Education. By JOHN GROVES. With corrections and additional matter by the American editor. 8vo. Sheep. $2.25.*

The object of the compiler has been to produce a work which young Greek scholars could use with ease and advantage to themselves, but sufficiently full to be equally serviceable as they advanced.

PICKERING'S GREEK LEXICON.

A Comprehensive Lexicon of the Greek Language, adapted to the Use of Colleges and Schools of the United States. By JOHN PICKERING, LL.D. New Edition, revised and corrected. Large 8vo. Sheep. $5.50.*

This work contains all the words in the Greek language, with their correct interpretation into English, and their different shades of meaning carefully distinguished and illustrated by citations from standard authors.

CHAUVENET'S
SERIES OF MATHEMATICS.

CHAUVENET'S GEOMETRY.

A Treatise on Elementary Geometry, with Appendices containing a copious Collection of Exercises for the Student and an Introduction to Modern Geometry. By WM. CHAUVENET, *Professor of Mathematics and Astronomy in Washington University, St. Louis.* Crown 8vo. Cloth. $1.75.

"I am glad to see at last an American text-book on this subject which is not from seventy-five to two thousand years behind the time, and which, without casting away what is good in the old, does not totally exclude the brilliant geometrical discoveries of the present century. I shall recommend its adoption as a text-book in this University."—PROF. J. W. SAFFORD, *Director of the Dearborn Observatory, Chicago, Ill.*

"At a late meeting of the Board of Public Schools in this city, Chauvenet's Elementary Geometry was adopted as a regular text-book in our High School course. Written by one who is so thoroughly a master, it everywhere in its details indicates in a suggestive form their bearings on the ultimate questions of Analysis. In publishing a work of the high character that the Geometry unquestionably bears, you have laid under obligation to your firm the friends of mathematical studies throughout the land."—WM. T. HARRIS, ESQ., *Superintendent of Public Schools, St. Louis, Mo.*

CHAUVENET'S PLANE AND SPHERICAL TRIGONOMETRY.

By WM. CHAUVENET, *Prof. of Mathematics and Astronomy in Washington University, St. Louis.* New and Revised Edition. 8vo. Cloth. $1.60.

CHAUVENET'S METHOD OF LEAST SQUARES.

A Treatise on the Method of Least Squares; or, The Application of the Theory of Probabilities in the Combination of Observations. From the author's Manual of Spherical and Practical Astronomy. By WM. CHAUVENET, *Prof. of Mathematics and Astronomy in Washington University, St. Louis.* 8vo. Cloth. $1.60.

CHAUVENET'S ASTRONOMY.

A Manual of Spherical and Practical Astronomy. Embracing the general problems of Spherical Astronomy, its special applications to Nautical Astronomy, and the Theory and Use of Fixed and Portable Astronomical Instruments. With an Appendix on the Method of Least Squares. Amply Illustrated with Engravings on Wood and Steel. By WM. CHAUVENET, *Prof. of Mathematics and Astronomy in Washington University, St. Louis* (*University edition.*) 2 vols. Medium 8vo. Cloth. $7.00.

GET THE STANDARD.

"It ought to be in every Library, also in every Academy and every School."—Hon. Charles Sumner.

WORCESTER'S

QUARTO DICTIONARY.

A large, handsome volume of 1854 pages, containing considerably more than 100,000 Words in its Vocabulary, with the correct Pronunciation, Definition, and Etymology.

Fully Illustrated. Library Sheep. $10.00.

"WORCESTER"

is now regarded as the standard authority, and is so recommended by Bryant, Longfellow, Whittier, Sumner, Holmes, Irving, Winthrop, Agassiz, Marsh, Henry, Everett, Mann, Quincy, Felton, Hillard, and the majority of our most distinguished scholars, and is, besides, recognized as authority by the Departments of our National Government.

THE COMPLETE SERIES OF

WORCESTER'S DICTIONARIES.

Quarto Dictionary. Illustrated. Library Sheep. $10.00.
Octavo (Universal and Critical) Dictionary. 8vo. Library Sheep. $4.25.
Academic Dictionary. Crown 8vo. Half roan. $2.00.
Comprehensive Dictionary. Illustrated. 12mo. Half roan. $1.75.
School (Elementary) Dictionary. 12mo. Half roan. $1.00.
Primary Dictionary. Illustrated. 16mo. Half roan. 60 cents.
Pocket Dictionary. Illustrated. 24mo. Cloth, 63 cents; Roan, flexible, 85 cents; Roan, tucks, gilt edges, $1.00.

Many special aids to students, in addition to a very full pronouncing and defining vocabulary, make the above-named books, in the opinion of our most distinguished educators, the most complete as well as by far the cheapest Dictionaries of our language.

"It follows from this with unerring accuracy that Worcester's Dictionary, being preferred over all others by scholars and men of letters, should be used by the youth of the country and adopted in the common schools."—*New York Evening Post.*

"J. B. Lippincott & Co. are most fortunate in having secured the plates, even though at great expense, of Worcester's Dictionaries. The best English writers and the most particular American writers use Worcester as their authority It is almost incredible the labor represented in Worcester's unabridged."—*New York Herald.*

BOOKS FOR TEACHERS.

I.

WICKERSHAM'S METHODS OF INSTRUCTION;

OR,

That Part of the Philosophy of Education which Treats of the Nature of the Several Branches of Knowledge and the Method of Teaching Them.

By J. P. WICKERSHAM, A.M.,

State Superintendent of Public Instruction of Pennsylvania.

12mo. Cloth. $1.75.

II.

WICKERSHAM'S SCHOOL ECONOMY.

A Treatise on the Preparation, Organization, Employments, Government, and Authorities of Schools.

By J. P. WICKERSHAM, A.M.,

State Superintendent of Public Instruction of Pennsylvania.

12mo. Cloth. $1.50.

SPECIAL CHARACTERISTICS.

I. These works are a philosophical exposition of that part of education of which they treat. Every division will be found in its proper place, and good reasons are always given for its statements.

II. They are practical. Every teacher can make an application of their principles. They are especially valuable as guides to young teachers.

III. Their style is clear and pointed. No rambling discussions, loose narratives, or nonsensical stories will be found within their pages. They claim rank with the more sober and solid treatises which form the standard works on law and medicine.

IV. They are exhaustive. Matter scattered through dozens of volumes on teaching is brought together and condensed in these, and nothing of importance appertaining to the subject is omitted.

V. They are now used as text-books with marked success in a number of State Normal Schools, Private Normal Schools, Teachers' Institutes and Associations.

VI. They contain matter which every parent and every school officer as well as every teacher should be acquainted with.

www.ingramcontent.com/pod-product-compliance
Lightning Source LLC
LaVergne TN
LVHW021321110826
845150LV00003B/633